The Single European Market
Prospects for economic integration

R. W. Vickerman

HARVESTER
WHEATSHEAF

New York   London   Toronto   Sydney   Tokyo   Singapore

First published 1992 by
Harvester Wheatsheaf
Campus 400, Maylands Avenue
Hemel Hempstead
Hertfordshire, HP2 7EZ
A division of
Simon & Schuster International Group

Typeset in 10/12 pt Times
by Keyset Composition, Colchester, Essex

Printed and bound in Great Britain by
BPCC Wheatons Ltd
Exeter

British Library Cataloguing in Publication Data

A catalogue record for this book is available from the British Library

ISBN 0 7450 1203 5 (hbk)
ISBN 0 7450 1204 3 (pbk)

2   3   4   5   96   95   94   93

The Single European Market

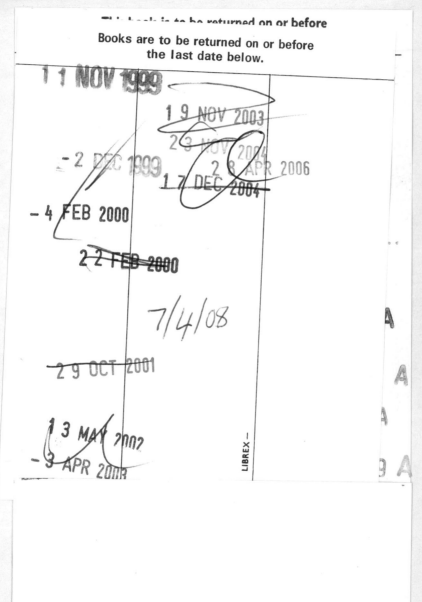

To Stephen, Jennifer, Karen and Thomas
the new Europeans

Contents

Preface

This book is about the process of economic integration in the
European Community. Over the last five years there has been an
upsurge of interest in the economic assessment of this process
associated with the move towards completion of the Single Market in
1992. The literature on the European economy has grown substantially in this period as well. There are now several good textbooks on
economic aspects of the European Community as well as an increasing
number of major research studies re-evaluating the Community's own
initial evaluations of the economic benefits of 1992. This volume aims
to fill something of a gap between these two types of book, and also to
provide a framework for assessing the future process of integration in
the 1990s.

Standard textbook treatments of the EC tend to treat the 1992
process as one, almost separable, element of study of the EC, rather
than as something central to the understanding of the Community as a
whole. This is because understanding the European Community
requires a wide range of economic knowledge, the basic economics of
Customs Unions, modern international trade theory, macroeconomic
and monetary theory, public finance, industrial economics, agricultural
economics, labour economics and regional and transport economics.
Pulling all of these strands together as well as conveying a rudimentary
knowledge of how the EC works is a major task for any textbook. The
danger is, however, that the reader gets a rather fragmented view of
the process of integration as a whole.

At the other extreme, research studies tend to concentrate on the
difficult issues of measuring and forecasting the process of change
under a varying set of assumptions. It has frequently been suggested

that the drive for integration in Europe, and especially the 1992 programme, is a purely political concept, for which an economic justification had to be found. The danger in the economic research studies is that they may tend to encourage the reader to overlook that wider dimension.

The concept behind this book is to try to link these various themes together – it is therefore a complement to existing textbooks and an introduction to the research studies. It does go beyond this, however, in its attempt to try to set the agenda for debate over integration in the 1990s. This is going to occur primarily at the regional level. A considerable amount of space is therefore devoted to assessing the regional distribution of gains and losses from the 1992 programme and the implications these might have for the structure of decision making within Europe, and the way that structure is financed. This issue has come to the fore in the political debate over the Maastricht Summit of December 1991 and the resulting Treaty. Some of this part of the book depends on findings from recent research by the author on regional impacts of change in Europe and the role of new transport infrastructure. Transport is seen as particularly important to this process since it is the transport system that provides the key links between the activities of the various regions.

How to use this book

The book is designed as a complement to standard textbooks on the economics of the European Community. The first part concentrates on the issues in economic integration. It rehearses the major economic arguments for the EC in the first chapter, placing stress on the development of an increasing degree of integration in the move from Free Trade Area through to full Economic and Monetary Union. Chapter 2 sets out the principal issues that need to be addressed in any study of integration: the location of economic activity, the role of transport in linking activities together and the development of trade at a national level in the EC. Chapter 3 goes a little further in assessing the determinants of competitiveness at a regional level. The current position is then drawn together in Chapter 4, which puts forward various ways of measuring the degree of integration that has taken place in the EC up to 1991. This is seen as a critical basis from which to understand the significance of the 1992 programme.

The second part of the book looks at future potential. Chapter 5 sets out in detail the 1992 programme, identifying the main components and how they will affect different industrial and commercial sectors, and different countries. Chapters 6 and 7 are the core of the second part. They look respectively at the impact on selected sectors and the impact on selected regions. One of the major concerns is, however, to avoid the temptation to look just at sectors and then use this to interpolate the impact on regions. Furthermore, it is important not just to predict forwards on the basis of the current structure of industry or its potential for scale economies, but rather to try to understand the way the challenges of 1992 will be responded to in varying ways in different sectors or in different regions. The final chapter considers how the process of integration will develop through the 1990s and strongly argues the need for an institutional structure which is flexible enough to cope with the pressures that will grow on regions.

Most readers will need to use this book in conjunction with a standard text on the organization of the EC. Those interested in particular sectors will also need to look at detailed research studies on those sectors. Useful complements are T. Hitiris, *European Community Economics* (2nd edition) and David Mayes (ed.), *The European Challenge: Industry's response to the 1992 programme*, both published by Harvester Wheatsheaf. The general reader will find this, however, a self-contained introduction to the issues in economic integration and their likely consequences.

Acknowledgements

This book has originated in three different teaching environments. First, it derives from an increasingly popular final year course on 'The Economics of the EC' which I have been teaching at Kent for some twelve years. I am grateful to successive generations of students on the course for their failure to understand issues which prompted me to try to set them down in a coherent way. I am also grateful for the helpful insights given in the early days by Stephen Holt and to my colleague Euclid Tsakalotos, who now shares the course with me. His obstinate refusal to let me get away with sloppy arguments has improved the thinking behind this book enormously, though I know there is still much in it that he does not agree with.

Secondly, I have had the opportunity to develop a summer course on the European Environment for Business for American and European MBA students over the past five years. There, too, I have found the need for a straightforward introduction to the issues, of relevance to the business world and to non-Europeans.

Thirdly, I have been asked on many occasions to address various local and business groups on what 1992 means and what effect it will have on their everyday lives. Here again it has been necessary to set the context for the detailed decisions, and the book has been written so that the non-specialist can see the way the various issues fit together.

To all of these groups who have been the experimental audience I am extremely grateful. I am also grateful to colleagues in various universities in France and Germany with whom I have had the opportunity to discuss some of the ideas in this book, and in DG XVI Regional Affairs, of the European Commission who have given me the opportunity to observe some policy making at the EC level. All of these have been helpful in allowing me to formulate my ideas; none of them should in any way be implicated in the final transmission of these into the final form of this book. Finally, I acknowledge with gratitude the faith of successive editors, initially Philip Allan and then Peter Johns and Mark Allin at Harvester Wheatsheaf who have shown exemplary patience and understanding.

Roger Vickerman
Canterbury, January 1992

1

Economic integration
an overview

1.1 From free trade to EMU: The five stages of integration

Economists have argued for most of the last two centuries that global free trade is beneficial. This benefit arises from allocating resources in such a way as to maximize world output, or conversely to minimize the resource cost of producing a given output. Hence goods are produced by individuals and in regions that have a comparative advantage in their production. Comparative advantage requires a comparison of the relative costs of producing goods in each region. The region should specialize in the production of those goods which it can produce relatively the cheapest – even if another region can produce all goods cheaper in absolute terms. Individuals, regions and countries then exchange or trade these goods in order to satisfy their range of wants.

For most of this period, however, free trade has not been the order practised in the real world because it is also the case that specific individuals or groups can secure at least short-term gains by restricting trade. Sometimes such restrictions may be justifiable on the grounds of encouraging the growth of new industries, where there is a potential future comparative advantage – the so-called infant industry argument. Often the restrictions are simply useful as revenue earners for governments through the use of tariffs or as bargaining counters to gain access to other protected markets.

Since universal world free trade has for much of this period become increasingly less likely, at various times regional groupings of countries have emerged with free trade as a basic principle of collaboration. However, free trade in goods and services within a regional grouping of countries poses certain difficulties. The first of these is that, although goods can quite easily be allowed to pass between countries within the group, unless they also agree on a common position with respect to goods entering the group from outside countries, controls will need to be maintained on internal frontiers. Without these, goods from third countries could overcome individual national barriers by finding the cheapest indirect route through a partner country. Hence, members of a Free Trade Area may decide on the need for a Common External Tariff to avoid these issues of sourcing and a Free Trade Area becomes a Customs Union.

The second difficulty is that even a Customs Union may have residual barriers to trade between its members. These are usually referred to as non-tariff barriers (NTBs). NTBs may range from border controls on the vehicles carrying goods (including quantitative restrictions on the vehicles of one country entering another within the Customs Union) to the detailed specification of standards on grounds of health, safety, etc., which are drawn up on an individual and not a collective basis. Furthermore, even where goods may pass freely between countries there may be substantial restrictions in trade in services and even more so on factors of production such as labour and capital. It is only when all these restrictions have been lifted that we can legitimately talk of a Common Market existing in the group of countries.

The third difficulty arises where, because of differing and inconsistent economic policies in the various countries, the movement of resources does not reflect the real, long-term economic advantages of particular areas, but the short-term speculative advantage gained through currency movements, differential interest and inflation rates, etc. In other words, the operation of a full Common Market leads to a need to fix exchange rates, at least in the short term, and this in turn requires the coordination of monetary policy and, by implication, the coordination of broad economic policy making objectives between the countries.

Finally, we may note that where currency exchange rates can still be changed and where, even if economic policy making is broadly coordinated, individual countries can pursue independent fiscal and budgetary policies, it is unlikely that a process of stable convergence will be achieved. Hence an ultimate implication is a move to a full Economic and Monetary Union (EMU). In an EMU the constraint of a single currency and unified monetary policy through a single central banking structure aims to force a convergence of economic performance throughout the whole Union. Here macroeconomic policy is unified rather than coordinated or harmonized. This would complete the formal handover of sovereignty over independent economic policy from the member states and thus typically carries with it a requirement for greater democratic accountability at the supranational level.

Hence in summary the five stages of integration can be represented as follows:

1. Free Trade Area (FTA).
2. Customs Union (CU) = FTA + Common External Tariff (CET).
3. Common Market (CM) = CU − NTBs + factor mobility.
4. Economic integration (EI) = CM + fixed exchange rates + macroeconomic policy coordination.
5. Economic and Monetary Union (EMU) = EI + single currency and central bank + unified economic policy.

1.2 The European Community and progress to integration

The distinctive feature of the EEC as established by the Treaty of Rome in 1957 is that membership implied an immediate move to a Customs Union with some aspects of a Common Market, and a commitment towards largely unspecified further integration. The original establishment of the EEC was against the background of a largely protectionist trading environment, prior to general world attempts to reduce tariff levels through the various rounds of the General Agreement on Tariffs and Trade (GATT). Hence the original six members of the Community (Belgium, Luxembourg, Netherlands, France, Italy and the Federal Republic of Germany) were committed to a gradual movement through stages 1 and 2 of integration over a transition period.

At the same time other European countries committed themselves to stage 1 (FTA) through the European Free Trade Association (EFTA) founded in 1959 in association with the EEC. These original seven (United Kingdom, Denmark, Norway, Sweden, Portugal, Switzerland, Austria) included several that eventually became full members of the EEC simply as a move from stage 1 to stage 2, FTA to CU. EFTA was later joined by Finland and Iceland with a special FTA agreement with Spain. However, a key feature of the EEC from the start was a commitment to elements of a Common Market using a gradualist sectoral approach. Hence Common Agricultural and Transport Policies were identified in the Treaty of Rome. These were two sectors that were seen to be central to the process of integration, albeit in different ways. It was this initial commitment to supranational policy making that deterred the United Kingdom and other EFTA members from making the full transition initially.

Agriculture presented the case of the typical problem sector which required coordinated action to avoid wasteful competition, whilst its social importance in a Community where around 20 per cent of the work-force was employed in the sector at the start of the EEC in the 1950s, although only producing some 8 per cent of the gross domestic product (GDP), raised the danger of continuing protectionist pressures. The Common Agricultural Policy (CAP) thus moved to a single agricultural market in which a CET would be established through variable levies on imports based on the relationship between domestic production prices and world prices. Community farmers would be protected from fluctuating prices by intervention buying at prices related to target prices set to guarantee acceptable incomes to farmers. In this way, the aim was for a single price across the Community and, with the help of funds for restructuring – so-called guidance expenditure – a reallocation of farming resources to improve self-sufficiency and efficiency on a Community-wide basis. That the reality was less impressive than this aim is perhaps the best known criticism of the EEC.

In transport the aims were rather different. Transport's real importance is as an input to production either by carrying finished goods or, increasingly as the pace of integration increased, moving inputs and intermediate goods. This required action on two fronts – the development of an adequate transport infrastructure for the EEC and the elimination of barriers to international transport. The latter arose partly because of differing technical, social and fiscal arrangements concerning transport – lorry weights, drivers' tests and hours regulations, and taxes on vehicles and fuel – and partly because of excessive regulation in the transport sector. This regulation was particularly prominent in the rapidly growing road haulage sector where restrictive regulations controlled competition with state-owned railways. Little real progress has been made on the last of these points, although the Community did go through a period of excessive harmonization of regulations with attempts to fix price brackets for freight transport from the late 1960s to mid-1970s. Progress was made on technical, social and fiscal harmonization and on discussing the basis for infrastructure investment, though not for implementing this at a Community level. In transport, therefore, no real Common Market was ever established to the extent that applied in agriculture.

Beyond these two sectors, however, the Treaty of Rome only suggested pious hopes towards future integration. The free movement of labour and mutual recognition of qualifications and social security entitlements is there as an ideal, but without practical means of implementation. In the most important sectors of manufacturing industry there is little substantive to promote the move from CU to CM, except for measures to promote competition and to control restrictive practices.

Largely, therefore, the common epithet of the EEC – the Common Market – was a misnomer for the Community as a whole for its first thirty years. The Community has tried to come to grips with this problem at various times. In 1970 the Werner Report recommended a move towards EMU over the decade of the 1970s. This was an attempt to resolve a long-running dispute between the so-called 'economists' who favoured the orderly progression via the achievement of a full Common Market, greater integration and convergence of economic performance, to EMU, and the so-called 'monetarists' who argued that only the strait-jacket of monetary orthodoxy in a full monetary union would ever force the Community through the painful adjustments of the CM and EI, stages 3 and 4 of our progression.

The Werner Plan misfired on two counts: the collapse of the world international financial system in 1971 and the preoccupation with expanding the Community itself in 1973 when the United Kingdom, Ireland and Denmark joined, followed by Greece in 1980 and Spain and Portugal in 1986. An attempt to salvage some progress towards a single financial market came again, however, in 1978 through the establishing of the European Monetary System (EMS) with its major initial feature being an Exchange Rate Mechanism (ERM) and a currency unit (ECU) based on a basket of European currencies. This recognized that a gradual move to fixed exchange rates could take place through stages 3 and 4 of the integration process.

Throughout this period, however, the Community often lost sight of the important goal of moving to the full Common Market before EMU could be tackled. It is true that in a piecemeal way the Commission busied itself with trying to suppress the various NTBs which sprang up to defend domestic industries from free trade in the absence of internal tariffs. This became the butt of anti-EEC propaganda as people wondered why Brussels bureaucrats should concern themselves with the size of eggs, the content of sausages, ice cream or chocolate, the noise emission of lawnmowers or the chemical content of beer. All of these, and many more, were seen as vital to ensure full and free competition, but the heavy-handed use of Directives to force harmonization was a bureaucratic and ineffective way of achieving this, and often misfired.

In the mid-1980s, therefore, the EEC seemed to have lost direction and purpose. Our typology suggests that this may not be unexpected.

In a sense no stage of the integration process is stable; its viability depends on maintaining some external pressures – largely through bureaucratic intervention. Stuck somewhere between stages 2 and 3 with odd bits of 4 and 5 in place it needed either to move much further down the road through CM to EI and EMU or to retreat towards a simple FTA. This latter would at least avoid the excessive bureaucracy needed to preserve the partial CM and the EMS. The route chosen was, however, more firmly forwards to the completion of the CM, now called the Single European Market (SEM) or Internal Market of the Community. Moreover, in 1987 a date for this completion was set of 31 December 1992, and 1992 became a mystical date in the development of the Community. Having set this process in train, the Commission under its President, Jacques Delors, determined to increase the momentum and produced a succeeding three-stage plan to completion of EMU, following on from completion of the SEM, albeit without a committed timetable beyond its first stage.

The Single European Act of 1987, a piece of legislation which passed virtually simultaneously into the laws of all the member states, was essentially a codifying of the various Treaties establishing and extending the Community. It was the legal basis for the subsequent five-year transition to the completion of the Single Market. However, it did not represent a fundamental change in the nature of the Community, rather a reaffirmation of principles that had subsequently become rather lost. Although there may still be arguments about the precise interpretation of some of the nearly 300 separate legislative items identified in the Community's White Paper of 1985, especially over such matters as border controls and fiscal approximation, it was largely accepted as a logical step. EMU, however, is very definitely another matter – a step beyond a Common Market.

The 'founding fathers' of the Community in the 1950s, such figures as Jean Monnet and Robert Schuman, and even national politicians such as Konrad Adenauer, clearly had the view that ultimate political union was the goal and that economic union was but one vital step along this road. However, the Community as it developed became more concerned with the minutiae of economic trading relations and less concerned with long-term visions. In one sense it was only when the original six had shown this commitment to pragmatism that membership became a practical proposition for the United Kingdom. EMU, however, goes beyond this largely pragmatic trading area – it implies a greater loss of control over basic macroeconomic policy instruments (sovereignty as it is popularly, but probably erroneously, called) and it involves a greater step into the unknown.

However, some greater democratic accountability of Community institutions and a better basis for formulating common policy objectives was clearly necessary. Thus, simultaneously with the establishing of an Intergovernmental Conference (IGC) on EMU (a necessary precursor to the essential new Treaty), a parallel IGC on Political Union was established – these both to deliberate during 1991. This raised again the question of whether the EC should move to a 'federal' political basis, but it rapidly became clear the word federal had too many contradictory meanings for it to be used as a basis for fuller discussion. To some it means yielding power to a centralized super-state; to others, the basis for greater devolvement of power to Europe's regions. This would follow the principle of 'subsidiarity' – that power should rest at the lowest most efficient level. Of course, either way, the nation state was most at risk and this raised understandable anxieties, compounded by the upsurge in regional nationalism in eastern Europe. The EC was faced not just with the applications to join from countries such as Hungary, Poland and Czechoslovakia (itself a federal state) following the revolutions of 1989, but also with the disintegration of Yugoslavia and then the Soviet Union itself in 1991, with emerging republics such as Slovenia and the Baltic States also seeking membership as a major policy objective. From the perspective of existing members this highlighted the question over 'widening versus deepening', whether the Community could cater for new, less developed, members if it had moved to greater integration, or whether only a Community that had established this more cohesive structure could cope with such new pressures.

Despite the '*non-Communautaire*' basis, it has been customary in the United Kingdom to try to construct cost–benefit appraisals of the steps towards integration. This is '*non-Communautaire*' in the sense that individual, sectoral, regional or national gains and losses should logically be subordinated to the consideration of the potential gain to the Community as a whole – redistribution of those gains is a subsequent and separate exercise. Such cost–benefit analyses of the moves towards free trade and greater integration in a Customs Union are extremely complex exercises since they depend on forecasting changes in economic relationships in a dynamic way as well as assessing the static benefits. We shall look at these issues in more detail in the following section.

EMU, however, is almost purely about dynamic changes in the long term, and this makes it extremely difficult to have any real economic basis for its assessment.

1.3 The economic basis of integration

Essentially, economic integration in a Customs Union is based on the fundamental principles of specialization and trade which stem from Adam Smith and David Ricardo. The rationale for a regional economic grouping is as a partial step back towards universal free trade through the dismembering of restrictions on trade between similar and nearby countries that either already, or potentially, have high proportions of their trade between each other.

The economic analysis starts from the presumption that some tariff barriers exist between the countries, and aims to show how both parties to a Customs Union can benefit in welfare terms from joining the union. This is depicted in Fig. 1.1.

Here it is assumed that the home country has a demand curve given by D_h and a domestic supply function S_h, which is upward-sloping given diminishing returns. The home country demand is assumed to be so small relative to world demand that it has no effect on the world price, hence world supply is perfectly elastic, S_w, at price P_w. Under free trade only $0q_1$ would be produced domestically and to satisfy demand at this price q_1q_2 would be imported. In order to protect the domestic industry a tariff of T is imposed, raising the domestic price to $P_w + T$. This increases domestic supply to $0q_5$ and reduces demand such that imports are q_5q_6. The government raises tariff revenue equal to the sum of the two areas $C + D$ in Fig. 1.1.

The essence of the CU is to enter a union with a partner country that, although possibly less competitive than the cheapest world price, has a comparative advantage over the home country and can supply according to S_p at price P_p. The effect of this is to reduce domestic supply to $0q_3$, but increase demand to $0q_4$, and now q_3q_4 is imported from the partner country. The welfare implications of this can be seen from Fig. 1.1. First, resources are released from high-cost domestic industry which can be redeployed in other sectors where this country has a comparative advantage over its partner – this is shown by triangle A. Secondly, consumers gain an increase in welfare from the increase in consumption from q_6 to q_4 – the consumers' surplus is given by triangle B. These areas together, $A + B$, are referred to as the gains from trade creation since they are unambiguous net welfare gains resulting from the new trade created between the partners. Consumers also gain from the lower price now paid on the existing consumption of $0q_6$, but area C is simply a transfer of welfare from the government in lost tariff revenue to consumers in the form of lower prices, and area E is a corresponding transfer from producers to consumers. This leaves the remaining area, D, which previously was tariff revenue to the

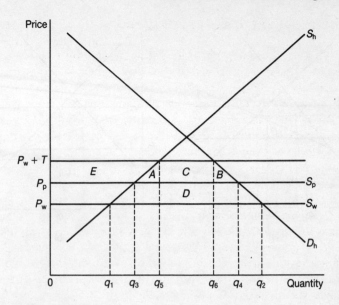

Figure 1.1

government, but is now lost as this trade q_5q_6 is diverted from the tariff-bearing world suppliers to tariff-free partner suppliers. This does, of course, represent a net cost to the home country as lower cost suppliers have been supplanted by higher cost ones and hence this is referred to as the loss from trade diversion.

The net gains from the CU thus depend on the relative sizes of the trade creation and trade diversion effects $(A + B - D)$. These will depend on the relative efficiency of domestic, partner and world suppliers and on the domestic elasticity of demand for the product.

There is also a loss of welfare to the rest of the world, countries outside the CU, which the new union will treat as irrelevant. It could be argued that the cost to these countries is particularly significant because, in the case of a European Customs Union, it includes Third World countries which thus bear the costs of the gains to Europe. This would argue that only a strategy that aims to reduce all tariff barriers is acceptable. Two arguments can be used against this. One is entirely pragmatic, that the chance of achieving global free trade is almost certainly zero. The other would argue that the welfare gain from the Union between the home and partner countries raises their incomes and hence their potential demands for the output of third countries – it may not be a first best position but will be a second best, certainly compared to doing nothing.

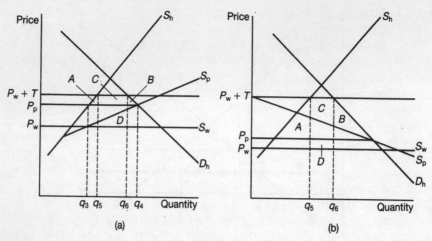

Figure 1.2

Much debate has centred on the relative sizes of the trade creation and trade diversion effects. Figure 1.2 shows these for slightly differing assumptions.

In Fig. 1.2(a) it is assumed that the partner country also faces decreasing returns to scale in supplying the product, but less seriously than the home country – this typically reduces the trade creation gains and increases the trade diversion costs, assuming that the common external tariff, T, is set at a fully protective level. In Fig. 1.2(b), on the other hand, the partner country faces increasing returns. As demand within the CU increases, scale economies can be exploited and the average cost will fall, thus increasing the trade creation gains and reducing the trade diversion costs.

These scale economy gains are part of a longer-term, more dynamic set of gains which the comparative static analysis of Figs 1.1 and 1.2 cannot capture. Increasing markets leading to scale economies and increasing incomes within the CU can lead both to further scale economies and to greater competition, which will help to eliminate residual inefficiencies within firms in the CU. Even where the static creation–diversion analysis leads to an ambiguity as to the overall net benefits, the scope for dynamic gains is often argued to clinch the argument in favour of the CU.

As we have seen, however, the assessment of overall net benefits depends critically on the relative elasticities of demand and supply in the home and partner countries. Both ex ante and ex post attempts at estimating these have been made, for the Community as a whole and for individual countries. Such measurement is always problematic. Ex ante measurement implies extrapolating elasticities forwards into a new situation. Ex post measurement implies disentangling trade creation from other simultaneous changes due to other completely exogenous factors, oil price shocks, wars, bad harvests, etc.

Table 1.1 records the ranges of ex post measurements that have been made for the Community at various times. These vary both in relative and absolute sizes of the effects, but are not all strictly comparable because of differences in their coverage (both of countries and sectors). The general picture seems to be one of net gain with trade creation benefits outweighing trade diversion costs for the group of countries as a whole and a tendency for the net gains to have increased through time.

Ex ante estimates are conceptually more interesting. Estimates were made at the time of the United Kingdom's entry into the Community in 1973, both officially to justify entry and as academic exercises. The White Paper of 1970 (Cmnd 4289) on the economic arguments surrounding UK entry into the EC looked at the effects of membership on agricultural prices, the balance of trade and budget contributions and gave a rather confused picture of expected overall gains or losses. Work by Miller and Spencer (1977) used a computable general equilibrium model to make a further ex ante assessment which put a figure of one-sixth of 1 per cent of income on the gains from trade creation, but an outward transfer of 1.5 per cent of national income on CAP, leading to an overall net loss of 1.8 per cent of national income. This work used an approach which aimed to capture the general equilibrium effects of UK entry, as opposed to the partial equilibrium model used in the simple diagrammatic exposition above, although the results were intended to be illustrative rather than definitive owing to the difficulty of defining the elasticities.

Table 1.1 Estimates of trade creation and trade diversion for the EEC.

Study	Year	Trade creation ($000 mn)	Trade diversion ($000 mn)
Truman (1969)	1965	4.5	−1.6
Balassa (1967)	1965	1.9	0.1
EFTA (1972)	1965	1.7	0.6
Truman (1972)	1967	9.2	−1.0
Major-Hays (1970)	1968	10.8	−2.9
Balassa (1974)	1970	11.4	0.1
Prewo (1974)	1970	18.0	−3.1

Source: Mayes (1978).

What these studies assume, however, is that there is a once and for all change in the implicit costs of trade between countries (through the reduction in tariffs) following which the countries' economies converge on a new equilibrium position. For those arguing against Customs Unions this is enough on the basis of the above evidence to urge caution. For those wishing to argue in favour, however, there is a further stage, the dynamic response of the economies.

The static analysis assumes simply that production adjusts according to the tenets of specialization. This will reduce costs both by producing in the cheapest location and by gaining from scale economies by concentrating production to serve larger markets. In addition, the increases in competition within the Customs Union will erode the power of national monopolies and reduce the losses from inefficient use of resources – so-called X-inefficiencies. The dynamic analysis then asks what will happen as a result of the increase in welfare that this gives rise to. Again, two complementary processes can be identified: increased incomes lead to an increased demand for goods and services, providing a multiplier effect on the economy, and secondly there is an inducement to greater investment so that firms can benefit from the lower costs of embodied technical progress – rather like the accelerator effect.

If we look at UK experience since 1973, however, the evidence tends to suggest that trade creation has been primarily at the cost of lost production in the United Kingdom and that the resources freed have not been sufficiently redeployed into areas of greater comparative advantage. As a result, dynamic effects have failed to arise to increase the beneficial outcome. But this is the very point at which we need to identify the failure to complete the Common Market implicit in the theoretical outline above. As tariff barriers have fallen in Europe, non-tariff barriers have grown up in their place. These NTBs have the effect of reducing trade creation benefits and preventing the onset of the dynamic factors.

1.4 The costs of non-Europe

Any failure to make the Customs Union a Common Market will act as a residual tariff, imposing costs on transactions between countries. These have become known as 'the costs of non-Europe', a concept explored in detail in a major Community study chaired by Paolo Cecchini. The Cecchini Report, its supporting research studies and subsequent detailed studies of individual sectors and countries have given us the best picture to date of the working of the Economic

Community. What they point to is a substantial annual cost of nearly 5 per cent of the Community's GDP.

These losses, how to recoup them, and the implications of this process are the central concern of this book, but briefly they arise from six principal sources:

1. The costs of crossing internal frontiers.
2. The failure to harmonize technical standards.
3. The failure to achieve fiscal harmonization.
4. The failure to exploit potential scale economies.
5. The potential for X-inefficiency.
6. The effects of preferential public procurement policies by government authorities.

We have already met the problem of scale economies and efficiency in utilizing resources. Public procurement, technical standards and fiscal policies (especially rates of VAT and Excise Duty) are all similar weapons by which governments protect their domestic industry from foreign, albeit other Community, countries. It is the presence of these factors, the real NTBs, that requires the continuing existence of controls on internal frontiers, to prevent the free movement of goods. These controls not only cost direct resources in their operation but impose costs of delay and bureaucracy on all crossing them.

Table 1.2 summarizes the main findings of the Cecchini Report on the contribution of these various factors to the overall costs and Table 1.3 indicates the macroeconomic consequences of their removal. We shall discuss the basis of these estimates more fully in Chapters 5 and 6. The argument is that the removal of internal frontiers will allow goods to move more easily and at lower cost. It will also remove the artificial protection which both prevented cross-border operations to exploit scale economies and gave protection from competition to inefficient domestic firms in all countries. The combined effect is to lower costs and stimulate demand. At the macroeconomic level this also has implications for levels of unemployment, for inflation and for public sector budgets. By making the EEC more efficient it can benefit the Community's aggregate trading position in the world.

Some critics have argued that the lower end of the possible band of results presented by the Cecchini Report is the most likely as residual NTB effects will persist. We have already seen reluctance over such factors as the degree of Community control over mergers, the removal of frontiers which serve to permit the control of terrorists and drugs as well as legally traded goods, and any harmonization of taxes which would remove governments' fiscal independence. One outcome of this

Table 1.2 Estimated gains from completion of Single Market.

Source of gain	Billion ECU	% GDP
Barriers to trade	8–9	0.2–0.3
Barriers to production	57–71	2.0–2.4
Economies of scale	61	2.1
Increased competition	46	1.6
Total EC-7 (1985 prices)	127–187	4.3–6.4
Estimate EC-12 (1988 prices)	174–258	4.3–6.4
Mid-point	216	5.3

Source: Cecchini (1988).

would be a so-called two-tier Europe with an inner group of fully integrated states and an outer group of states retaining some barriers – these inner and outer groups would to a large extent reflect both geographical lo..tion and length of EC membership, with the outer group being the geographically peripheral members that joined in the various expansions of the Community.

On the other hand there is also a view that by only taking the initial once for all effects and their short-term working through the economy as a multiplier effect, the Cecchini study has underestimated the potential impact by a substantial amount. Dynamic benefits arising from the accelerator effect as firms are induced to replan their actions, to invest further in more efficient equipment, etc. could generate at least as great an additional level of benefits.

These studies also highlight a further point – that even a completed internal market is itself only a stage on the road to a fuller Economic and Monetary Union. The question is raised, therefore, whether all the potential benefits of a Single Market can, or will, be realized whilst member states are free to follow independent monetary or macroeconomic policies. These may continue to distort the allocation of resources in the Community and depress the overall level of economic activity in the interests of maintaining some specific policy objectives in one member state which are incompatible with those in other countries. EMU raises a set of extremely complex issues, many of which lie well outside this study, but these cannot be totally ignored. Any decisions taken following the intergovernmental conference on EMU in 1991 will influence real decisions of potential investors about what and where to invest. Since issues of sovereignty over economic policy making are more jealously guarded for macroeconomic and monetary policy than for microeconomic and sectoral issues, this is likely to prove more difficult to resolve.

Table 1.3 Estimated macroeconomic consequences of completion of Single Market.

Source of gain	GDP % change	Consumer prices % change	Employment change (mn)	Budget balance change (% points of GDP)	External balance change (% points of GDP)
Customs barriers	0.4	-1.0	0.200	0.2	0.2
Public procurement	0.5	-1.4	0.350	0.3	0.1
Financial services[1]	1.5	-1.4	0.400	1.1	0.3
Supply effects[1]	2.1	-2.3	0.850	0.6	0.4
Aggregate[2]	4.5	-6.1	1.800	2.2	1.0

[1] Economies of scale and competition effects.
[2] Average estimate – the study reports a spread of ±25–30% around these values.

Source: Cecchini (1988).

1.5   Understanding the Single Market: Gainers and losers

In the subsequent chapters we shall be taking various of the key themes identified here, developing them and presenting evidence as to what has been achieved, and what remains to happen. One of the key extensions is a disaggregation of the process of integration to see who within the Community gains and who loses. Sometimes these gainers and losers will be in terms of groups in society, producers, farmers, consumers; sometimes they will be sectors of the economy, foodstuffs, pharmaceuticals, automobiles, road hauliers; but they will also be geographical areas and not specifically at a national level, but rather at a regional or local level.

The restructuring of the European economy implicit in the Single Market means fundamental changes in the location of industries, changing the nature of production and moving goods (finished or intermediate) and resources around. This the key focus of what follows. It does not result in simple answers such as more centralization; or more gains to the most developed regions and losses to peripheral areas and less well-developed regions. There is a difference between the potential for gain and the actual achievement of that gain, and in the nature of which source of gain applies where. This provides a complex matrix of influences which we need to unravel, first by looking at a simplified structure of the workings of the economy in a spatial context and then by looking at evidence for different sectoral and regional dimensions.

2
Location, transport and trade

2.1 Introduction

The core analysis of a Customs Union and the transition to a single internal market presented in Chapter 1 is based arbitrarily on the integration of *national* economies. This has convenience for understanding many aspects of the transition from a non-free trade situation to a Single Market. Nation states are the level on which economic policy is established and around which the usual defensive walls of tariffs and NTBs are constructed. Hence it is national frontiers that assume significance. However, within a completed Single Market such spatial units become much less significant and we should begin to look more fully at interactions between regions.

There is a political significance to this move also. Several unified nation states within the Community have important regional issues within their frontiers which remain unresolved. Obvious examples are Scottish or Welsh claims for devolution within the United Kingdom, and the friction between Flemish and Walloon communities in Belgium. Germany is already a Federal Republic, but tensions between the federal level and certain *Länder* have been emphasized by the incorporation of the former GDR into the Federal Republic. Regionalism in France, Spain and Italy is becoming increasingly important. These issues are highlighted by the fragmentation of the former Soviet bloc and the break-up of countries within it on ethnic, linguistic and economic grounds.

To understand the economic basis and implications of these changes we need to undertake a closer analysis of the spatial organization of the economy of the Community at a regional level. This involves three interrelated elements: the choice of location by industrial and commercial enterprises, the role of transport in linking producers and consumers, and trade in finished products, intermediate goods and factors of production. Perhaps the key issue is to understand the recursive links in this process, the way transport, location and production technologies interrelate both as causes and effects. It is not just a question of determining an optimum production technology and then deciding where to locate it to minimize locational costs, but of recognizing that different technologies may be appropriate in different locations. Moreover, the choice of transport may influence both of these decisions as well as be influenced by them. Thus firms do not simply have to determine the cheapest way of moving inputs and outputs to and from the best locations of optimal production technologies. Transport, and particularly changes in transport, may influence how goods are produced, e.g. in one location or many, and where each process is located.

2.2 Industrial location in the European Community

The view that has dominated the development of the EC is that there are benefits to be gained from trade. The corollary of trade is specialization. The gains, in terms of lower resource costs of producing a given level of output (and hence of increasing welfare), arise because firms are able to gain more through specialization and exchange than is lost through the greater costs of transporting goods which this might imply. Specialization at the level of the enterprise is essentially about maximizing scale economies. At the level of the region, however, it is about geographical specialization – the increasing localization of industries.

Increasing regional specialization carries with it further potential economic advantages – in addition to internal scale economies to the firm come external economies of agglomeration and urbanization. Skilled local labour forces, specialist suppliers, dedicated transport facilities and supporting service sectors are all examples of the former. The creation of a local infrastructure which lowers unit costs accounts for the latter. The rationale for the organization of production in large urban areas derives from the existence of such external economies and this gives a cumulative twist to the process of urbanization as both a cause and consequence of economic development.

Such specialization as a consequence of trade liberalization in a Common Market could therefore imply the movement of firms or entire industries from many existing locations, in all member countries, to concentrate in a smaller number of preferred locations. This will be particularly pronounced where there are very substantial scale economies to be sought in the Common Market. Table 2.1 details the extent of such potential scale economies in the EC. The measurements, based on the study of Pratten (1988), use the concept of the minimum efficient technical scale of production (METS), i.e. the size at which unit costs are minimized. Two indicators are given: the METS as a percentage of production to show the extent to which firms are likely to be too small, and a measure of the possible burden in terms of the percentage increase in unit costs faced at a size equal to one-half METS. Some 27 per cent of plants in the Pratten study had a METS greater than 5 per cent of total EC production, i.e. there would be space for only twenty plants of optimum size. Thirty-one per cent of the sample faced cost penalties at one-half METS of 10 per cent or more in excess of those at METS. In the automobile industry, for example, METS is found at 20 per cent of the EC market and 200 per cent of the UK market, with firms at one-half of this size facing a costs penalty of between 6 and 9 per cent. Achieving scale economies might imply a drastic reduction in the number of car firms and hence in the number of regions where this industry is represented.

However, despite the evidence on scale economies, such a process, which would apparently lead to increasing concentration at both firm and regional levels in key industries, is not inevitable. The globalization of industry, in what some writers refer to as a post-Fordist society,

Table 2.1 Measures of scale economies in selected sectors.

Sector	METS as % production UK	METS as % production EC	Increase in unit costs (%) at ½ METS
Cars	200	20	6–9
Trucks	104	21	7.5
Computers	≥ 100	n.a.	5
Aircraft	≥ 100	n.a.	20
Dyes	≥ 100	n.a.	17–22
Tractors	98	19	6
Refrigerators	85	11	4
Steel	72	10	6
Electric motors	60	6	15
Telephone exchanges	50	10	3–6
Television sets	40	9	9
Synthetic rubber	24	3.5	15
Petrochemicals	23	3	12

Source: Commission of the European Communities (1988), after Pratten (1988).

has been based on using increasingly efficient transport in a world of more open economies and less restrictive trade to take advantage of localized efficiency in one part of a production process. At a world level this has meant devolving labour-intensive tasks to low wage economies in South-East Asia whilst retaining the high wage, high value-added tasks in the home country. At a European level this same process is seen in the high levels of investment by German firms in peripheral regions of Ireland, Spain and Portugal and now in eastern European countries. The car industry again provides useful examples of this process at work: Bosch have invested in a new automotive electronics plant in Wales, Volkswagen have invested both in Seat in Spain and in Skoda in Czechoslovakia as well as their commitment to the renovation of the former Trabant concern in the new *Länder*. The major investments by Japanese producers Honda, Nissan and Toyota in the United Kingdom fall into a similar category. We shall have a closer look at the car industry in Chapter 6.

Essentially, an industry achieves the economies of specialization at the process level. Even if there are ultimately fewer car producers, the industry can remain represented in many regions. More trade, however, takes place at the level of intermediate goods within a sector than at the level of finished goods being exchanged between sectors. This fits into the increasingly important phenomenon of intra-industry trade with now represents over 70 per cent of all trade between some of the more developed countries of the EC, although it has only attained levels of 20–30 per cent of trade between the less developed countries, and intermediate levels in trade between the more and less developed. This suggests a greater degree of integration between countries such as France, Germany and the United Kingdom than between Spain and Greece or Spain and the United Kingdom, a point we shall return to in Chapter 4.

Limits to concentration and specialization at the regional level will be set by limits to the urbanization economies, which beyond a point may become diseconomies as resources become fully employed and infrastructure becomes congested. Previously falling average costs will thus start to rise. Although this appears an essentially neoclassical economic view of a theory of self-balance in which diminishing returns will always come to the rescue and limit divergence, it is clear that this type of process is beginning to cause concern to traditional core regions of Europe as they are losing out, if not to peripheral regions, at least to newer industrial regions outside the traditional core. Hence, although the Paris, London and Frankfurt regions remain amongst the richest of the EC (Fig. 2.1), the fastest rates of growth are found in regions such as Rhône-Alpes (Lyon) in France, East Anglia (Cam-

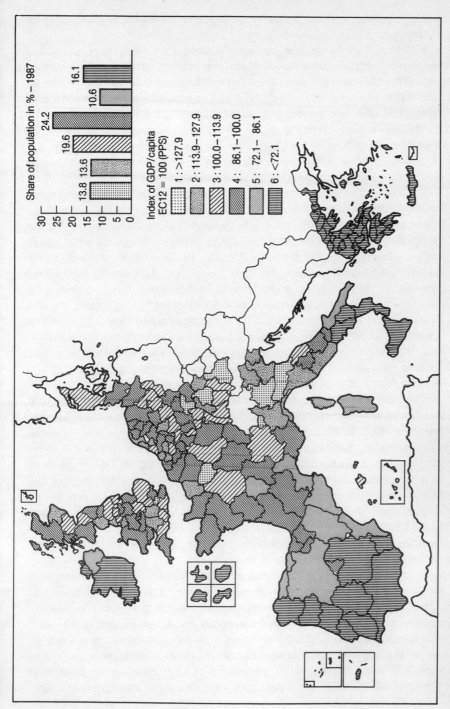

Figure 2.1 Regional distribution of income per capita.

bridge) in the United Kingdom, Baden-Württemburg (Stuttgart) in Germany.

Figure 2.1 presents the existing situation of GDP/capita, as one measure of the distribution of economic activity around the Community. We could also choose alternative measures such as proportion of industrial employment, unemployment or changes in the labour force, but these do not produce a substantially different picture of the existing situation. What none of them does adequately, however, is measure the potential for change in the region. Nevertheless, Fig. 2.1 is a useful starting point since it gives a good overview of the way economic activity has developed in the Community.

It shows the richest regions to be associated with the major metropolitan centres of Europe or the fast-growing regions of southern Germany and northern Italy. The poorest regions are clearly on the periphery. There is also an important group of regions with GDP/capita generally below the average for the Community as a whole which lies towards the geographical centre of the Community. These are regions which are often peripheral within the context of their own member state, and lie along internal frontiers of the Community and hence experience elements of both peripherality and the shadow effects of a border. Although there have been some important changes over the years in the fortunes of some individual regions, the broad pattern shown in Fig. 2.1 is one that has remained substantially unchanged over the life of the European Community.

This is not to suggest, however, that a process of change such as that brought about by economic integration in a CU or Common Market will not have substantial impacts on industrial location and regional development. Any process of change is going to imply some firms declining and others replacing them. Within a region this may mean that traditional highly localized sectors die, a process that implies the loss of demand for particular resources or skills. Such a process of change may be traumatic for that region and its residents. Many traditional industrial regions may thus face a process of effective deindustrialization whilst erstwhile rural regions face an influx of new demands and new pressures.

This issue of deindustrialization is a difficult one. For some it is simply measured as the loss of employment in sectors that form the export base of the economy. The export base is that group of sectors where comparative advantage is used to create an income-generating surplus. Manufacturing industry is seen by this school as being the only sector that possesses the characteristics of productivity growth that can generate such a process of growth. On this basis, it is clear that deindustrialization is a widespread phenomenon throughout Europe.

The manufacturing sector declined in terms of employment between 1966 and 1983 by between 14 per cent in France, 16 per cent in West Germany and 33 per cent in the United Kingdom (Rowthorn and Wells, 1987). The only exception to this general fall was in Italy where it rose by 5.3 per cent. The percentage share of manufacturing fell by between 1.6 percentage points in West Germany and 8.9 percentage points in Belgium, but had a rise of 0.3 percentage points in Italy.

However, this may give a misleading impression of the nature and scale of the problem. One difficulty is the use of employment as a measure of deindustrialization, since productivity growth can imply increasing value added with static or falling employment. As Cheshire (1991) has shown, the rank order of member states differs according to whether one uses changes in employment, output or the ratio of output change to employment change (Table 2.2). The United Kingdom, for example, was eighth (out of the nine members for which full data were available for changes 1983–87) in terms of employment change, fourth on output change and third (behind Ireland and Luxembourg) on the ratio measure. West Germany in contrast was third in terms of employment, but sixth in terms of output and eighth in terms of relative productivity change.

Secondly, for regions at or near full employment, some employment loss from these sectors will be necessary to create the space into which new sectors can move, and increasing output of the base sector will generate increasing demands for other more dependent sectors. Thirdly, it is not clear that only manufacturing industry possesses the characteristic of increasing productivity; much of the marketed services

Table 2.2 Industrial production and employment in selected EC countries 1983–87.

	Output 1987 (1983 = 100)	Employment 1987 (1983 = 100)	Ratio: $\dfrac{\text{Output change}}{\text{Employment change}}$
Belgium	110.3	91.8	1.20
Denmark	119.1	105.7	1.13
W. Germany	111.7	95.7	1.17
France	106.1	88.7	1.20
Ireland	139.0	87.8	1.58
Italy	107.5	89.2	1.21
Luxembourg	132.3	94.2	1.40
Netherlands	113.8	96.3	1.18
United Kingdom	116.3	87.9	1.32

Source: European Economy, February 1989 (after Cheshire, 1991).

sector has displayed similar increasing returns. Finally, a loss of employment that is matched by a loss of population for a region can be part of a process of restoring a better balance between metropolitan and non-metropolitan regions in an urban system. Large cities, and particularly the cores of large metropolitan regions, have typically been losing population both to their own hinterland, a process of decentralization of population, and to smaller cities in the urban hierarchy, a process of deconcentration of population. Clearly on an absolute basis this involves deindustrialization, but this may be an essential means of restoring the competitiveness of such a city region.

Camagni (1991) has suggested a continuum of changes on the basis of cross-classifying regions by their relative employment growth and their relative productivity growth. On this basis, only those in the vicious cycle of falling employment and productivity would be truly deindustrializing. Others with falling employment would have rising productivity. If this rise were insufficient to balance the fall in employment, output would fall and the regions would be seen to be falling behind, but if the rise in productivity outweighed the fall in employment, output would be rising and the regions could be thought of as simply restructuring. Similarly, there may be regions with rising employment which give as much cause for concern because of falling productivity. For example, regions classified as displaying 'industrial conservation' would have productivity falling faster than employment rose, such that output would fall. Such regions would typically be deliberately trying to protect their industrial employment, but at the cost of preventing needed restructuring. Others may still be gaining some growth in output despite the fall in productivity, but again this very sheltered development may not be sustainable in the long term. The real problem is seen as failing to classify these latter types of regions as deindustrializing whilst including those where valuable restructuring in terms of rising productivity is occurring.

Cheshire (1991) has demonstrated how in terms of employment both deindustrializing and industrializing regions are scattered across the EC. The worst examples of deindustrialization are found in the Walloon region of Belgium, Northern Ireland and Liguria, with other deindustrializing regions in Scotland, Wales, northern England, central and eastern France, and southern Italy. Industrial growth is found in central and western France, south-western France, northern and central Italy and both northern and southern Germany.

The basic problem for the regions is how to allow this process of transition to occur without suffering some of the costs of adjustment. One of the major reasons why countries install NTBs is as a means of protecting industries and regions from too rapid an adjustment.

Regional problems in member countries of the EC have been seen as arising partly because of the failure to be able to compete owing to a lack of initial advantage – so-called structurally deficient regions – and partly because of the decline of traditional industries in regions heavily dependent on them – the declining old industrial regions. The structurally deficient regions are found mainly in the south and west of the Community. Old industrial regions are found towards the heart of the Community in France, Belgium and West Germany, but predominantly in the United Kingdom. As recent attempts by the European Commission to define the regional problem of the Community demonstrate, there is no easy way to classify regions. Factors such as demographic structure, occupational structure and location all contribute to a region's potential and its problems.

The role of the EC in removing NTBs thus requires a regional policy to ensure an orderly transition. This is not just a short-run problem as the persistence of long-term structural problems clearly shows. Furthermore, it can be argued that some persisting regional problems are the result of inappropriate regional policies in the past which have sought to prevent the process of change rather than to manage it effectively. The 'regional problem' is not just a question of regions, it is a question of understanding sectoral change. Sectoral change, in turn, is not just a question of regional industrial structure, but also of the performance of firms within each sector within a region. What determines the competitiveness of firms in a given location thus becomes a key question and will be discussed in detail in the following chapter.

Competitiveness involves more than just a static comparison between regions at a given point in time, determined solely by factors internal to each region. We need to consider the dynamics of the transmission of impacts between regions. The theory of comparative advantage recognizes the existence of initial disparities in levels of productivity. One trade partner could be absolutely less efficient in producing all goods, but still gain from specialization in producing those goods where it was relatively least inefficient. However, such a result depends on two critical assumptions about resource mobility – that resources are internally mobile between sectors but externally immobile between trading partners.

Particularly in a period of considerable change, resources such as labour may only be slowly mobile between sectors. Skill disparities may make it difficult to reabsorb redundant labour from one sector easily into another. The recent history of industrial restructuring in the United Kingdom shows clearly how the growth sectors have typically not absorbed the redundant labour from the sectors of declining employment, but rather employed new labour, especially female labour. This happens within regions, but it occurs even more dramatically between regions where it is not just skill barriers, i.e. a failure to reskill redundant labour, but also geographical immobility reinforced by cost-of-living differentials which produces widening individual and regional disparities.

In the simple model, the transmission of welfare between the residents of the trading partners takes place through trade in goods and services. These embody the skills and relative efficiency of the trading partners which themselves reflect differences in initial resource endowments. All trading partners are individually better off than they would be without trade, but the less well endowed or less efficient partners may not automatically achieve the same level of welfare as those that are better off. Such convergence of economic welfare involves a further step and has been a source of major controversy throughout the history of the European Community. In terms of the simple model, there is an equalization of factor prices throughout the trading area.

If goods do embody the initial factor endowments of the exporting area then implicitly labour-intensive goods are being exported from labour-abundant areas to those with relative labour scarcity, i.e. from implicitly relatively low wage to relatively high wage areas. This embodied labour could have the same effect as a movement of labour from an abundant area to a scarce area, depressing wages in the receiving area by reducing labour's relative scarcity and increasing wages in the exporting area by increasing demand for it. Empirically, we face the difficulties both of defining factor abundance and of relating factor prices directly to this relative abundance. Labour, in particular, poses problems because of variations in skill which represent a form of capital embodiment in labour.

This is how the model applies to a pure free trading situation, but what about the case of the Common Market where there is a free market in the factors themselves as well as in an embodied form in goods? Initial views might be that the adjustment can simply happen faster. Variations in productivity lead to differences in factor prices and factors will simply move to higher-priced areas. Instead of increasing discrepancies this acts as an equilibrating force in a traditional neo-classical way, depressing productivity and factor prices in the receiving areas and increasing them in factor-exporting areas. However, we have to remember two features: that trade in goods is taking place in parallel to any trade in factors and that factors have differential mobility. Both of these require us to think more carefully about the production element in the model, which has so far been largely ignored by assuming a single technology for each good (represented by its factor composition).

Considering production, we have two main points. Essentially the same good to the consumer can be produced by very different technologies, and secondly, factors have very different propensities of mobility. Further to this second point, immobile factors can be either ubiquitous or locationally very specific. We deal with each of these issues in turn.

Traditionally industrial location models work in two stages. In the first stage an optimal production technology is chosen, and in the second stage this is located in space by considering the space cost curve. This is based on the assumption that demand is fairly evenly spread. If demand is concentrated in particular locations, e.g. cities, then we need to overlay the space cost concept with the notion of market areas. In both of these the cost of transport is critical. This involves both the cost of moving inputs to the point of production and the cost of moving outputs to the point of consumption. Transport costs are typically assumed proportional to distance and weight or bulk. Hence a production process can be characterized as either weight- or bulk-gaining or weight- or bulk-losing. In the former case (many assembly industries of consumer goods) the finished product is more expensive to transport than the inputs – hence production will gravitate towards centres of consumption. In the latter case (process industries, iron- and steel-making), the reverse is true and such industries gravitate to sources of the materials. This can be measured by the Materials Index, which expresses the weight of material inputs to that of the finished product as a ratio: high values imply a location dominated by inputs; a value that is a fraction of one, a location dominated by the market; and a value of about one a relatively footloose industry not subject to overriding influences of either.

However, suppose that we allow location to be traded off against other factor inputs directly (see Vickerman, 1984, Chapter 3 for a more detailed discussion of this point). What this means is that factor inputs that are locationally specific are available at different prices at different delivered locations owing to different transport costs. Hence at different locations, different combinations of inputs may be used. In effect, the locationally specific input has been traded off against transport. One of the interesting consequences of this is that as output expands, the preferred location may change – this is a possible consequence of seeking scale economies in an enlarged market and therefore of considerable interest to us here.

Thus we have seen that transport can be traded against other factor inputs to change optimum technology. It can, of course, also be traded against output as a means of enlarging or reducing market area. Again, traditional space cost models tend to assume a given output which can be sold at a given price in the market. However, output might be determined jointly with technology. Peripheral regions might have small markets optimally served by small producers using one technology, whereas core regions have large markets which need a different optimal technology. Changing transport costs may thus change both the technology and the optimal market area.

The mobility of factors of production is the next critical issue. Where factors are fixed, like land, differential demands at different locations must be met by price changes. Such price changes will then affect optimal technology. Where factors are mobile, the price changes can lead to a migration of factors reducing the impact on possible changes in technology. If factors were perfectly fixed or perfectly mobile this would present no real problem, but that is clearly not the case. One reason is NTBs; thus capital has for most of the history of the EC faced controls on its free movement in and out of many member states. Similarly, labour has faced controls on its free movement from both administrative and cultural barriers. The latter may be the continuing most important barrier to a full Common Market. The continuance of language barriers provides a disincentive from both the demand and supply sides of the labour market, whilst Europe's ethnic questions remain unsolved in many areas. Increasing political fragmentation and regionalization therefore present a threat to this essential mobility. Increasing the freedom of movement in a unified market for labour is, therefore, a key priority for the Community. One factor in this is removing the remaining physical barriers to movement, which brings us to the question of the role of transport.

2.3   Transport

We have suggested above that transport should be considered as one of the factors of production, determining the choice of technology as well as location, but it has a rather special role which requires further consideration. Transport is ubiquitous in the sense that some form of transport must exist at every possible location. However, measured in terms of the cost of overcoming a unit of distance, transport is clearly not ubiquitous and depends both on the provision of infrastructure and the organization of transport services on that infrastructure. Recognizing the importance of transport as a factor binding the Community together, the Treaty of Rome identified the transport sector, along with agriculture, as being in need of a common policy. The Common

Transport Policy (CTP) has never been so comprehensively developed as the Common Agricultural Policy (CAP), but it has made some progress, albeit slowly, over the provision of infrastructure and the creation of a common market in transport services.

The basic problem of transport is that it is not a single homogeneous sector, but can be provided by a number of modes. These different modes of transport can be both competitors and complements. Each mode requires its own dedicated infrastructure: rail tracks, roads, ports and airports. These infrastructures are both expensive to construct and tend to display considerable economies of scale. Only where there are large flows between two points will it be possible to provide efficiently more than one infrastructure mode. There is therefore a strong tendency towards monopoly in the provision of infrastructure – indeed transport infrastructure is often taken in economics as the classic example of the natural monopoly. Both of these aspects, scale economies and monopoly, have led to substantial state intervention in the provision and control of transport infrastructure.

Transport services are slightly different. Once the infrastructure has been provided, services are rather less costly to provide. There may be some scale economies in the provision of services; for example, rail services only become worthwhile where there are larger flows, given the greater technical complexity and capacity of rail vehicles. Rail also poses greater problems of controlling vehicles on the infrastructure than most other forms of transport, which has typically led to a single authority controlling both infrastructure and service (though this is not universally true and certainly not essential). At the other extreme, road offers great flexibility and scope for competition within fairly broad constraints on safety and traffic control.

The major issue in road transport is the extent to which uncontrolled entry to the market for providing services leads to destructive competition. Transport services can be not only privately, but also individually, supplied. The problem for the operator of the large vehicle is to find a sufficiently large flow to fill the vehicle to an economic level. Where people or goods have common origins and destinations this is not difficult, but once either or both origins and destinations become more dispersed, and the common element in these flows smaller, individual transport (private cars, vans, etc.) become more attractive. These use the infrastructure less efficiently however, leading to congestion at lower levels of flow and are more costly in total resources. To the individual user, the time savings and convenience of scheduling make them appear more attractive. What is not perceived is the deviation between these private marginal costs and the true social marginal costs.

It is this combination of issues that any transport policy needs to address. How it does this will affect both the location of industries and how they produce at that location. The objective must be to provide transport that enables the economy to function, at a given level of activity, at the minimum possible aggregate cost. Certainly the CTP has had this broad objective in view, but it has tackled it in a very piecemeal way.

The infrastructure issue has been approached mainly through an attempt to exhort to best practice. Hence substantial studies on investment appraisal have had the aim of a common method of evaluation, particularly of items such as time values and accident costs in road investment. There have also been moves towards harmonization in railway accounting practices. Clearly substantial national differences in these areas could lead to implicit subsidies to users of infrastructure which would act as an NTB. Indeed transport costs have often been characterized as having the same effect as a tariff.

What has not been fully addressed is the supranational issue in infrastructure. The Community has tried to identify missing links in the Community infrastructure. They tend to be associated either with physical barriers, such as the Channel or the Alps, or the incidence of national frontiers. What has been less forthcoming is a means of providing finance for such links of Community importance or of Community decision taking about them. The Commission proposed, on a number of occasions, a new financial instrument which could address this problem specifically, but this was repeatedly rejected by the larger countries of the Community. The financial benefits of such an instrument could accrue on the one hand to small countries heavily engaged in transit traffic such as Belgium, but the economic benefits would be more widespread to all users of Belgian infrastructure. On the other hand, small peripheral countries of the Community need to use infrastructure in other countries more than those at the core of the Community. Total flows may be small on the infrastructure, but proportionately very significant for the users from the peripheral regions. A particular case in point is that of Irish traffic using infrastructure in the United Kingdom which is of lesser importance from a UK perspective but vital to the Irish traffic.

Although the Community has had powers to make financial assistance to transport infrastructure projects of Community significance via infrastructure funds, these have involved relatively small contributions to major projects. Like regional development grants from the ERDF, such grants raise the difficulty of needing to be activated by member countries and not by the Commission. Despite the presumption of 'additionality', i.e. that EC financing is additional to that normally provided by the member government, whilst it is true that governments must contribute in a matching grant manner to that project, the EC financing can typically be regarded as displacing an equivalent amount of national finance and thus of not increasing overall infrastructure investment. This view has particularly plagued the usefulness of EC money in UK transport because of the definitions of public money used by the Treasury. The problem is that it fails to provide additional funding to cope with the additional needs presumed to be incurred by European integration (for a fuller discussion of this see Vickerman, 1991a).

By the end of 1990, however, the Community had agreed a much reduced programme of assistance to transport infrastructure of Community importance. An action plan of 240 million ECU over the period to 1992, less than 40 per cent of that proposed by the Commission, was agreed by the Council of Ministers. This would support seven specific programmes:

1. High-speed rail links along three main corridors: Paris–Brussels–Köln–Amsterdam–London; Sevilla–Madrid–Barcelona–Lyon–Torino–Milano–Venezia–Trieste; Madrid–Lisboa–Porto.
2. The Brenner Pass Alpine route.
3. Road and rail connections to and within Ireland.
4. Road and rail links with Scandinavia.
5. Road and rail links with Greece.
6. Road links across the Pyrenees.
7. Development of combined transport networks.

A further proposal of a master plan for a 25,000 km network of new and upgraded railways was also presented by the Commission in December 1990. This would concentrate on fifteen key links, predominantly in border regions, which would be consistent with the priorities of the general transport infrastructure plan. The cost of 150 billion ECU for this ambitious plan would come largely from national governments and the private sector; the EC's contribution was proposed at just 60 million ECU.

Provision of infrastructure is not, however, the sole role of the EC in the transport sector. From the point of view of achieving the Common Market, achieving a Common Market in transport services is probably of even greater significance. This has involved intervention in a number of areas to achieve a degree of harmonization, on technical, social and fiscal matters. Technical considerations relate to such matters as lorry weights and dimensions and other aspects of construction and use of vehicles, including proposals to regulate and standardize speed limits. Social considerations deal with such matters as restrictions of drivers' hours. Fiscal matters are concerned with vehicle and fuel taxation, particularly in terms of reciprocal recognition of other member states' vehicles as not being liable for additional taxation when being used on a member state's roads.

Harmonization in all of these areas is necessary to prevent operators from one member state having an unfair competitive advantage in operating either to and from or within another member state. If one member state had, for example, no restrictions of drivers' hours, larger vehicle weight limits and lower vehicle and fuel taxes, its transport firms would have much lower costs of operation whilst at the same time imposing higher social costs on other member states. It also helps towards providing a more common basis for modal competition within each member state which has implications for the cost of transport to its users.

Road haulage has, in most countries, been a highly regulated sector, mainly to provide protection to state-owned railway sectors. This regulation, through both taxation and quantitative controls on operation, has been the principal interference with the development of a free market in transport. Often this is reinforced by subsidies to rail transport which themselves have a national bias in that they can artificially reduce the transport costs faced by firms within the member state. An example of this was where the Deutsche Bundesbahn offered extremely favourable, subsidized, tariffs to haul coal from the Saarland to other parts of Germany, thereby undercutting otherwise cheaper imported coal. In this case the transport subsidy did not simply divert traffic from road to rail but acted as a regional subsidy to the Saarland coal industry, and a general subsidy to those industries using Saarland coal.

Within the road haulage sector, the existence of differing national regulations in an otherwise open European market would lead to problems of vehicles operating between member states. If, for example, Italian operators were less constrained than German operators, then goods moving between Germany and Italy would be more likely to be carried in Italian lorries which would not be controlled in Germany. More problematic would be if Italian lorries started to carry loads entirely within Germany or between Germany and France. As a consequence a system of bilateral quotas developed which in effect allowed the movement of lorries between states on a one-for-one basis, thus maintaining the total numbers in any one state constant. In order to promote greater freedom the Community initiated a system of Community Quotas which allowed lorries to move anywhere within the Community. However, the numbers of permits was kept at a very low level, despite consistent attempts to increase the numbers.

For a short period the Community tried to initiate a system of much more widespread control over the road haulage sector, reminiscent of structures in the CAP. In this, control was extended to pricing, fearing the problems of instability which so often characterize transport. This instability is between the two extremes of destructive competition, in which low entry costs lead to excessive entry to the industry, depressing rates to a non-economic level and causing bankruptcies on a massive scale, and monopoly. The solution was to impose price controls which fixed both minimum and maximum rates in the so-called bracket rate or forked tariff. Since freight rates depend both on the commodity being carried and the length and nature of the route, the imposition of the forked tariff led to enormous administrative problems. This policy was only enforced for a short time from its introduction in 1968, although the rates have remained as a reference tariff in many instances, since by the early 1970s opinion in the Community was shifting towards a more liberal regime in transport. The United Kingdom had abolished quantitative controls in 1968 with broadly beneficial effects on the industry.

Nevertheless, it has been a slow process to get agreement on a general relaxation of controls in the industry especially towards permission of cabotage (carriage of goods solely within another member state). This has probably led to gross inefficiency in this sector with an excess of capacity over that needed by industry, with consequent upward pressure on freight rates, inefficient operators being protected from competition. The cost of empty lorry movements has been estimated at 1.2 billion ECU, of which it is suggested that 20 per cent relates to regulatory restrictions, and the black market rate for Community-wide licences has been estimated at 17,000 ECU, equal to 23 per cent of the annual operating costs of a truck.

This suggests that from the perspective of transport services as well as from that of infrastructure, transport is far from being ubiquitous in the Community. Again, peripheral regions suffer from the need of their goods to cross more frontiers and hence to fall foul of more shortages of permits, especially where loads sometimes need to wait at frontiers to avoid a bilateral quota being exceeded. Conversely, however, there is some suggestion that deficit regions in trade terms can benefit from cheap transport for their own exports as otherwise empty trucks seek back-haul loads – this depends crucially on the markets being in regions to which the lorry can return since generally second to third country trade as well as cabotage has been prohibited.

We have characterized transport thus far principally as involving competition between road and rail, with rail requiring protection from aggressive competition by road given its need to maintain its own infrastructure. Conversely, there is a problem of allocating road track costs adequately to road users to ensure users pay a share of the infrastructure costs that reflects their physical impact on that infrastructure. The period of development of the EC since 1957 has, however, coincided with major technological change in transport and the emergence of new modes which have increased in importance as the Community has grown larger.

In freight transport the increasing unitization of traffic, especially in containers, has led to greater possibilities of multi-modal transport, exploiting the economic advantages of each mode of transport, but minimizing the costly trans-shipment of goods. This process has been aided by the development of the roll-on roll-off (ro-ro) ferry enabling either complete road goods vehicles or train loads to be loaded and unloaded simply and effectively. Thus far this has mainly benefited road transport. Traffic carried by road in Europe as a whole doubled in terms of tonne–kilometres between 1970 and 1988 whilst that by inland waterway remained roughly constant and that by rail fell by nearly 5 per cent. Road now carries nearly 50 per cent of tonnage and 55 per cent of tonne–km in intra-EC international traffic (over 70 per cent of total intra-EC tonne–km), compared to 13 per cent of tonnage and 17 per cent of tonne–km by rail, the remainder being by water.

The trend towards unitization and multi-modal transport eases the position of more peripheral locations since they can have access to the major networks without needing specific access points within the region. Truly multi-modal traffic, where, for example, road vehicles provide local collection and delivery to and from a railhead and are then carried piggyback by rail between major centres, has been limited in its development. This is primarily because of problems of incompatibility between the maximum size of road vehicles and the constraint of rail loading gauges. The importance of this, however, is that the change of mode can occur without the major investment in cranes, overhead gantries, etc. which are required for loading and unloading of containers. Again, the less the investment necessary in fixed capital, the more easily and flexibly a transport system can penetrate peripheral regions and serve less dense traffics.

In passenger transport, but also in high value, low bulk freight (especially parcels traffic), the major change has been the growth of air and road transport, largely at the expense of rail. An increasingly undermaintained and outdated European rail system has found it impossible to match the speed offered by air transport for journeys over about 300–400 km and the convenience of the private car for shorter journeys. Passenger kilometres increased by about 75 per cent by private car between 1970 and 1988, but only about 20 per cent by rail. World air traffic probably almost trebled in this period. It is estimated that for international journeys air had about 30 per cent of the total market in 1986/87, with road (car and bus) taking 54.5 per cent and rail just 7.5 per cent of the market.

The growth of air transport is also reflected in the falling off of investment in all surface transport modes, from around 1.5 per cent of GDP in 1975 to around 0.9 per cent by 1984. As total road traffic grew by 30 per cent, annual investment levels fell by 30 per cent.

But the growth of air transport has also coincided with, and had some influence on, the decentralization of major metropolitan centres. Airports as major transport modes have become magnets for new industries and this has led to first urban and later national rail systems being connected to them. Hence airports such as Frankfurt, Amsterdam, Zürich and Genève are all on their countries' national inter-city rail networks and Paris Charles de Gaulle and Lyon Satolas will be linked to the French TGV system in the early 1990s. This linking is a further type of multi-modal transport development accentuating the hub effect of major international airports at the possible cost of regional air routes.

However, airlines in Europe have been highly regulated and this has served both to limit the growth of air travel owing to high fares and to restrict the entry of carriers prepared to develop regional routes. The restrictions on various air freedoms have, as in road haulage, prevented adequate development of competition and efficient linking of second and third order centres. The role of state-owned national flag-carrying airlines has been important here.

Increasingly, dissatisfaction with inefficiency in airline operation, coupled with excessive congestion of both major airports and airspace, have prompted firmer action at a European level. The final influence may not, however, be the relaxation of regulation agreed in 1992 – although the liberalization of UK–Netherlands and UK–Ireland traffic demonstrates benefits to both trunk and regional traffic – but of competition from new high-speed rail routes.

High-speed rail has two major influences. First, it can provide for both city centre and suburban traffic at a time of renewed interest in city centre development. Secondly, by using new purpose-built infrastructure for passenger traffic it can liberate capacity which speeds up freight traffic on existing lines. The final impact of high-speed rail remains to be seen, but it is already clear from experience in France that it can have important locational influences on business, although these are far from being clear and straightforward.

Transport, thus, defines the shape of the Community – changes in transport may redefine this shape by changing accessibility. What we must recall from earlier sections of this chapter, however, is that accessibility is not a clear objectively measurable phenomenon since transport is not fixed in its relationship to production. Faster transport or cheaper transport or, most importantly, reliable transport may change what (or who) is carried and how it (or they) is (are) carried and in which direction. This is why we have to consider transport in context and not attempt to solve transport questions in isolation.

2.4   Trade

The third principal issue in this discussion, trade, is both a cause and effect of the other two. The location of industries and the existence of transport require and permit trade to take place, but that trade provides the demand for transport and allows specialization and hence the localization of industries.

Typically, we start by looking at the broad macro trends in trade as an indicator of the degree of integration between trading economies. There are three elements to this: the importance of trade in the economy as whole, the importance of trade with particular countries and the importance of trade in particular commodities. Table 2.3 shows both how trade has increased in its importance as a part of GDP for all countries over recent years, but also how the importance of trade differs between different countries. The smaller, more open economies such as Ireland, Belgium and the Netherlands have the greatest dependence on trade, the more developed and larger economies have a lesser dependence as do the less developed economies of southern Europe, although here it is increasing rapidly. Table 2.3 also shows how much more important trade is to European countries than to the United States or Japan. This would still be true in comparison with the United States even if we excluded intra-EC trade since this accounted for 58.7 per cent of all EC trade in 1988, leaving extra-EC trade equal to 11.2 per cent of EC GDP, a reduction from around 12 per cent in the 1960s.

Table 2.4 shows in summary the pattern of trade between member states of the Community and a comparison of the change in overall importance of intra-EC trade over the past thirty years, for the EC as now constituted. All members have seen an enormous increase in the importance of such trade which has increased from 37.2 to 58.7 per cent of all EC trade, a point we shall return to in Chapter 4. This is particularly true for countries such as France and the United Kingdom which had much wider trade networks prior to this. For the United Kingdom, the transition can be related to around 1970, just prior to UK entry to the Community: growth prior to that time was relatively

Table 2.3 The importance of trade in relation to GDP, EC, United States and Japan, 1960–90.

	B	DK	D	GR	E	F	IRL	I	L	NL	P	UK	EC-12	USA	J
1961–70	44.4	28.6	19.2	9.8	10.8	13.5	35.7	13.8	81.3	43.2	23.5	20.5	19.1	5.3	9.9
1971–80	55.7	29.2	24.1	16.0	14.6	19.4	43.9	20.1	89.4	48.7	23.7	26.5	24.5	7.9	12.2
1981–90	72.2	34.9	30.0	21.5	20.3	22.6	59.1	21.4	100.1	57.8	33.2	26.6	28.5	8.2	13.2

Source: Eurostat.

Table 2.4 Trade flows between EC countries in 1988 (as percentage exports of exporter).

Importer	BL	DK	D	GR	E	F	IRL	I	NL	P	UK	EC-12
							Exporter					
BL	–	2.0	7.4	2.8	3.1	8.7	4.4	3.4	14.9	3.1	5.2	6.5
DK	0.9	–	2.0	1.0	0.6	1.0	0.8	0.8	1.7	2.2	1.4	1.4
D	19.5	17.7	–	24.3	11.1	17.3	11.2	18.1	26.6	14.7	11.6	12.3
GR	0.5	0.8	1.0	–	0.6	1.2	0.4	1.6	0.9	0.3	0.6	0.8
E	2.2	1.6	3.0	1.4	–	4.7	1.7	4.1	1.8	11.3	3.3	2.9
F	20.0	5.7	12.5	8.6	17.2	–	9.1	16.6	10.6	15.3	10.1	11.0
IRL	0.3	0.5	0.4	0.2	0.4	0.4	–	0.3	0.5	0.5	4.9	1.0
I	6.2	4.6	9.0	16.1	9.0	12.5	3.8	–	6.4	4.1	5.0	7.1
NL	14.7	4.2	8.6	3.8	4.4	5.3	7.0	3.1	–	6.0	6.8	6.7
P	0.6	0.5	0.8	0.3	5.2	0.9	0.3	1.2	0.6	–	1.0	0.9
UK	9.3	12.0	9.3	8.2	8.9	9.6	35.5	8.0	10.6	14.2	–	8.1
EC-12 1988	74.2	49.8	54.1	66.8	60.5	61.6	74.1	57.1	74.7	71.5	49.8	58.7
EC-12 1958	55.4	59.3	37.9	50.9	46.8	30.9	82.4	34.5	58.3	38.9	21.7	37.2

Source: Eurostat.

modest, but the transition from the trade pattern of a non-member to that similar to those of the other large Community countries essentially occurred over the period 1970–82.

This table also shows how the pattern of trade for all countries is dominated by relations with the single largest economy of Europe, Germany. This is the largest trade partner, for both exports and imports, for all but three countries, Ireland and Portugal, whose peripherality leads to their being dominated by a larger immediate neighbour, and Belgium which is equally dependent on trade with France and Germany. This has centralizing tendencies within the Community; for example, note how Portugal's trade with Greece, Ireland and Italy is less than those countries' average shares in EC exports, whilst the figures for France, Germany and the United Kingdom are above the average. The UK figure reflects an important historic link between Portugal and the United Kingdom. There are also asymmetries in this since Portugal's share of each of the more central country's exports is about equal to its average share of EC exports.

Table 2.5 illustrates the variations in the composition of export trade by SITC (Standard International Trade Classification) for each member state. This is a reflection of the degree of specialization in production. We can clearly pick out the more agriculturally based countries, Denmark, Greece, Ireland and the Netherlands, which specialize in agricultural and agriculture-based products. A further group is of those more specialized in the typically more technically advanced manufactures of SITC Group 7, such as Germany, France, Italy and, perhaps more surprisingly, Spain. The United Kingdom and Ireland fall a little way behind this group in specialization in this key manufacturing sector. Except for the expected lower than average importance of SITC 0 and 1 and the above average importance of SITC 3, fuels, the United Kingdom has the most average trade pattern in terms of commodities, suggesting perhaps a failure to achieve dominant comparative advantage and specialization in any one sector.

Macro trends in trade are interesting and illustrate the general conclusion that trade creation has outweighed trade diversion effects in Europe, but we shall need to look behind these to ascertain more about both sectoral and geographical patterns of trade. Such sectoral and geographical patterns are biased by remaining barriers to trade of all types and it is necessary to understand these in order to examine how patterns of trade will respond to the removal of these barriers. The principal finding here will be that of the amount of intra-industry trade occurring in the EC. Contrary to our a priori expectations about specialization according to comparative advantage, a large amount of

Table 2.5 Composition of intra-EC trade by country in 1988.

SITC group		BL	DK	D	GR	E	F	IRL	I	NL	P	UK	EC-12
						% intra-EC exports by value							
0-1	Food, drink and tobacco	11.3	31.2	6.2	26.2	15.6	16.7	26.2	7.3	20.4	6.9	7.6	12.0
2+4	Raw materials	3.4	6.8	2.5	6.6	5.8	5.8	4.8	1.8	7.6	11.3	3.0	4.1
3	Fuels	3.0	1.5	1.1	3.2	3.1	2.1	0.6	1.2	10.0	1.2	8.7	3.5
5	Chemicals	14.1	6.7	12.0	2.0	7.5	13.1	11.4	7.0	15.6	5.4	11.0	11.7
6	Manufactures by material	28.6	11.1	18.7	26.5	19.2	17.8	9.2	23.5	15.0	23.7	15.6	19.1
7	Machinery and transport equipment	27.2	21.8	46.4	2.7	39.4	36.0	32.1	35.4	17.6	19.4	32.8	34.6
8	Miscellaneous manufactures	8.5	12.5	10.2	29.9	9.0	8.2	13.7	23.2	7.9	32.1	11.2	11.5
0-9	Total	100.0	100.0	100.0	100.0	100.0	100.0	100.0	100.0	100.0	100.0	100.0	100.0

Source: Eurostat.

40   *Location, transport and trade*

trade in the EC involves an exchange of products within industry
groups rather than between them. Such cross-hauling of commodities
carries with it an implicit waste of transport resources, but it also
suggests scope for resisting excessive centralization of activity in the
Community and therefore is a key issue in our approach. We shall look
at this in more detail in Chapter 4, but first we need to make some
assessment of the determinants of competitiveness, since this will
determine both the degree of integration achieved and the scope for
further integration, both at the regional and national levels.

3

Measuring regional
competitiveness

In this chapter we turn to the nuts and bolts of the exercise of assessing the potential gains and losses from completing the internal market. In an ideal world we would simply take measures of input prices and, given existing technology, assess what should be produced where after making allowance for the costs of spatial separation. The discussion of the previous chapters has shown how far we are from such an ideal world – is there therefore anything we can say about competitiveness which is of any value?

First, it will be clear that, since technology is not given, the exercise of comparing prices in different regions is itself much more complex. We need to know about a range of prices and a range of technologies. Secondly, our understanding of the process of specialization and trade is based on the conventional notion of trade flows between countries and regions being in different products, i.e. inter-industry trade. In practice, however, most trade in Europe (over 60 per cent of trade between the larger economies) is in terms of trade within industries, intra-industry trade. Here specialization occurs in terms of quality, design or other detail specification. This also reflects the way multinational companies distribute their production around different locations to take advantage of local competitive advantages and/or to spread risks. Thirdly, we have to allow for the way regional and other spatial policy initiatives influence decisions on location and production since these are a central part of competitiveness.

Of these points, the first and the third involve ex ante observations, and we deal with them in this chapter. The second, intra-industry trade, can only be assessed and dealt with ex post, although we shall need to consider if there are any stable determinants of the relative intensity of such trade. We defer this to the next chapter where it is better considered in the context of the degree of integration between the economies of the EC.

3.1 Measuring input prices

In a simple model we shall assume three basic inputs to any production process: labour, land and capital. It is also worth while distinguishing between different levels of labour skill since the higher the skill, the more likely is labour to have similar characteristics to capital. Of these three inputs, land is spatially fixed and capital the most mobile. We should expect greater variations in the price of the less mobile factor since the lack of mobility will lead to separate markets in which prices do not equalize. Capital as the more mobile factor would be expected to behave more like a single market. That this is not necessarily true is a major factor to be accounted for.

We also need to distinguish carefully between prices and factor costs. Variations in wages or land prices, for example, do not necessarily reflect variations in unit wage or land costs to the user since differing tax and legal regimes can lead to substantial variations in actual costs. These apply not just at a national level, but often at a regional or local level. Furthermore, productivity differentials, reflecting working hours, training or the amount of capital available per worker, imply major differentials in the unit costs of labour.

A glance at the national situation (Table 3.1) shows substantial variations in hourly labour costs in industry. Using the United Kingdom as the benchmark, hourly costs vary from only 26 per cent of this level in Portugal to 160 per cent in Germany. However, since value added/employee is on average 50 per cent higher in Germany than in the United Kingdom (Table 3.2), most of this differential is removed.

It is difficult to distil evidence on regional variations into a simple form because of the wide variations in influencing factors, but useful guidance can be obtained from a comparison of adjacent regions in different member states. For this purpose we shall make a number of comparisons in this chapter between the regions of Kent and Nord-Pas de Calais. This has particular relevance because of the way these two regions are likely to be brought closer together as a result of the completion of the Channel Tunnel in 1993 as well as the Single Market (Holliday *et al.*, 1991b).

A comparison of unit labour costs in Kent and Nord-Pas de Calais (Table 3.3) reveals a difference on average of between 40 and 60 per

Table 3.1 Index of hourly labour costs in industry, 1984 (UK = 100).

	Index	Indirect costs as % of total costs
Belgium	148	24.8
Denmark	135	7.5
W. Germany	160	23.3
Greece	45	19.0
France	138	31.3
Ireland	99	15.9 (1981)
Italy	118	26.4
Luxembourg	124	16.2
Netherlands	154	26.9
Portugal	26	24.9
UK	100	16.9

Source: Eurostat.

Table 3.2 Productivity levels (value added/ employee) 1985 (US = 100).

	Total	Range
UK	42	40–66
France	65	43–79
W. Germany	65	43–92
Japan	100	37–236
US	100	100

Source: Emerson (1988).

Table 3.3 Comparison of average monthly labour costs in Kent and Nord-Pas de Calais, all employees (ECU per month).

	1981	1984	1988	1990 est.
Kent				
Wages and salaries	1 179	1 325	1 234	1 332
Total labour costs	1 356	1 524	1 419	1 532
Nord-Pas de Calais				
Wages and salaries	1 315	1 734	1 551	1 540
Total labour costs	1 841	2 428	2 171	2 156

Sources: Eurostat, OECD.

cent, with wages themselves showing a rather narrower differential of between 10 and 30 per cent. The widening which occurred in the early 1980s on the basis largely of differences in national government policy has been substantially eroded during the later 1980s.

It is more difficult to assemble evidence on land prices, and they are even more susceptible than labour to local, regional or national variations in the conditions surrounding use. Thus, density of population will affect availability and also the degree of severity of land-use controls and planning. But density of land use can also be important: hence, for example, in regions where residential land use occurs at higher density owing to the wider use of high-rise apartments, the pressure on commercial land uses and prices will be less.

There is a recursive relationship between land use and price. In regions of high specialization it becomes simpler to zone land use and hence the effective supply from a given area of land is increased.

Using our cross-border example again reveals substantial variations between Kent and Nord-Pas de Calais, but this time in the favour of Nord-Pas de Calais. Land prices may be as much as twenty times greater in parts of Kent than in Nord-Pas de Calais. Industrial rents vary by a factor of between three and ten and office rents are up to three times as much in Kent.

It is estimated, however, that taking into account differences in labour costs, land costs and local taxes, assuming other input prices remained the same, a typical small industrial plant employing about 100 people on 2800 m^2 (30,000 square feet) would be about 10 per cent cheaper to operate in Kent than in an equivalent location in Nord-Pas de Calais.

It may be thought initially that financial capital would be the least problematic input, showing little variation between regions because of its mobility. In practice, however, this is not the case. There are still substantial barriers to capital mobility between countries within the EC. Formal controls on capital movement are supposed to be in the course of removal, both as part of the creation of the Single Market and as part of the first stage of the Delors Plan towards Economic and Monetary Union. However, there are residual controls and it is a major step from removal of controls on the export of capital to the creation of a Single Market in financial services which ensures the supply of financial capital on the same terms anywhere in the Community.

The spatial impacts of financial flows are not well documented, even within countries. It is clear that one of the consequences of the movement to national banking systems is a tendency to concentrate outflows from poorer regions into richer regions. The banking system acts efficiently to transfer funds from areas of low marginal rates of return to areas of high rates. However, it is not just a question of the simple maximization of rates of return. Investment managers will also gravitate towards areas of greater dynamism, leaving those less willing to take risks in charge in the more depressed regions. Hence the effective demand for funds is also lower in these areas.

Could this situation be transferred to an EC-wide context, however? There could clearly be strong rate of return pressures for increasing centralization. However, the implicit competition between funds could reduce capital productivity and act as a brake on the centralizing tendency. Essentially the problem is that we cannot consider capital independently of the availability of other less mobile factors. In the United Kingdom, the equivalent drying up of investment opportunities in the core areas of the economy has led to an increasing search for foreign investment opportunities, both within and without the Community. Ironically as British capital seeks investment opportunities outside the United Kingdom, foreign capital has been taking advantage of the opportunities perceived within the United Kingdom. This reflects the essentially different priorities implicit in the behaviour of financial institutions in different markets.

One of the possible sources of specialization available in a single market for financial services is a specialization in types of investment by different national financial sectors. What remains to be seen is the way in which financial institutions respond to this in terms of their geographical coverage. To the extent that, for example, German industrial firms wish to make investments in Ireland and they continue to be advised and financed by German banks, there is an implicit transfer of investible funds from the customers of those German banks into Ireland. The Irish local economy thus benefits. The relationship between bank and immediate client has not changed. But does this acquired knowledge of Ireland mean that now the German banks start lending directly to Irish firms in Ireland (or indeed to firms in other member countries wishing to establish in Ireland)? This seems less likely since it requires the bank to gain specialist knowledge of new clients operating in different systems. The geographic relationship between financial institution and client seems to be likely to dominate.

On the deposit side the different practices governed by different banking regulations in different countries mean that the type of service offered and the conditions under which it is offered often vary considerably. A move to completing a single market in financial services would reduce these variations, but would this improve the availability of funds for investment in certain regions and would it change the competitive position of those regions?

It seems likely that the position of some of the more backward regions of Europe would be improved by giving the financial institutions of those regions access to both a wider range of funds and to improved banking technology. The risk in such a situation is always going to be that funds flow out rather than in, but any improvement in the efficiency of the financial system is to be welcomed.

There is one further aspect of the financial sector which does affect competitiveness – the relative quality of service given to firms trading in other national markets. This affects not just the investment potential already discussed, but transfer of funds, foreign exchange dealing and provision of insurance for goods in transit and against default by foreign suppliers or customers. This is perhaps the major area where provisions of the Second Banking Directive will be critical. However, whether this is achieved by harmonization of standards, by joint venture operations or by the expansion of the major banks into other member states remains to be seen. It is clear that this is one area where Japanese industries have had major advantages since Japanese banks have set up in most major customer countries specifically to serve their own clients in those markets.

There is a further dimension to financial integration, however, that is provided not just by free movement of capital, but by a common currency or fixed exchange rates with no exchange controls. Traditional theories of national competitiveness note that an uncompetitive country will suffer a balance of payments deficit which will put downwards pressure on its currency until the devaluation restores competitiveness. If the currency cannot move downwards then this equilibrating mechanism is not available and equilibrium can only be restored by an outflow of resources. More likely is that the equilibrium is not restored, but unemployment of the least mobile resources occurs. This argument has frequently been used to show, on the basis of continuing regional disequilibria within countries, that currency union is a bad thing for weak or uncompetitive regions.

This would be to oversimplify the situation, however. In practice, weak regions benefit from regional policy that aims specifically at imitating the consequences of a devaluation. Instead of reducing the prices of output in terms of foreign currency, it reduces their prices in terms of domestic currency by subsidizing the costs of inputs.

Both devaluation and regional subsidies provide a protection to less competitive areas, but, it can be argued, at the cost of not increasing their competitiveness. If producers know that their uncompetitiveness will be compensated, they lack incentives to become more competitive. This would not apply if all producers were simply price takers and users of standard technology. However, where they are not simply price takers and where they can use discretion in the efficiency with which they utilize inputs, there is an argument that in a Single Market with currency union, regional producers will perform more efficiently than where they are protected.

Two arguments still remain in this context, however: whether regions themselves face balance of payments constraints on their growth in a macroeconomic context and whether there is a need for some form of fiscal redistribution to allow for imbalances. Dixon and Thirlwall (1979) argued, on the basis of a model of export-led growth, that balance of payments problems will provide a constraint on growth. Export growth depends both on the composition of output (via the income elasticity of demand for a region's products) and on the price competitiveness of those goods. Further, Thirlwall (1980) argued that the constraints on growth imposed by the need to meet balance of payments difficulties will operate differentially on struggling regions.

This argument can, however, be turned around. Despite not having formal balance of payments problems, a lagging region will have imposed on it exactly the same burdens as a deficit nation – the main difference is that the absence of balance of payment statistics provides no early warning indicator of difficulties. The speed and extent with which these difficulties occur will depend on the degree of openness of the regional economy and the extent of inter-industry integration within the region.

A lagging region's difficulties are typically compounded by the extent to which its fiscal burdens increase. The same has to some extent also been true of budgetary finance within the EC. Two things happen: one is that direct tax payments tend to reduce more slowly than the reduction in growth of the tax base; the other, that indirect tax burdens rise in relative terms during a slowdown as proportionately more income is devoted to taxed consumption and less to untaxed saving. Also, to the extent that receipts from government sources depend essentially on continuing activities, where activities cease there is no basis for making payments. Hence the gap between revenue contributions and receipts widens. This impinges severely on the capacity of the competent government authority to act since it sees revenues falling, but expenditure needs rising. Most countries have in place some form of grant redistribution system which attempts an equalization of the fiscal burden, both on individuals and on the competent authorities, across the country. Since the Fontainebleau Agreement of 1984 the EC has also had a partial correction mechanism of this type in place.

Federal structures usually have a more sophisticated system enshrined in their constitutions providing for a visible means of redistribution. This would seem to lie at the heart of the matter as far as a move to a currency union in Europe is concerned. It seems vital to achieve a situation where the fiscal environment in which firms operate is not working counter to needs. It seems more effective in policy terms to ensure neutrality in fiscal pressures than having to pay out direct subsidies to firms or to unemployed resources. (See Eichengreen, 1990, for a more detailed discussion.) We shall return to this argument more fully in Chapter 7.

3.2   Regional policy instruments

Any attempt to assess competitiveness meets the problem of the use of government policy to compensate for perceived lack of competitiveness and its consequences. Hence both non-spatial industry policies and regionally specific policies cloud the true situation and upset the operation of local factor markets.

Most industry and regional policies operate on the principle of subsidizing factor prices. Within the EC, direct subsidies to labour are prohibited, but indirect subsidies through training, etc. are allowed and indeed are operated at the Community level. The main source of subsidy is capital subsidy through grants, incentives, etc. to new investment. There is also widespread use of infrastructure as a means of reducing the external costs faced by industry in assisted regions. Indeed, nearly 90 per cent of EC spending through the European Regional Development Fund has gone on infrastructure of some form. The advantage of infrastructure grants are that they appear not to offer differential assistance to individual industries which would conflict with the broad aims of the Community competition policy.

We need to distinguish four types of aid to industry: Community aid through its regional, social and agricultural funds; national regional assistance; Community policies on individual industries; and national assistance to industry.

Since its inception, the Community has recognized the need for aid to its disadvantaged regions. Initially this was operated through the agricultural fund (EAGGF) for rural regions and the Social Fund for helping the retraining, etc. of displaced workers in such industries as coal mining. Since shortly after the United Kingdom's accession to the Community, a separate regional fund, the European Regional Development Fund (ERDF), has operated to redistribute resources to the Community's problem regions. The scale of the problem can be seen in the fact that the richest region, Hamburg, had a GDP/capita five times that of the poorest, Calabria, in 1970. This ratio increased to 6.5 by 1977.

The ERDF operates on the basis of the principle of additionality. It is thus intended to increase aid to problem regions not to replace national assistance. The idea is that problem regions typically suffer from problems arising at the national level which national governments should respond to; the Community is making a contribution to the additional pressures which operating in the Common Market occasions. The Thompson Report which led to the establishing of the ERDF in 1975 recognized that there was no single set of characteristics of problem regions, and hence no single set of solutions. Some regions faced problems because of their reliance on ineffective and unproductive agriculture, others because of the decline in their traditional industries, others simply because of their peripherality (including formerly regions along the eastern frontier of West Germany). Peripherality was certainly not a necessary characteristic of a problem region in the enlarged Community; such regions as Nord-Pas de Calais in France and Hainaut in Belgium are, in fact, central in the Community.

National governments were left originally to nominate designated regions on the basis of criteria laid down by the Commission, available funds in the ERDF were allocated on a quota system according to the intensity of regional problems. On this basis Italy and the United Kingdom were to receive the major allocation of ERDF funds, but all member states had some entitlement. Since the Fund was a very small share of the EC Budget, typically less than 5 per cent, this meant only a tiny fraction (less than one-tenth of 1 per cent) of Community GDP was going to solve structural problems.

Furthermore, the quota system, which applied until the reforms introduced in 1985, prevented the EC from concentrating all the effort on the poorest regions. Most of the ERDF budget was allocated on the basis of the quota between all the member states. Generally, the size of the state's regional problems was to be reflected in the size of the quota, but this ignored the extent to which being a poor region in a rich state posed a different order of problems from those of being a poor region in a poor state. It was left to member governments to propose projects to the Commission, which then had the duty of vetting and either approving or rejecting them. Since EC approval also committed the national government to expenditure, funding to regions could fall in times of national government expenditure costs. Thus the United Kingdom was often in the position of not using up all of its quota allocation and considerable mismatches between expenditure and need arose (Armstrong, 1985). The non-quota section, which could be allocated by the Commission to address wider issues, was far too small to have any real impact.

The ERDF was also itself in potential conflict with other EC policies. Although the Guidance section of the Agriculture Fund was also supposed to assist structural change in rural areas, in practice this was a tiny amount since the Guarantee section which supported farm prices dominated expenditure and typically was transferring resources from poor agricultural regions to richer ones. Regional policy also conflicted with the Community's competition policy in so far as regional policy aid was directed at individual industries. This is why more neutral infrastructure projects dominated ERDF aid, to the extent of nearly 80 per cent of total expenditure (Table 3.4).

Recognizing these problems, the Commission repeatedly proposed from 1980 onwards a reform of the ERDF which would scrap the quota systems and concentrate more power into the Commission to enable it to focus spending on areas of greatest need. As ever, a compromise formula had to be found. Although the formal quota system was abolished, indicative ranges of expenditure were retained, along with some entitlement to assistance for every member state in a reform that became operative in 1985. By this time Greece had joined the Community and in 1986 Spain and Portugal were due to join, all three of which would clearly have strong claims to the ERDF for assistance. The Commission did manage to gain greater control over a larger section of the ERDF which it used mainly to initiate new forms of integrated programme. The intention was to demonstrate how concentrating the limited resources on a narrower geographical area could achieve much more effective results.

At the same time it was clear that completion of the Single European Market by 1992 envisaged in the White Paper of 1985 would itself have spatial implications. Whatever these were likely to be in actuality, the fear of greater centripetal concentration dominated thinking. The main cost of the 1992 programme was seen to be greater exposure of the Community's structural weaknesses. Thus a commitment to double the so-called Structural Funds of the Community was given. This required a common approach to the Agricultural Guidance, Social and Regional Development Funds. It also required a redefinition of problem regions, particularly since the success of integrated programmes showed how much tighter definitions should be used for greater success.

This time the Commission itself undertook the definition of the regions using data supplied by member countries, some of which were not previously available and not published. This was used to identify six basic objectives, as follows:

1. Lagging regions – defined as those NUTS (Nomenclature of Territorial Units for Statistics) Level II regions with a GDP per head at least 25 per cent below the EC average; up to 75 per cent

Table 3.4 ERDF allocations, 1975–89 (million ECU).

	Programmes			Projects				Studies	Total
	Community programme	National Programme of Community Interest	Total	Industry	Infra-structure	Indigenous potential	Total		
Belgium	–	45.33	45.33	42.39	134.47	1.35	178.21	2.19	225.73
Denmark	–	11.75	11.75	25.34	140.42	0.57	166.33	6.14	184.22
W. Germany	23.06	53.95	77.01	511.14	353.97	–	865.11	0.19	942.31
Greece	27.33	357.10	384.44	42.10	2,594.76	–	2,636.86	0.37	3,021.66
Spain	130.35	249.98	380.33	11.67	2,591.38	2.36	2,605.42	0.09	2,985.84
France	9.63	338.73	348.35	382.77	2,145.90	11.04	2,539.72	11.60	2,899.68
Ireland	42.54	111.44	153.97	311.19	843.86	3.70	1,158.75	1.14	1,313.86
Italy	29.27	591.43	620.69	977.49	6,949.49	0.59	7,927.57	24.06	8,572.33
Luxembourg	0	1.94	1.94	0	14.69	0	14.69	0	16.63
Netherlands	0	14.18	14.18	32.24	200.85	0.01	233.28	0.19	247.65
Portugal	51.41	124.85	176.26	–	1,269.63	1.49	1,271.12	0.57	1,447.95
United Kingdom	11.59	533.35	544.94	1,003.46	3,686.27	3.36	4,693.08	10.84	5,248.86
EC-12	325.18	2,434.03	2,759.19	3,339.97	20,290.14	24.47	24,290.14	57.38	27,106.72

Source: European Commission.

of the cost of a project and at least 50 per cent of the public
expenditure will come from the EC.
2. Declining industrial areas – defined at NUTS Level III or labour
    market areas on the basis of unemployment rates being above the
    EC average for at least three years (at least 1.25 percentage points
    higher on average), the share of industrial employment above the
    EC average and an observable fall in this industrial employment.
    Only 27 of 131 such regions are entirely eligible; grants will be to
    a maximum of 50 per cent of the cost of the project with a minimum
    of 25 per cent of public funding from the EC.
3. Measures to combat long-term unemployment, defined as those
    over 25 unemployed for more than twelve months.
4. Measures to assist young peoples' integration into the labour
    market.
5. (a) Adjustment of agricultural structures.
    (b) Rural areas – outside Objective 1 regions, with a high share of
    agricultural employment, low level of agricultural income and a
    low level of socio-economic development; similar grant arrange-
    ments apply as for Objective 2 regions.

Objectives 3 and 4 are met from the European Social Fund (ESF)
alone and are not regionally restricted, but are supposed to be
determined within the overall framework for Structural Funds. Similarly, Objective 5(a) is the sole remit of the Agricultural Fund (EAGGF).
Objectives 1 and 5(b) are met from a mixture of the ERDF, ESF and
EAGGF and Objective 2 from ERDF and ESF, but in each of these
three cases the ERDF provides most of the funds.

The fund providing the major share of funding would coordinate the
policy. A broad allocation was then made between member states on
the basis of the incidence of regions in each objective (Table 3.5). It
can be seen that the basic policy stance taken was that since it was
Objective 1, lagging regions, that needed the greatest assistance, this
limited the total assistance available to a country such as the United
Kingdom which had a high incidence of Objective 2, declining
industrial regions. Despite being allocated nearly 40 per cent of
Objective 2 funding and 25 per cent of Objectives 3 and 4 funding, the
United Kingdom is allocated less than 8 per cent of total structural
funds compared to the nearly 20 per cent of ERDF funds received
between 1975 and 1989.

One useful change, however, is the move towards a more
programme-dominated approach within which each member state has
to agree a Community Support Framework (CSF) with the Commission. This will enable the Commission to improve the coordination and
efficiency in the utilization of the funds.

Table 3.5 Structural fund allocations 1989–93 (million ECU).

	Objective 1 1989–93	Objective 2 1989–91	Objectives 3 and 4 1990–92	Objective 5 1989–93	Total
Belgium	–	195	174	33	402
Denmark	–	30	99	23	152
W. Germany	–	355	573	525	1,453
Greece	6,667	–	–	–	6,667
Spain	9,779	735	563	285	11,362
France	888	700	872	960	3,420
Ireland	3,672	–	–	–	3,672
Italy	7,443	265	585	385	8,678
Luxembourg	–	15	7	3	25
Netherlands	–	95	230	44	369
Portugal	6,958	–	–	–	6,958
United Kingdom	879	1,510	1,025	350	3,678
Total	36,286	3,900	4,128	2,607	46,835

Source: European Commission.

The total allocation of funds to regional problems rose gradually during the 1980s. Compare the total sum of nearly 43 billion ECU allocated under Objectives 1, 2 and 5 for 1989–93 with the total of 27 billion ECU from the ERDF for the whole period 1975–89. This is a direct result of the commitment to double the allocation from the Budget to Structural Funds over the transition period to the Single Market and bringing all the funds dealing with structural problems under a single heading.

However, the magnitude of the problem has also increased. This was partly because of the accession of countries such as Greece, Spain and Portugal which were poor, but also had substantial internal regional disparities, but partly because the existing poor regions of the Community had failed to make any progress against the richer regions. Even after nearly fifteen years of EC regional policy through the ERDF, GDP/capita in terms of purchasing power parity (i.e. adjusted differences in price levels) in Hamburg remained 3.1 times that in Calabria and compared to the poorest, Voreio Aigaio in Greece, the ratio was 4.59. Even Calabria had an absolute per capita income level (not adjusted for purchasing power) 2.5 times that of Voreio Aigaio. In terms of unemployment the gap is even greater: even excluding the Community's offshore territories there was an unemployment rate in the worst region (Andalucia) a massive 15.6 times that in the best (Luxembourg). However, as Table 3.6 shows, some regions have made some progress: note in particular the way in which northern Italian

Table 3.6   The community's richest and poorest regions 1970 and 1988 (index, EC = 100).

1970	EUA/head current prices		1988	ECU/head PPS
1 Hamburg D	197.5	(2)	1 Groningen NL	183.1
2 Ile de France F	167.4	(3)	2 Hamburg D	182.7
3 Bremen D	162.3	(6)	3 Ile de France F	165.6
4 Storkobenhavn DK	157.7	(11)	4 Greater London UK	164.0
5 Düsseldorf D	142.1	(18)	5 Darmstadt D	148.9
6 Oberbayern D	140.1	(8)	6 Bremen D	146.8
7 Stuttgart D	138.4	(9)	7 Lombardia I	137.3
8 Darmstadt D	138.0	(5)	8 Oberbayern D	135.1
9 Berlin (West) D	136.9	(13)	9 Stuttgart D	133.8
10 Karlsruhe D	136.5	(20)	10 Val d'Aosta I	133.8
1 Calabria I	39.4	(21)	1 Voreio Aigaio GR	39.9
2 Molise I	42.7	(43)	2 D.O.M. F	41.6
3 Basilicata I	43.0	(24)	3 Norte P	41.9
4 Sicilia I	50.4	(31)	4 Ipeiros GR	41.9
5 Puglia I	51.2	(35)	5 Alentejo P	45.9
6 Campania I	51.7	(27)	6 Algarve P	46.0
7 Abruzzi I	52.3	(66)	7 Dytiki Makedonia GR	46.7
8 Ireland IRL	52.3	(25)	8 Kriti GR	48.5
9 Sardegna I	58.4	(36)	9 Extremadura E	49.0
10 Umbria I	65.2	(101)	10 Dytiki Ellada GR	50.0

The figures in parentheses indicate the relative position of these regions in 1988 counting from either top or bottom as appropriate. Some regions are affected by changes in the level at which regions are defined, e.g. Greater London was part of South-East in 1970.

Source: European Commission.

regions have entered the top ten of EC regions whilst some of the central regions have made major gains.

This has now set the pattern of Community assistance for the next few years. It is clear that the funds available as ever are not large enough to make any major inroad on the problem in the absence of other forces redressing the imbalance in the Community. This is where close monitoring of the impacts of the Single Market will be required.

Although most aid has been given through major programmes, some regions may still be eligible for some assistance, even if not designated. Thus Article 10 of the ERDF Regulation allows for aid to urban areas which are not Objective 2 eligible (areas such as London and Marseille will benefit) and border regions can be designated under the INTER-REG programme (parts of Kent are receiving aid here, principally because neighbouring regions across the internal Community border are eligible). Furthermore, there are a substantial number of other programmes dealing either with specific problem industries, such as

RECHAR (coal), RESIDER (steel) and RENAVAL (shipbuilding), or in promoting new technologies and communications such as LEADER (for local rural development) or STAR and its successor TELEMATIQUE (for improving access to advanced telecommunications).

National governments all continue to give aid to their own regions, both as part of the additionality requirement alongside EC funds and independently. Over this the only controls which the EC has are the Treaty provisions limiting specific assistance to industry on competition grounds. Certain measures, such as the creation of Enterprise Zones, therefore require clearance by the Commission before their introduction. In many cases the aid is given to areas that do not qualify under the EC's rules, such as specific assistance under the urban programme in the United Kingdom, especially to areas in London which the Commission would not accept as designated areas. However, in this latter case the Commission has recognized the need for some assistance as noted above.

The total extent of this aid is difficult to estimate for the EC as a whole. In the United Kingdom spending on regional assistance fell markedly during the 1980s from around £1.5 billion in 1979 to less than half that figure by the end of the decade. This reflects a shift in both policy stance and emphasis. The Action for Cities programme in the United Kingdom had a budget of just over £4 billion (5.6 billion ECU) for 1990–91.

Turning to industry-specific aid we have a more complex picture. At the Community level financial aid has not typically been made because of conflicts with competition policies. However, the Community has involved itself in both the protection of specific industries from world competition and attempts at the orderly reduction of capacity in certain other industries.

The most developed case of industrial protection is in the Multi-fibre Arrangement (MFA) which aims to limit imports of textiles and clothing from the newly industrializing countries of SE Asia in particular. Since textiles are a classic regionally concentrated industry, the MFA has had important consequences for protecting certain regions in the United Kingdom, Germany and France. Voluntary export restraints (VERs) have also been used as a means of controlling imports and protecting Community industries. Whilst more used independently by member states, the EC collectively has agreed a VER on video recorders with Japan. Here the VER is essentially being used in an infant industry way. Agreement has never been reached Community-wide on the use of VERs in the automobile industry, however.

It must not be forgotten that spatially very significant sectoral effects are produced by the Common Agricultural Policy which has the effect both of an external trade protection system, subsidizing domestic producers and imposing levies on imports, and of supporting different products, and hence their regions of production, differentially. If the CAP operated essentially as a transfer mechanism from rich consumers to poor producers it might be an acceptable, if inefficient, transfer system from rich to poor regions. In practice, the differential support given to different products and the, until recently, unlimited support to production, has meant that the system actually transfers more to richer farmers in richer regions of the Community. Essentially it is the dairy and grain farms of northern Europe who have gained. Since the support system requires consumers to pay the high supported prices and since food forms a larger part of the budget of poorer people, it is the poor and hence poorer regions that contribute differentially large amounts to the system.

In other areas the Community has tried to limit the extent of wasteful subsidy to declining sectors, by trying to negotiate orderly reductions of capacity in such sectors as steel and shipbuilding whilst also using Social Fund provisions to help in the retraining and resettlement of displaced workers from the coal industry in particular. This has had limited success, but is an area where the EC should be playing a strong coordinating role by providing a more certain environment in which planning can take place.

If Community assistance to non-agricultural sectors is on a relatively modest scale this is more than made up for by national assistance to industry. Between 1981 and 1986 the level of subsidy given by member states to agriculture, industry, energy and transport grew steadily to a level of 100 billion ECU, about 3 per cent of Community GDP, almost three times the total EC Budget. Table 3.7 shows the extent of aid to manufacturing industry in this period. Italian aid actually increased fourfold in this period, whilst that in Britain reduced by a third, Italy was spending 23.8 billion ECU against the United Kingdom's 2.8 billion ECU. Generally, problem areas were greater where the public sector was larger and more difficult to control. The Commission's increasingly tough line on this in cases such as the aid to Renault and Rover is indicative of the worry.

Even this is an understatement, however, since it typically covers only national aid. Often local government gives substantial industrial aid which is difficult to identify. In Germany, for example, despite the Federal Government's generally restrained policy, the *Länder* and local authorities were spending much larger amounts. A study by Jüttemeier (1987) suggests that total aid to manufacturing industry in

Table 3.7 National aid to manufacturing (Av. 1981–86).

	% value added	ECU/worker
Italy	15.8	5,951
Greece	13.9	–
Ireland	12.3	3,741
Belgium	4.5	1,373
Netherlands	4.1	1,419
France	3.6	1,223
Luxembourg	3.5	1,079
UK	2.9	757
West Germany	2.9	940
Denmark	1.7	609
EC average	5.5	1,774

Source: EC Survey of State Aid.

Germany in 1984 was twice the size of that given by the Federal Government (see Pelkmans, 1989, for a more detailed discussion).

As already mentioned, quotas and VERs have been much more enthusiastically imposed by national governments and should be taken together. Italy, for example, has a quota on Japanese car imports, France uses a VER. Short of a quota or VER, countries can distort trade patterns effectively by manipulating either technical standards or administrative practices to make imports more difficult.

3.3 Conclusions

Knowing where and how aid operates presents us with an extremely difficult problem in determining regional competitiveness. Because of differential aids to industries one region may be a cheap location for one industry, but not for another. Increasingly, national regional aid programmes have moved from blanket subsidies to specific aids, dependent not just on precise geographical location and industry, but also on type of firm. Some policies are geared specifically at assistance to small- and medium-sized firms, such as Enterprise Zones. Others are specifically aimed at securing major inward investments into regions such as the revised *Prime d'Aménagement du Territoire* since the 1986 reforms of regional policy in France.

This complexity has shown no sign of being reduced within the Community and it seems likely to increase within the Single Market as pressures for action to cope with feared competition take hold at both local and national political levels. There is a great danger that whatever the real competitive situation, any chance of really allowing resources to optimize their spatial allocation within the Community seems doomed to failure in the light of political expediency. This is a self-fulfilling prophecy – the distortions created by market intervention at the local/regional/national level have a tendency to produce the expected consequences and hence to be used as a justification for further protection. We thus have to be extremely careful in making assessments of the competitive situation in any one region just on the basis of input prices or unit costs. Typically assessments of optimal location will have to be made on the basis of full information about the specific investment being contemplated, since it is only at this level that accurate information on both input prices and regional aid can be incorporated. The potential gains from a single market require a greater freedom of movement of resources, free from local policy interference, and not just opening up the markets in goods, to stand any chance of being realized.

4

The existing order
Integration to 1991

In Chapter 2 we made an initial assessment of the extent to which trade patterns were related to location and transport. In Chapter 3 we assessed the factors that determine the competitiveness of different regions. Now we need to make an overall assessment of the extent to which integration has occurred in the Community up to 1991. The first part of this involves a more detailed look at the process of trade integration.

4.1 Trade and integration

Much of the evidence on trade and integration is of the broad macro type which we examined in Chapters 1 and 2, essentially the measurement of the extent to which trade creation within the EC has dominated trade diversion. One of the problems with this approach is that it tends to ignore the spatial dimension of the EC itself.

Simple assessments of this spatial dimension have used the economic potential approach initially developed by Clark *et al.* (1969), but more recently reworked by Keeble *et al.* (1982a, 1988). Economic potential is essentially the assessment of market area size for any location on the basis of the incomes of potential markets deflated by their costs of access. Thus if a region j has a regional income of Y_j and the costs of transport between region i and region j are c_{ij}, then the economic potential of region i is given by adding up the incomes of all other regions, j, deflated by the cost of the intervening distance c_{ij}:

$$P_i = \Sigma_j \frac{Y_j}{f(c_{ij})}$$

The transport cost element $f(c_{ij})$ comprises direct and indirect transport costs (such as congestion, waiting time, etc.) and also the costs of crossing frontiers which included customs checks and tariffs.

Thus Clark and Keeble were both able to show (a) predicted absolute changes in economic potential arising from the removal of tariffs as the Customs Union provisions of the Treaty of Rome became operative and as the EC was enlarged, and (b) the distribution of such gains between different parts of the Community. Keeble *et al.* (1982b) also demonstrated the effect which a major change in transport infrastructure could have, in the case of a Channel Tunnel.

Interpreting the results of these potential studies is a little difficult. Two basic measures of changes through time are needed: the change in the absolute level of potential and the change in the regional potential relative to the highest potential in the EC. Thus Keeble *et al.* (1982a) have demonstrated how there was a generally downwards trend in the latter measure for peripheral regions in the original six members of the EC as the process of integration and accessibility improvement favoured the more central regions. Hence the index for Calabria fell from 12.7 per cent of the maximum to 10.9 per cent between 1965 and 1973, and that for Bretagne from 28.3 per cent to 25.4 per cent. The 1973 enlargement increased the absolute potential of these regions by 15 and 17 per cent respectively, but much larger percentage increases were gained by the new peripheral regions, e.g. 40 per cent for Scotland and 76 per cent for the Danish region of Vest for Storebaelt. Whilst smaller percentage increases were identified for more central regions, 6 per cent for the highest potential region of Rheinhessen-Pfalz, 7 per cent for Ile de France, these of course represented much larger absolute increases which constituted a widening of the absolute regional differential. The estimated changes over the period of integration of the three new 1973 entrants also favour the more central regions with the relative position of the more peripheral regions generally slipping whilst that of the central regions was maintained or increased, although the changes in this period were less marked than for the earlier periods given the rather lesser impact of tariff changes.

The conclusion clearly to be drawn is that the process of integration through removing barriers to trade engenders a widening of regional disparities and hence a lesser degree of overall cohesion. There is an important caveat in the study's findings, however: they are based on the assumption that increases in accessibility are revealed in reduced costs of distance and consequent decisions on investment. They do not have a strong foundation in a full economic model since they only draw inferences from changes in market areas, and not from any complementary changes in supply side factors such as factor markets or technology.

A more comprehensive evaluation of this question can be drawn from a series of studies conducted by Peschel and her associates (e.g. Peschel, 1981, 1982, 1985, 1990; Bröcker and Peschel, 1988; Bröcker, 1988). These are of particular interest because they focus on the changes in the key core economy of Germany. There are three principal stages in the development of this work: first, to identify changes in the aggregate patterns of trade; secondly, to examine how regional economic development is affected by a period of trade integration; and thirdly, to focus on the differences between regions showing different patterns of integration.

The first stage of these studies uses bilateral trade flows between a set of Organization for Economic Cooperation and Development (OECD) countries over a long period from 1900 to 1981, but with a specific focus on changes from 1955 to 1981 covering the period of trade integration within the EC. These flows are normalized to overcome the problem of differing volumes to give what is in effect a set of measures of the intensity of trade relationships between each pair of countries. These measures are taken as indicative of the strength of interdependence between the economies and hence as a measure of their degree of integration. Increases in this measure for one pair of countries will imply a reduction in the value of the index for the relationship between each of those countries and certain other countries. Thus the value of the index expresses a measure of changing trade preferences through time.

However, the principal interest is not just in these bilateral flows, but in the way which these can be assembled to give an indication of multilateral trade connections by which certain sets of countries appear to be more bound together than other sets, either on a hierarchical or overlapping basis. These clusters of countries are identified by finding the critical value of the smallest (normalized) bilateral flow in the set, the weakest link in the chain: this provides a measure of the degree of integration in the cluster. Peschel (1985) demonstrates the extraordinary stability of the trading patterns over the very long term from 1900 to 1975 except for the inter-war period. These patterns seem to reflect two sets of influences: distance and political factors.

Looking just at the period since 1955 the emergence and strengthening of the EC as a trade block can be seen quite clearly. Within the original six, the Benelux countries obviously show the dominant clustering with around 25 per cent of their trade as a critical value. France, Italy and Switzerland provide another cluster at a rather lower level of integration, but with the non-EC members being gradually loosened away from the others through time into stronger links with Austria and other southern European non-members. West Germany displays the most interesting pattern with a relatively low degree of integration initially reflecting its earlier reliance on its natural markets in eastern Europe, then becoming linked with the more southerly members before becoming more firmly linked to its closest neighbours, the Benelux countries. The United Kingdom, despite the rapid growth of its EC trade throughout the period, remains much more firmly linked with the United States and the Scandinavian countries. This is especially seen with the use of an extended data set of more countries for the later periods when the United Kingdom's traditional world-wide trade flows show it to be integrated at only a relatively low critical value (Fig. 4.1).

This pattern is quite consistent with earlier findings on the role of distance. Giersch (1949) demonstrated that distance did appear to explain a considerable part of the observed variations in inter-country trade flows, with the exception of the case of the United Kingdom. Here, Giersch argued that the relative cheapness of sea transport led to a lesser concern with transport costs and that this was reflected in the prevailing analyses of trade which were content to assume that countries could be treated as points. Beckerman (1956) too identified that distance assumed a rather different significance for different countries. In a study which measured the rank correlation between distance and flows of imports and exports for European countries between 1938 and 1953, Beckerman showed that the association was strongest for small economies such as Belgium, that there was a generally downwards trend in the degree of association and that the United Kingdom had a generally lower level of association than other countries. He also identified a rather different pattern of German trade which led to his presenting German results separately for a case including and excluding trade with Turkey and Greece.

To try to capture the specific effect of distance in more detail, Bröcker (1980; and see Peschel, 1981) estimated the implicit deterrence effect observed in intra-EC interregional trade flows for fifty-seven regions of the original six member states. This implied a much lower level of flow across national borders than would be expected for given distances, but with rather different patterns in different directions (Table 4.1).

The simplest interpretation of this is to suggest that on average each internal border of the EC represents a cost equivalent to the transport costs associated with a road distance of 375 km, that for Franco-German trade implies a barrier equivalent to as much as 586 km, whereas for Belgian–Italian trade it is as low as 39 km. This cost is additional to the actual costs of distance. Note that trade with Germany involves on average rather higher costs than this average, trade with Italy rather lower costs. This is consistent with the rather greater integration resulting from the orientation of growing Italian

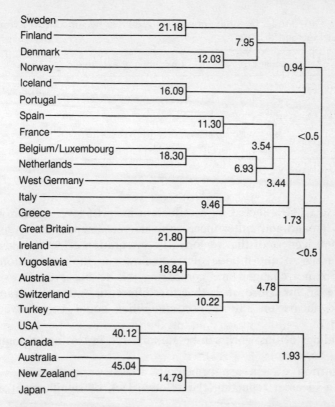

Figure 4.1 Patterns of trade integration for OECD countries, 1981. (*Source:* Peschel, 1985.)

trade with the rest of the EC, whilst Germany, despite its domination of overall trade patterns, was less integrated than would at first appear. This is claimed by Peschel (1981) to demonstrate that distance as such is less important than political and other impediments to trade, thus providing a counter view to the potential model which was not based on actual trade flows.

To substantiate this thesis further it is helpful to look at the results of a detailed study of the process of integration in the regions of the Federal Republic of Germany and the Scandinavian countries (Bröcker and Peschel, 1988). This added the further disaggregation into industrial sectors so that the differential supply and demand conditions in each sector could be allowed for. The choice of countries enabled consideration of the separate development trends of the EEC and EFTA in the period up to 1970. This study made an attempt to identify regional demand and supply functions for the various sectors and to

Table 4.1 Estimated impediments to trade between EC-6 countries (equivalent km road distances).

	Germany	Belgium	Luxembourg	Netherlands	France	Italy
W. Germany	0					
Belgium	431	0				
Luxembourg	376	−16	0			
Netherlands	341	123	566	0		
France	586	208	226	419	0	
Italy	539	39	182	36	440	0

Source: Peschel (1981).

allow these to be affected by a reduction in tariff levels which would increase demand and either increase or decrease supply depending on the competitiveness of that region. The integration effect is calculated by estimating an anti-monde of trade flows on the assumption that tariffs were not changed and comparing this to observed flows. The advantage of this approach is that the differential effects of transport costs and tariffs on different commodities could be allowed for specifically.

The findings of this work can be summarized in two main points:

1. Integration effects are principally industry-specific rather than region-specific, reflecting the relative lack of significance of distance.
2. At neither individual industry nor aggregate levels is there a bias towards regions in a particular location: sometimes peripheral regions suffer at the expense of more central regions, but sometimes they may gain. For example in Sweden the gains were usually felt by the less agglomerated regions and the agglomeration nearest to the core of Europe, the Malmö region, fared relatively badly. In Germany there was a balance between gainers and losers, although it was here generally the more agglomerated regions that gained most.

A more detailed study of fifty-eight German regions compared actual EC-related trade flows with hypothetical trade flows for those regions estimated on the basis of the development of their trade with EFTA regions for the 1960–72 period (Peschel, 1982). This confirmed the gains of the more agglomerated regions and that the biggest gains were felt by those regions closer to the centre of the EC. However, the study did not suggest that this was at the expense of more peripheral German regions – and it must be remembered that some German regions were extremely peripheral to the EC at this time, namely those on the border between the FRG and the former GDR. It also suggested that the regions closer to the centre of the EC benefited less than might have been expected on the basis of their existing industrial structure and trade patterns.

To explore this finding further, Peschel and Bröcker (1988) (see Peschel, 1989, for a summary) examined the regional pattern of manufacturing employment change for eighty-eight employment zones of the FRG for the period 1970–87. Generally, this showed that faster growth and less decline took place in newer industrial areas than in the traditional old industrial areas, that peripheral and rural areas grew generally faster than large agglomerations, and that districts in the south grew faster than in the north. This set of findings is unsurprising to British observers who had generally come to the same conclusions (Fothergill and Gudgin, 1982; Begg and Moore, 1987). The major difference, however, is that from the UK perspective it was easy to draw the conclusion that a process of centralization within the EC was draining industrial activity southwards in the United Kingdom towards some core area of activity in the EC. The removal of barriers such as the Channel by completion of the Channel Tunnel, which possibly kept up import costs more than they did export costs and thus acted as equivalent to a tariff barrier (equal to about 130 km of road distance according to Keeble *et al.*, 1982b), would only accelerate this process. Such a view seems to underlie the more pessimistic views of UK prospects in an integrated European economy (e.g. Cutler *et al.*, 1989). Bröcker and Peschel's work has demonstrated that this process is repeated in other EC countries in a way which is not centralizing in any overall sense.

Vickerman (1987, 1991b) has explored this theme in the specific context of the Channel Tunnel and the impact on the nearby regions in the United Kingdom, France and Belgium. This has noted the extent to which the lack of regional development in Belgium is itself contradictory to any expectations of centralizing development, but argues that the main problem with new transport corridors is that they act as closed tubes of communication, only bringing together major nodes, but potentially leaving deserts of inadequate economic development between. There is little evidence of interest in industrial relocation in these regions, despite considerable investment in new infrastructure and the high profile of the Channel Tunnel, suggesting that there is little sign of any change in this situation.

Thus far we have looked at trade as the main indicator of the process of integration, consistently with the general presumption of trade creation as the main consequence of the removal of trade barriers. However, this tends to assume a maintenance or even a reinforcement of the comparative advantage basis of specialization into inter-industry trade. That this has not occurred is the subject of the next section, but this will require us to think more fully about the convergence of the process of production itself.

4.2   Intra-industry trade and integration

Trade theory has traditionally concentrated on the process of specialization according to relative factor abundance within the so-called Heckscher–Ohlin–Samuelson framework. Such a theory would predict that trade within a trading block would tend to be dominated by flows of goods between countries which represented their specialization in different industries. The export of capital-intensive goods from capital-rich countries and of labour-intensive goods from labour-rich countries would work towards the equalizing of factor rewards in different countries as part of the process of convergence. Indeed, the initial tests of convergence within the EC were made on the basis of such a framework (Tovias, 1982; Gremmen, 1985). These were not convincingly conclusive because of the problems of both measurement and assumption involved. This was at least partly caused by the lack of variation in capital intensity of the original members of the EC.

The major feature of the growth of EC trade between essentially like countries has been of the growth of trade in similar products. Such cross-hauling of goods appears initially to be essentially inefficient, since it involves the incurring of higher transport costs, whilst potentially preventing the enjoyment of scale economies. However, various authors have argued that such trade emanates from the search for greater product diversity which confers benefits of greater choice and variety on consumers (Dixit and Stiglitz, 1977; Lancaster, 1979). This was consistent with a view that the perfectly competitive firm assumption of the Heckscher–Ohlin model was less appropriate than one of monopolistic competition, but nevertheless a monopolistically competitive world for which an optimal equilibrium state could be identified.

In a useful review Greenaway and Milner (1987) identify that intra-industry trade is associated with imperfectly competitive product markets where consumers have diverse preferences and the production function is subject to increasing returns to scale and/or the markets can be segmented. Whilst it is intuitively obvious that certain markets are likely to be dominated by such trade, what is less clear, until placed in a general equilibrium framework, is that both inter- and intra-industry trade can co-exist – and given that capital intensities may vary between optimal production techniques for differentiated products, initial endowments of factors may still be important.

One of the principal difficulties is of measuring intra-industry trade satisfactorily – the principal problem is clearly in deciding what constitutes an industry, but, since the essential principal of measurement is to identify significant two-way flows in a given product, there are also problems caused by aggregate trade imbalances. A basic index of intra-industry trade (IIT) adjusts for these imbalances in total trade and can be expressed for trade in product i between countries j and k as:

$$\text{IIT}_{jki} = 1 - \frac{|(X_{jki}/X_{jk}) - M_{jki}/M_{jk})|}{(X_{jki}/X_{jk}) + (M_{jki}/M_{jk})}$$

where X_{jki} represents exports of i from j to k and X_{jk} total exports from j to k. Similarly, M_{jki} represents imports of i from j to k and M_{jk} total imports from j to k. This index will take values between 0 and 1, increasing as intra-industry trade increases.

Table 4.2 shows the extent of intra-industry trade within the EC as measured by Neven (1989). This shows in particular the greater concentration of such trade in the dealings of the more advanced northern countries of the community, whilst dealings between the southern countries show much less intra-industry trade, as do dealings between the north and south, where trade would appear to be based on more conventional inter-industry comparative advantage criteria.

It can be noted here that the United Kingdom, which is often seen

Table 4.2 Average intra-industry trade indices (%).

	UK	D	B	F	NL	I	DK	E	IRL	P	GR
UK		73	73	79	77	64	63	57	70	40	41
D	73		74	74	63	58	71	58	59	36	35
B	73	74		72	77	54	55	59	50	40	36
F	79	74	72		63	63	50	63	48	39	37
NL	77	63	77	63		41	67	53	52	39	44
I	64	58	54	63	41		46	60	47	47	31
DK	63	71	55	50	67	46		39	55	29	28
E	57	58	59	63	53	60	39		40	46	19
IRL	70	59	50	48	52	47	55	40		25	25
P	40	36	40	39	39	47	29	46	25		31
GR	41	35	36	37	44	31	28	19	25	31	

Source: Neven (1989).

as being less integrated than other countries, has some of the consistently highest rates of intra-industry trade. There is also a stronger orientation to some economies, the traditional trade partners of Ireland, the Netherlands and, to a lesser extent, Denmark, but also the United Kingdom has the highest levels of intra-industry trade for trade with both France and Italy. Other notable examples are the strength of the Franco-German trade axis in similar goods and the degree of integration of the Benelux economies.

Balassa and Bauwens (1988) have attempted to explain the value of this index for intra-European trade on the basis of two sets of variables representing the characteristics of the countries and of the industries. On the former it is hypothesized that the growth of intra-industry trade represents consumers' increasing preference for variety and product differentiation and hence such trade will increase with GDP per capita, but also with similarities in the size and income levels of pairs of countries. Size is important because it allows the achievement of scale economies despite the degree of product differentiation. The relative degree of orientation of the economy towards trade would also affect the degree of potential for participating in intra-industry trade. It is also hypothesized that the distance between countries will reduce the importance of such trade whereas common cultural ties, e.g., of language, will increase it. Industry characteristics are represented by measures of scale economies, which *ceteris paribus* would reduce the scope for intra-industry trade, of product differentiation (measured by variation in the unit value of exports), of marketing costs, as a further measure of product differentiation, and of the degree of industrial concentration which would also tend to increase product standardization and reduce intra-industry trade.

Empirical testing of such a model, based on 152 product categories for trade between eighteen European countries in 1971, produced the hypothesized results with highly significant coefficients with the expected signs for income, size, inequality, trade orientation, distance and product differentiation. Other particularly significant determinants were the existence of a common border, common language (especially English) and the existence of scale economies and industrial concentration. Interestingly, the two dummy variables representing membership of the two trade groups, the EC and EFTA, were positive but rather less significant, especially the former.

Balassa and Bauwens also introduced the determinants of inter-industry trade as measured by the relative physical and human capital endowments of each country, adjusted by the intensity of factor use in the production of each commodity. A separate test of just inter-industry trade showed that these variables had the expected positive signs, indicating trade between European countries observing the comparative advantage hypothesis. Putting the two sets of variables together confirmed all the expected hypotheses; indeed, only the common French language variable was insignificant and under the combined specification, membership of the EC, and especially of EFTA, became highly significant.

Trends in such trade patterns have been explored by Jacquemin and Sapir (1988). Using a set of variables representing determinants of inter-industry (factor endowments) and intra-industry (scale economies and product differentiation) trade, plus measures of trade barriers and industry growth, they set out to explain the share of EC imports in the total imports to France, FRG, Italy and the United Kingdom in 1973 and 1983 on the basis of disaggregated industry data. The results tend to confirm those of Balassa and Bauwens in identifying both inter- and intra-industry effects as determinants of intra-EC trade patterns, with some evidence that the latter are becoming more significant through time in terms of the degree of product differentiation. These EC countries show a continuing and increasing inability to supply demands in fast-growing demand areas through time, however. The Common External Tariff had a roughly stable effect through time, increasing intra-EC trade, but the Common Agricultural Policy appears to have increased its significance as a determinant of such trade creation. The peculiar position of the United Kingdom as a new entrant in 1973 was picked up by use of a dummy variable for the United Kingdom which had a negative effect on intra-EC trade, but one which reduced substantially in significance by 1983. Generally, the results indicate support for the hypothesis of convergence through trade.

Globerman and Dean (1990) have suggested that the growth of intra-industry trade stabilized in the 1980s, although Greenaway and Hine (1991) suggest that the reduction in its growth may have been less pronounced and occurred rather later. Greenaway and Hine also suggest that the move towards greater integration in the Single Market may change the nature of this convergence of trade patterns somewhat as there is a search for gains from further inter-industry specialization.

4.3   Integration in the production process

The evidence from trade data clearly points to a process of convergence as both intra-EC trade and, within the total, intra-industry trade increase reflecting a growing similarity in patterns of demand and in patterns of production. This process of convergence should also be identifiable in terms of the way products are produced in the community. Two processes are at work here. One is the movement of factors of production between member states in response to differences in productivity which would reduce the differences in factor endowment. The second is that the increase in competition between producers should lead to a convergence in technology. This will be reinforced by the relocation of manufacturers between countries, or the setting up of branch plants as a means of exploiting remaining differences in the costs of production or of reducing transport costs.

One way of examining such trends is through the input–output tables of the EC. These measure the flows of goods between industries and the input requirements of each industry in terms of its demands for the outputs of others. Ideally such tables could be joined together to give a complete picture of both intra- and inter-country inter-industry flows. This would demonstrate both differences in technology between countries in their relative use of different inputs and the sectoral demands for trade flows into each country. A major difficulty in this, however, is the degree of inconsistency between the classifications used in each country's input–output tables, which typically means that only relatively aggregated tables can be joined together in a consistent way.

It has also been discovered that there are major inconsistencies in the aggregates when these are added up. In theory we should expect the sums of intra-EC exports to equal the sums of intra-EC imports, but national input–output tables tend not to disaggregate trade flows by their origin and destination so we need to add in trade data, usually collected on a different basis, to allow for this. Schilderinck (1984) attempted to reconcile these differences between the export and import flows in terms of a so-called 'expenditure balance' for each commodity. However, in some cases these balances are extremely large, both in absolute terms (frequently in billions of ECU) and as a proportion of the estimated export flows (more than 100 per cent). There is no systematic bias to under- or over-recording, although in some sectors the balances are typically positive (agriculture and services) and in others typically negative (energy and manufacturing). Recently, Boomsma *et al.* (1991) have shown that the sources of error come from discrepancies in information on prices and volumes in both input–output and trade data.

Table 4.3 shows a simple comparison of the technical coefficients (i.e. the coefficients that measure the input required from each sector per unit of final output of a given sector) for the manufacturing sector in the eight EC countries for which there exist 1980 input–output

Table 4.3 Input–output coefficients for manufacturing, 1980.

Supplying sector	DK	D	E	F	I	NL	P	UK
Agriculture	0.17	0.54	0.11	0.09	0.07	0.13	0.16	0.06
Fuel and power	0.03	0.04	0.04	0.04	0.04	0.07	0.05	0.05
Manufacturing	0.32	0.40	0.37	0.32	0.41	0.40	0.38	0.40
Construction	0.004	0.001	0.004	0.004	0.003	0.01	0.002	0.001
Market services	0.11	0.13	0.10	0.12	0.09	0.09	0.08	0.14
Total intermediate inputs	0.62	0.63	0.62	0.58	0.65	0.69	0.68	0.65
Wages, salaries	0.26	0.27	0.17	–	–	0.18	0.19	0.24
Operating surplus	0.09	0.05	0.14	–	–	0.03	0.13	0.06
Consumption of fixed capital	–	0.04	–	–	–	0.04	–	–
Gross value added	0.38	0.38	0.37	0.43	0.35	0.30	0.32	0.35
Total resources	1.00	1.00	1.00	1.00	1.00	1.00	1.00	1.00
Of which imports	0.45	0.20	0.14	0.24	0.20	0.58	0.29	0.28

– figure not available for this element; the scope for error in the estimates means that the individual elements do not sum to the totals in all cases. The figures for Spain are estimates due to the lack of total output figures. The figures for the UK relate to 1979, those for all other countries to 1980. Tables were not available for Belgium, Luxembourg, Ireland or Greece.

Source: Eurostat (1991).

tables (Eurostat, 1986). These are intended, however, only as a first indication of the degree of difference and similarity in production technologies in the various countries, and should be treated with caution.

One or two elements can be identified in this table which are worthy of comment. We can note how the import component of the manufacturing sector is higher for the smaller economies such as Denmark and the Netherlands and somewhat higher for Portugal and the United Kingdom than for the other four larger economies. The contribution of value added is also lower for those countries with the highest import coefficient. Detailed estimates of primary inputs are not available for all the economies, but we can note the tendency for wages and salaries to be lower in the poorer countries, Spain and Portugal, although also in the Netherlands, and for operating surpluses to be rather higher in these countries. The latter would be consistent with a generally lower marginal product of capital in these countries, requiring a compensating rise in profit levels to attract necessary capital. We can also note how the technical coefficients vary somewhat; for example, the higher coefficients on agricultural inputs in Portugal and Denmark reflect the structure of manufacturing with more emphasis on food products in these economies. In the Netherlands there is an exceptionally high contribution of construction, which, coupled with that for agriculture, gives the highest value for intermediate inputs. The use of marketed services as an input to manufacturing was somewhat higher in the United Kingdom, Germany and France than in the other economies.

Over time there is some tentative evidence of a narrowing of the variations in coefficients between the six countries for which data are available. Table 4.4 presents the standard deviations of the coefficients across the six for aggregate manufacturing for 1975 and 1980. With the exception of construction, these show a reduction, although this appears to be primarily driven by a convergence between the UK and German figures. Further work is clearly needed on the evidence on production technologies.

Our conclusions from this section have to be rather tentative, the data are imperfect and rather difficult to distil into simple comparisons. It suggests that there are substantial divergences in technology between EC countries, and that the evidence of convergence is rather weak. However, this is quite consistent with the trade evidence in that we should expect countries to continue to use differing technologies to reflect both their differing resource endowments and factor prices, and their emphasis on product differentiation.

Table 4.4 Variations in technical coefficients for manufacturing 1975 and 1980.

	Standard deviation of coefficients	
	1975	1980
Agriculture	12.00	10.24
Fuel and power	14.30	9.90
Manufacturing	31.36	30.88
Construction	7.08	9.23
Market services	12.16	7.29
Total intermediate inputs	27.73	25.28
Gross value added	25.63	22.22

4.4 Overall convergence in the EC

Thus far we have been dealing with indicators of convergence which suggest changes in welfare. We conclude this discussion with a look at some more direct measures of convergence: those that result from the changing patterns of trade and production on which we have so far focused – namely prices and income levels. If we had a completely integrated common market with free movement of all goods, services and resources, then we should expect the prices of these to converge. As such prices converge, reflecting converging marginal factor productivity and optimal allocation of resources, per capita incomes should also converge.

We have referred above to the difficulties involved in examining factor prices as a measure of such convergence because of the difficulties of controlling for variations in factor quality. We turn now to a consideration of the prices for commodities and services. Table 4.5 summarizes some of the evidence from Emerson (1988) on prices. This is shown for most sectors in terms both of prices net of taxes and including taxes. Clearly in most cases there is a greater divergence when taxes are included, but this does have relevance for the domestic markets of those countries in terms of the way it impacts on consumers' relative final demands and hence on market conditions in that sector. This is particularly true of those products subject to excise duties such as alcohol and tobacco.

The interesting features of this table are the increase in divergence during the 1970s, followed by some convergence in the 1980s; the fact

Table 4.5 Price dispersion in the EC-9 by product group.[1]

Product group	Without taxes			Taxes included		
	1975	1980	1985	1975	1980	1985
1 Total consumer goods	–	–	–	22.7	23.9	22.2
A Consumer goods, excluding energy and services	16.5	17.1	15.1	20.4	20.9	19.4
1.1 Food	16.3	15.2	14.3	19.2	18.0	17.3
1.2 Food products subject to excise duty	18.9	21.1	17.0	31.3	38.3	32.6
1.3 Textiles, clothing, footwear	13.6	16.3	12.8	15.8	17.7	13.5
1.4 Durable goods	12.4	13.9	12.2	17.6	17.6	17.4
1.5 Other manufactures	21.3	21.3	19.3	21.7	19.9	20.0
B Energy	–	–	10.4	20.4	21.9	15.4
C Services	–	–	–	27.3	29.1	27.2
2 Equipment goods[2]	13.6	13.7	12.4			

[1]Coefficient of variation.
[2]Prices net of deductible VAT.
Source: Emerson (1988), Table 7.1.1.

that food was not different from the average for consumer goods despite the existence of the Common Agricultural Policy; that energy and services had rather higher levels of divergence than other consumer goods except for those subject to excise duty, although there was a relatively strong convergence in the 1980s in energy; but that price divergences were generally relatively smaller in equipment (intermediate) goods than for final consumption.

Clearly, however, there was a relatively low degree of convergence in prices in the Community by the mid-1980s, reflecting a lack of achievement of a genuine Single Market in products. This is of course one of the principal factors lying behind the push towards the Single Market in the 1980s.

This reflects a lack of integration in individual markets. A measure of overall integration at the more macro level is provided by evidence on comparative rates of inflation, and on the indicators for the financial markets. This is particularly true of the 1980s because of the discipline of the exchange rate mechanism (ERM) of the European Monetary System (EMS), introduced in 1979 and of which all EC countries except the United Kingdom, Greece, Spain and Portugal became members (although Spain joined in June 1989 and the United Kingdom joined right at the end of the period in October 1990). EMS implied a need to secure monetary convergence whilst allowing the weaker countries to gain credibility in their monetary policy from the stronger, Germany in particular. Table 4.6 examines the behaviour of consumer prices. These do show some evidence of convergence, especially in comparison with what was happening to those countries outside the ERM. Thus although the coefficient of variation of inflation rates rose on average between the 1970s and 1980s for those countries which entered ERM in 1979, it remained fairly stable during the 1980s, whereas the non-ERM countries showed a more substantial rise, greater volatility and even a slight trend upwards during the 1980s. Individual countries outside the ERM, the United Kingdom in particular, showed the most dramatic movement towards convergence, but it is clear that the ERM countries did experience a more stable environment than those outside. Using unit labour costs as another indicator driven by ERM membership suggests rather less convergence. Without the possibility of adjusting competitiveness through exchange rate adjustments, except in the periodic realignments of ERM, members should be forced to curb inflationary wage settlements and seek productivity improvements. As Table 4.7 shows, the convergence was less marked than in non-ERM countries up to 1985, but the increasing discipline of ERM since then, especially on France and Italy, suggests an important increase in the convergence process.

Table 4.6 Movement of consumer price indices: ERM and non-ERM countries (1974–90).

	Average 1974–8	Average 1979–85	1986	1987	1988	1989	1990	Average 1986–90
Germany	4.7	4.1	−0.2	0.8	1.3	3.2	2.8	1.6
France	10.7	10.3	2.9	3.3	3.0	3.3	3.4	3.2
Italy	16.4	14.9	5.7	5.0	4.8	6.0	6.1	5.5
UK	16.1	9.6	4.4	3.9	5.0	6.1	7.0	5.3
ERM members								
Arithmetic average	10.7	8.9	2.2	2.4	2.7	3.9	3.8	2.9
Standard deviation	3.8	3.9	2.0	1.7	1.4	1.1	1.5	1.3
Coefficient of variation	0.35	0.43	0.91	0.71	0.53	0.28	0.39	0.45
Non-ERM members								
Arithmetic average	14.1	12.1						
Standard deviation	8.2	11.1						
Coefficient of variation	0.58	0.87						

Sources: Ungerer *et al.* (1986); *European Economy*, No. 46, Dec. 1990.

Table 4.7 Movement of unit labour costs; ERM and non-ERM countries (1974–90).

	Average 1974–8	Average 1979–85	1986	1987	1988	1989	1990	Average 1986–90
Germany	6.0	2.5	2.5	2.1	0.1	0.9	2.8	1.7
France	10.9	7.9	2.3	1.9	1.3	2.4	4.1	2.4
Italy	17.9	11.5	5.5	6.8	6.1	6.0	7.1	6.3
UK	18.4	8.2	4.1	3.6	6.3	9.0	10.9	6.8
ERM members								
Arithmetic average	9.8	5.0	3.6	3.6	1.7	1.2	4.1	2.8
Standard deviation	4.0	3.7	1.3	2.9	2.3	2.4	2.0	1.7
Coefficient of variation	0.41	0.74	0.37	0.81	1.33	2.00	0.48	0.61
Non-ERM members								
Arithmetic average	10.1	3.9						
Standard deviation	4.5	3.0						
Coefficient of variation	0.44	0.77						

Sources: Ungerer *et al.* (1986); *European Economy*, No. 46, Dec. 1990.

A further indicator of increasing stability has also been taken to be the reduced frequency of realignments within ERM, implying both a greater familiarity with the system as a framework for policy and a greater convergence between the behaviour of the members' economies (Table 4.8). Finally the behaviour of monetary aggregates

Table 4.8 Realignments of ERM 1979–90.

Date of realignment	Currencies changed and realignment relative to central rate (%)
24 Sept. 1979	Germany (+2.0), Denmark (−2.9)
11 Nov. 1979	Denmark (−4.8)
22 March 1981	Italy (−6.0)
5 Oct. 1981	Germany (−5.5), France (−3.0), Netherlands (−5.5), Italy (−3.0)
22 Feb. 1982	Belgium (−8.5), Luxembourg (−8.5), Denmark (−3.0)
14 June 1982	Germany (+4.25), France (−5.75), Netherlands (+4.25), Italy (+2.75)
21 March 1983	Germany (+5.5), France (−2.50), Netherlands (+3.5), Belgium (+1.5), Luxembourg (+1.5), Italy (−2.5), Denmark (+2.5), Ireland (−3.5)
20 July 1985	Germany (+2.0), France (+2.0), Netherlands (+2.0), Belgium (+2.0), Luxembourg (+2.0), Italy (−6.0), Denmark (+2.0), Ireland (+2.0)
7 Apr. 1986	Germany (+3.0), France (−3.0), Netherlands (+3.0), Belgium (+1.0), Luxembourg (+1.0), Denmark (+1.0)
4 Aug. 1986	Ireland (−8.0)
12 Jan. 1987	Germany (+3.0), Netherlands (+3.0), Belgium (+2.0), Luxembourg (+2.0)
8 Jan. 1990	Italy (−3.7)

themselves is an indicator of convergence in both overall economic performance and in economic policy making (Table 4.9). Perhaps this shows the clearest evidence of convergence within that group of countries belonging to the ERM.

If there is convergence in operation then we should expect to see over the long run a move towards greater cohesion in the economies of the EC. Table 4.10 presents some data on per capita GDP, measuring both regional and national disparities. One of the concerns we have highlighted in earlier chapters is the extent to which the process of national convergence may emphasize the existing regional disparities in member countries. Clearly if there is to be real integration in the EC we should expect to see a marked reduction in both national and regional variations in economic well-being, lest the costs of integration are seen to be borne excessively by certain poorer groups in the Community. Table 4.10 suggests that regional disparities have reduced by similar relative amounts over the long period 1950–85, but this implies continuing and widening absolute differentials between the regions as average income levels have risen. Within the long period we can also note a widening in disparities during the 1970s, principally as the effects of the first oil shocks led to different national policy responses and differential behaviour in the various macroeconomic indicators considered above.

Table 4.9 Movements of monetary aggregates.

	Narrow money			M1 + quasi money		
	1974–78	1979–84	1985–88	1974–78	1979–84	1985–88
Germany	10.9	4.4	8.5	9.4	5.3	6.6
France	11.5	11.0	4.4	14.5	10.6	8.8
Italy	17.8	14.7	9.6	21.2	13.9	8.4
UK	15.5	11.4	19.1	11.1	15.8	18.5
ERM members						
Arithmetic average	13.1	8.8	8.1	14.5	9.8	8.0
Standard deviation	3.6	4.4	3.8	4.1	3.5	1.7
Coefficient of variation	0.27	0.50	0.47	0.28	0.36	0.22
Non-ERM members						
Arithmetic average	13.1	12.5	17.8	15.1	16.8	14.5
Standard deviation	7.1	14.2	12.9	7.0	12.6	8.2
Coefficient of variation	0.54	1.14	0.73	0.47	0.75	0.57

Source: Eichengreen (1990).

Table 4.10 Indices of regional disparities of GDP/capita 1950–85.

	1950	1960	1970	1980	1985
Index of regional disparity	0.124	0.102	0.078	0.098	0.071
Index of national disparity	0.095	0.081	0.061	0.082	0.056
National disparity as % total disparity	76	79	79	84	79

Source: Molle (1990).

At an even more localized level the work of Cheshire *et al.* (1986) and Cheshire (1990) has demonstrated the lack of convergence in the problems faced by the EC's major urban regions. Again, the 1970s saw a general increase in the problems faced by urban regions with a slight improvement during the 1980s. The process of integration nationally has, however, tended to polarize the urban regions into those that have benefited and those that have suffered from the increased competition. The latter include both urban areas in traditional industrial regions of northern Europe and the poorer cities of southern Europe. However, the economic progress of the national economy is not an indicator of performance since there is a general and substantial worsening of the performance of most traditional industrial German cities over the longer period.

4.5 Conclusions

We set out in this chapter to examine the evidence for, and progress towards, integration by 1991. It has become clear that although there are clear signs of convergence in many indicators, trade, prices, monetary aggregates and even levels of GDP, there is still a long way to go before it can be argued that there is, in any real sense, economic cohesion within the Community. One of the principal reasons for this is that there are always strong pressures to compensate for moves towards greater integration with policies designed to protect those parts of an economy that are especially vulnerable. It is this continued existence, and even reinforcement, of non-tariff barriers to trade through subsidy, variations in standards, border controls, preference in public procurement, etc. which constitute the 'cost of non-Europe', which the Commission's 1992 programme is oriented to eliminate, and which the remainder of this book addresses.

5

Realizing the Single Market

So far we have considered the process of integration in a rather abstract way, as a theoretical concept of free trade and in terms of the completion of a 'single market'. We turn now to the more practical problem of determining what would define such a single market, how it was proposed to achieve it and what the gains were expected to be. This chapter concentrates on the broad aggregate issues in the debate, identifying the gains to the Community as a whole. The following two chapters take up the more difficult issues of who gains and who loses from this process in terms of both sectors and regions. First, however, we need to review the way in which the Community approached the problem of defining the parameters of a genuine European Single Market.

5.1   Background to the Single Market debate

Increasing dissatisfaction had emerged, even after the introduction of the European Monetary System in 1979, with the extent of and pace of movement towards a genuinely common or single market. The obvious barriers of borders, customs posts and need to change currencies remained. So did a wide range of differences in technical standards, restrictive public procurement policies and fiscal provisions which necessitated the border controls and themselves restricted both the achievement of scale economies and the increase of competitive pressures in Europe.

It was the European Parliament which started the pressure with a series of reports on what became known as 'the costs of non-Europe'.

Various estimates of the impact of continuing border controls emerged, in terms of both the impact on average prices in Europe and on the Community's GDP.

In 1985 a new Commission, under the presidency of Jacques Delors, took office and began to devise a programme necessary for the achievement of a Single European Market. A White Paper was produced, setting the target date of the end of 1992 for the programme's completion, and identified 282 policy measures that would be required to achieve this. The task and the timetable required were legislated for in the Single European Act which finally passed into each member country's laws in July 1987. This committed the member states to enact the necessary Directives into national legislation after their agreement by the Council of Ministers.

The Commission started in an essentially dirigiste mood. The way to the Single Market was to achieve agreement on harmonizing all those national rules and regulations that stood in the way of a border-free single internal market for the Community. The problem with this approach was that it clearly antagonized some national governments, notably the British, who saw it as an essentially illiberal attempt at centralizing decision making in Brussels. Moreover, it required detailed agreement on some areas of national policy that had hitherto been regarded as sacrosanct, such as the proposal to 'approximate' (i.e. harmonize within two broad bands) the permissible rates of VAT.

Increasingly, therefore, it was seen that the desired end product could just as easily be obtained by a less bureaucratic means. Most variations between countries would only survive if competitive pressures allowed them to do so. As long as all citizens of the Community were allowed free movement and freedom to move goods, insupportable differences in taxes or regulations would be forced to be harmonized.

This was a re-enactment of an old debate in the Community which had started in the 1960s over early attempts at Economic and Monetary Union. Was it essential to get harmonization and convergence before a real economic union could take place, or would a simple decision to open borders, make all money convertible at fixed exchange rates, etc. force the economies into this position?

The final outcome was, logically, something of a compromise: harmonization is necessary in a number of areas for reasons of public safety, etc., as is the transfer of some power in certain areas to Brussels, e.g. merger policy, but the recognition of the lack of need to harmonize every last detail was an important step forward.

Clearly it was also necessary to support the view that there were substantial benefits to be gained from completing the Single Market;

that it was not a zero-sum game but one with enough net benefits to compensate any losers whilst leaving the gainers better off. This job was entrusted to a group of experts under the chairmanship of Paolo Cecchini, who reported in 1988. The Cecchini study was itself a massive exercise involving not just an attempt to make an overall macroeconomic assessment, but also to include case studies of the most important sectors and independent assessments of the scope for gain in some of the more critical areas such as scale economies and public procurement. Both the strength and the weakness of the Cecchini studies lie in the putting of numerical values on the gains. The strength is in the quantitative assessment of the costs of non-Europe which is comprehensive and thorough. The weakness is in assuming that this measures the gains that can be achieved. Clearly quantification was necessary, but at the same time gives a hostage to fortune – how far does the final conclusion depend on the acceptance of each individual measurement?

This issue surrounds both the economics and the politics of the Single Market programme. Are the benefits only available as a complete package or can any one part of them stand on its own? Clearly, politically, the Commission required acceptance of the whole package. 1992 à la carte would not have been desirable, both because it would have led to prolonged wrangling about compensation and because failure to accept certain critical parts of the package would have seriously damaged the whole programme. Essentially the programme identifies the ways in which member states have frustrated the move to a genuine common market in all goods, services and resources markets. Tightening controls on any one area would typically mean the search for continuing escape routes in other areas. The economic modelling also only holds up on the assumption that the full programme is achieved; partial rather than general equilibrium modelling could be done, but was not in this case and would undoubtedly have produced rather different results.

Against this background, we now outline the main features of the 1992 programme and its economic assessment before returning to a critique in the final section of the chapter.

5.2   Elements of the Single Market programme

The Single Market programme addresses the following five broad areas discussed in the Cecchini study:

1. The cost of border controls.
2. The harmonization of technical and other standards.

3. Achieving scale economies.
4. Improving competition and efficiency.
5. The cost of public procurement policies.

In addition there is the question of harmonizing the business operating environment in terms of taxation, company law, regulation and other matters in the hands of member states. We look at each of these in turn.

5.2.1 *The cost of border controls*

Border controls, both for immigration and customs checks, impose costs in four ways. First, they impose extra administrative burdens on firms given the complexity and diversity of paperwork involved in moving goods between countries within what is supposed to be a Common Market. Secondly, the need to check this paperwork causes delays at frontiers, which raises the cost of transporting goods. Thirdly, there is a welfare cost of business which is simply not done because the perceived cost of the above is too high. Finally, there is the cost to governments of maintaining the controls effectively.

The administrative formalities used to require numerous different forms for each country such that a consignment going by lorry from the United Kingdom to Italy would require documentation relating to its export from the United Kingdom and its import into Italy, plus different documentation for its passage through intervening countries which itself would necessitate the route being decided in advance. Any discrepancies in the forms would hold up the consignment – sometimes until corrected forms could be supplied from the original exporter. This has been simplified from 1988 with the introduction of a Single Administrative Document which is valid for all countries. Even here, however, the specific requirements of each country for different information led to the need for an eight-page document.

The cost to firms is the cost of having experienced staff to complete this documentation quickly and accurately. This is a particular burden for small firms who either do not export enough to warrant having expert staff or not enough to individual markets to understand particular local requirements in those markets. Specialist freight forwarders can help in this process, but nevertheless the average cost per consignment will be higher by an estimated 30–45 per cent for smaller firms, which are thus discouraged from adding to the level of competition in cross-border trade in the Community.

Delays at frontiers are, of course, largely caused for freight by the need to check all the documentation. It is not just the time to check the documentation and the further delay if it is wrong, but the congestion this causes. It is estimated that at Dover, the main exit and entry point for British trade with continental partners, the average delay for a lorry is of the order of 4–6 hours. Furthermore, this delay is unpredictable, especially at land frontiers. Border crossing-points do not always have coordinated opening hours so any delay en route can lead to missing one of these and a further delay. In addition, regulations on drivers' hours mean that time spent queuing cannot be counted as a break and hence an exceptional delay leads to the need for an extra rest period and imposes further costs of the haul. It has been estimated that taking a lorry from London to Milan takes 60 per cent longer than an equivalent length of journey wholly within the United Kingdom, even after discounting the Channel crossing. This is all due to frontier delays and the necessary extra rest periods these require.

The total cost of administration and delays is estimated at around 8 billion ECU or about 2 per cent of the value of cross-border trade. This is reflected therefore in higher prices and gives an element of protection to less efficient domestic producers. If the costs were roughly the same throughout the Community this may be an annoyance but not such a worry. In fact, they vary considerably and not just between countries, but often between exports and imports for one country (Table 5.1). This shows how much more costly it is for firms to trade with Italy than with other member countries, and even more difficult for Italian firms to export. None of this has taken account of further costs due to the lack of a Single Market in the transport sector itself. Border controls are, of course, a necessary requirement where different regulatory regimes exist and to police the quota system which still dominates the road haulage sector.

Table 5.1 Administrative costs to firms per consignment in EC trade.

	Imports (ECU)	Exports (ECU)
Belgium	26	34
W. Germany	42	79
France	92	87
Italy	130	205
Netherlands	46	50
United Kingdom	75	49
Average	67	86

Source: Emerson (1988).

However, a potentially even greater welfare loss arises because this cost dissuades firms from attempting to operate in other markets even if they can meet regulatory standards and get round public procurement restrictions. The cost of simply getting the goods delivered reliably to their destination at an acceptable price will often be too great. Studies for the Cecchini Report suggest this could amount to anything between 4.5 billion and 15 billion ECU.

Finally, the cost of maintaining the controls is put at 0.5–1 billion ECU to member states. Of course, border controls are not justified solely on the basis of frustrating cross-border trade; this is often a by-product of other purposes. As long as technical standards and regulatory environments differ, goods entering and leaving have to be checked to make sure they are what they are claimed to be and conform. Customs and other border officials are also concerned with the passage of drugs and other banned products, criminals and terrorists, and differing excise duty and VAT regimes lead to the need to restrict parallel importing or cross-border shopping. But this becomes essentially a question of principle. The enforcement of technical standards can be undertaken for untraded goods at the point of sale and not by stopping consignments at roadside checkpoints. The enforcement of the criminal law is not administered at county boundaries in the United Kingdom, nor even at *Land* boundaries in Germany, despite nominally independent police forces. The United States manages to live with variations in state consumption taxes without controls at state frontiers. Ultimately, either one accepts the logic of a Single Market with full reciprocity or one rejects it. The problem is that one is essentially having to cost the price of terrorism against the losses in the market. It is possible that the gains from the market would more than pay for more effective and less visible policing – whether that would be more effective in controlling cross-border crime and terrorism is a question to which an answer is needed.

5.2.2 Technical standards and regulations

A major constraint on free trade across internal frontiers arises from the adoption of differing technical or regulatory standards in different countries. Sometimes these reflect deliberate attempts to protect domestic firms; often, however, they are simply the result of different traditions. We need to distinguish between true technical standards affecting such things as electrical safety, automobile construction or the permissible content of vegetable fat in ice cream, and regulatory standards that affect in particular the trading of professional and financial services.

The essential argument affecting both of these areas is that of top-down full harmonization versus mutual recognition and competition. Safety in the construction of domestic electrical appliances is an area where some degree of harmonization and agreed standards is probably necessary. It is much less clear that preventing Belgians from eating British chocolate because it contains excessive vegetable fats by Belgian standards, or preventing Germans from drinking Belgian beer because it contains additives, until all Europeans can agree on a definition of chocolate or beer, is so essential. In the latter case, agreement on the form of presentation of contents so that consumers can make informed choices is clearly a preferable way forward.

Despite the clear shift away from a policy of harmonizing, it is nevertheless true that the major part of the 1992 programme does involve directives on standards – over 160 of the planned 279 Directives relate to harmonizing standards in veterinary, phytosanitary and pharmaceutical areas alone. These are clearly areas where public safety concerns are greatest and a simple policy of mutual recognition would not suppress widespread calls for maintaining barriers by individual countries because of specific health and safety fears.

The Community has established two organizations to oversee technical harmonization: CEN (Comité Européen de Normalisation) and CENELEC (for electrical standards). Their basic task is to determine the minimum standards that are acceptable to all countries. Clearly there is scope for national bodies to develop higher standards and for producers to use these and allow the market to make its choice, but the minimum standards would have to be met by all Community producers and the presumption is that this would allow products to enter any other country.

Beyond this setting of minimum standards, a principle of mutual recognition would determine whether goods could be sold. As long as they met the criteria laid down in one member state then goods could freely pass between member states and be sold in them. We now look briefly at three sectors where technical and regulatory standards are particularly important – food and drink, pharmaceuticals and financial services. The first and last of these are given fuller treatment in the following chapter, but it is useful to identify the main points here.

Food and drink

The basic principle of mutual recognition is the one annunciated in the now famous Cassis de Dijon case of 1979 which could be claimed to be the basis for the move to completion of the Single Market. In this an importer was refused permission to import and sell Cassis de Dijon, a liqueur spirit made from blackcurrants, in West Germany since the alcohol content did not meet the minimum requirements laid down for spirits in Germany. Cassis contains around 16 per cent alcohol; spirits in Germany are expected to contain 30 per cent (or by special recognition 25 per cent). Similarly, the 16 per cent figure was too high for the product to be classified as wine. German courts upheld this decision, but on reference to the European Court of Justice it was held that no member state could rightfully withhold a product from the market if it was legally saleable in another member state unless overriding health or safety considerations could be shown.

Interestingly, the Germans later tried to use the health consideration to enable them to assert the traditional *Reinheitsgebot* of 1516 as a reason for excluding imported beer. The *Reinheitsgebot* prescribed that beer must contain only barley, hops and water and therefore any beer containing chemical additives would fail to meet this requirement. This would exclude most non-German beer from being sold as beer in Germany, since the additives are typically to increase the life and ability to travel of the product, and would protect the highly localized, inefficient, breweries in Germany. Whilst presumably based on the fact that beer consumption in Germany is substantially higher than in other member countries and that German beer drinkers would risk building up higher levels of chemical content through drinking foreign beer than other Europeans, the view of the Court was that as long as clear labelling of contents took place it was up to the consumer to choose and not to individual governments to exclude goods that could be bought over the border in Belgium, France or the Netherlands.

Perhaps not surprisingly the food and drink sector offers other examples of similar restrictions on products which are aimed at protecting domestic producers. Italian regulations prohibit mineral water from sale in plastic bottles, thus increasing costs of transport for foreign producers. Danish regulations require beer to be sold in returnable bottles with refundable deposits. Again, the foreign producer faces higher costs and almost all beer consumed in Denmark is consequently produced locally. Several countries have regulations prohibiting the use of soft wheats in the preparation of pasta; only the more expensive (but locally produced) hard durum wheat may be used. Others restrict the use of cheaper vegetable fats in chocolate products or ice cream.

The full cost of these restrictions is not easy to estimate; it depends on how much prices of the protected products are raised by the protection and the extent to which economies of scale could be realized in the production of the cheaper, but excluded, products. The Cecchini Report suggests a figure of 0.5–1 billion ECU for these. The foodstuffs sector has in any event seen considerable restructuring and merger and acquisition activity in recent years. This might suggest that with fewer regulations more concentration could emerge with a reduction in consumer choice. It is a sector where there is not large scope for natural growth since income elasticities of demand are low. However, it could provide scope for product development into new markets which would compensate for these problems. In the final analysis, the extent to which this can occur depends essentially on whether European tastes will converge to allow for EC-wide products to become the norm. Probably Germans will continue to prefer German beer and Italians traditional pasta products, but they may find less choice of producers as a result of lower prices.

We shall note some further points relating to the foods and drink industry in the context of tax harmonization later.

Pharmaceuticals

Pharmaceuticals represent a further important area where technical standards provide a critical restriction on the development of European markets. Drug registration procedures differ considerably between member states and typically have to be repeated state by state. Although this is a sector where European firms have shown great innovation and where they have potential for world markets, within Europe the market is fragmented and suffers from a wide range of regulation. This produces a situation in which prices for generically similar drugs can vary by a factor of ten between countries. Even between Germany and France prices (exclusive of taxes) are 2.5 times the latter in the former.

With a common system of registration, which would enable any drug recognized and approved in one member state access to any other member state, it is estimated that unit costs could fall by up to 0.8 per cent (which would amount to a saving of over 270 million ECU), and if prices converge towards the European average, total expenditure could fall by three times that amount (equivalent to 3 per cent of current expenditure).

Pharmaceuticals do, however, present a slightly different problem since large quantities of drugs, particularly prescription medicines, are not sold directly to the final consumer. Instead they are prescribed by an intermediary, the doctor. It is the doctor who is a focus, therefore, for the marketing of drugs. Moreover, neither the patient nor the doctor typically pays directly for the drug, given the widespread use of national or fully funded insurance-based health care systems in

Europe. Neither, therefore, has any real interest in using the cheapest drug available for any condition. National, branded drugs will always have an advantage over anonymous generic drugs, and therefore again the realization of savings will depend on a shift in preferences as well as a liberalization of regulations.

Financial services

A slightly different incidence of regulatory problems arises in the financial services sector although the problem is similar in its effect. As with pharmaceuticals, financial services institutions have to be licensed by the appropriate regulatory authority for each country in which they operate. The range of services allowed and the way in which services can be offered differs markedly between countries. In banking, Belgium did not allow variable-rate mortgages, France prohibited interest-bearing current accounts. Except in the United Kingdom there was generally control over the mortality rates used in life insurance and these were typically set much more conservatively, based on population averages rather than the life insured, leading to premiums varying by a factor of more than two.

Here, however, as well as providing a form of regulatory protection for domestic operators, financial services regulation is also used to support domestic monetary policy. Whereas foreign banks have not been precluded from being established in other countries, they can only be so if they operate essentially like domestic banks. Economies of both scale, in terms of size of transactions, and scope, in terms of range of transactions, are thus limited since cross-border transactions are no easier.

Capital controls have been widespread in the EC, even since introduction of the European Monetary System in 1979. In fact some commentators have suggested that the Exchange Rate Mechanism of the EMS, in which currencies are kept within a limited deviation (±2.25 per cent for most currencies) of the cross rates in a fixed parity grid and of a basket of all the currencies (the ECU), has only been sustained by capital controls which serve to prevent short-term speculative movements of funds. However, the evidence seems to suggest that in practice capital controls have been much diminished over the period since introduction of EMS (Eichengreen, 1990). Two major historical users of capital controls, France and Italy, had removed remaining restrictions by July 1990 in line with the plans of the first stage of the 1989 Delors plan for Economic and Monetary Union. Major restrictions were then only in place in the weakest economies of Greece and Portugal, and to a lesser extent in Spain.

Capital controls are not only a hindrance to a single monetary space within the EC, but also to the single market for capital. But does this require a Single Market for financial services? In one sense the answer is no. The United States, for example, has a financial system which operates without widespread inter-state banking. There is clearly a single monetary space controlled by the Federal Reserve Board, and a single capital market with free flows of financial capital, but detailed banking regulations differ from state to state and the system depends on essentially local institutions.

The proposals for financial services in the EC allow for the continuance of some diversity in the way financial institutions operate, but also allow for mutual recognition of the right to operate. The analogy has been made with a driving licence system in which each state fixes the rules under which a licence is obtained, which is then recognized by all other states, but local rules govern when driving in another state. Germans cannot claim exemption from motorway speed limits in the United Kingdom on the basis that they have none in Germany, nor can UK drivers insist on driving on the left in France. Similarly, banks and insurance companies will not need separate registration in each country. Subject to certain minimal harmonized standards governing deposit ratios each country can fix its own rules for registration (which will essentially govern its own nationals) and for operation (which will govern all institutions when operating within its borders).

Obviously there is some pressure for national rules of registration to move towards the basic standard so as not to disadvantage national institutions, or to encourage them to register elsewhere. There is also some pressure to fix local rules of operation to suit national institutions. However, the final outcome is a case of imposing minimal harmonization and allowing competitive forces to provide the pressure towards a Single Market.

Scale economies may be more relevant in insurance and scope economies in banking, but either way the Cecchini Report suggests that price reductions of between, typically, 4 and 20 per cent could be achieved in the sector. The more regulated economies may see greater falls, the less regulated, like the United Kingdom, may see less. The importance of the sector in the economies of the major countries, and the scope for cross-border operations, does imply the possibility of substantial gains, of the order of 0.7 per cent of GDP in the EC as a whole, but as much as 1.5 per cent in the most regulated sectors such as Spain. More important, however, is the role which financial services play in allowing other sectors to develop in the Community, and this requires some further thought.

There are two basic ways in which integration of financial markets can work to the advantage of other sectors. One is that a wider range of competitive services will exist throughout the Community, possibly with some continued national specialization. German banks have often been credited with having played a major role in the success of German companies by being prepared to take a long-term stake in return for some direct control. Similar close links can also be found in Japanese industry. British insurance companies have a wide experience of world-wide risks. Such specialization could help companies looking for specific types of service. The second way preserves the close relationship between banker and client built up in a home environment, but allows banks to offer services to their clients directly in all other member states, at a lower cost than currently implied by the need to set up under local regulations. One option already becoming increasingly likely is to try to gain the best of both of these by banks entering into formal cross-national links, including reciprocal equity swaps. This ensures both the knowledge of local operating conditions is not lost whilst offering cross-border services to clients.

Clearly the balance of advantage for the Community as a whole depends on how much of the potential gains from deregulation and greater efficiency are passed on to the Community's other sectors, plus the scope for the Community's financial sector to benefit in world competitive ter.ns from its greater efficiency.

In total the move towards harmonization of technical standards and the consequent elimination of the barriers to the free movement of goods and services in all sectors is estimated to result in a benefit to the Community of 60–70 billion ECU or 2–2.5 per cent of GDP.

5.2.3 *Achieving scale economies*

The fragmentation of the European market and the inability of firms to serve it as a whole leads to a loss of the benefits of scale economies. The US economy with 220 million consumers or the Japanese with 120 million are smaller than the EC with 340 million, but are respectively 3.5 or 1.5 times the size of the Community's largest single separate economy, the German with 78.5 million. What is particularly interesting about the US and Japanese economies is their greater dependence on home markets: the United States exported only about 6 per cent of its GDP and the Japanese 10 per cent in 1987; the Community's individual economies exported between 12.5 per cent (Spain) and 60 per cent (Belgium), an overall figure of 22 per cent (42 per cent of which was external trade). This substantial homogeneous home market gives rise to the potential for scale economies which, by reducing costs, increases external competitiveness.

The problem that European producers face is that even within the

Community they do not have a single market within which they can develop such scale economies. Since markets have developed in a fragmented way, firms in many sectors cannot reach the least possible costs, a minimum efficient technical scale. We have already identified (see Table 2.1) the extent to which scale economies are not being realized in a selection of sectors, following the work of Pratten (1988). If all industries could achieve their minimum efficient technical scale, this could produce a further total Community-wide saving of 60 billion ECU or a further 2 per cent gain in GDP.

Economies of scale have effects in two ways. They will lead to lower costs and prices within the EC which release resources and generate demand. They also have an effect on the competitiveness of EC industry in world markets and hence on the ability of firms in such industries to secure greater exports with a consequent impact on EC output and incomes.

Economies of scale can be realized as a result of changes in the rules governing trade within the EC, such as public procurement restrictions or technical standards; changes in the degree of hindrance to trade, such as border controls and fiscal regimes; and changes induced by increases in income. The first of these affects individual sectors differentially, the second and third effects operate on all sections. However, it is clear that not all sectors are in a position to benefit equally from the effects of scale economies. It is only in sectors where the output with the least cost of production (minimum efficient technical scale) is large relative to the domestic market that substantial gains can be made, since it is only in these sectors that external trade growth will be essential as a cause of market growth.

Clearly the achievement of lower costs through scale economies has implications for existing firms and their regions of location. The growth of some firms to achieve scale economies, even in a growing market, will imply the disappearance of smaller units. This also affects attempts at statistical explanation since the removal of the smallest firms automatically increases the average size of units. More seriously in the longer term, however, is the impact on competition of an increase in the average size of units and a reduction in their number. Here the balance will be between the reduction in competitive pressures between small firms in each domestic market and the increase in competition between larger firms in the wider European market. The latter is essential to ensure the dynamic benefits from the continuing search for greater efficiency which some authors claim is overestimated by the Cecchini studies (Neuberger, 1989; Cutler *et al.*, 1989) but others claim is grossly underestimated, by as much as 30–50 per cent (Baldwin, 1989).

This argument is not easy to resolve on a priori grounds. We can show the industries where scale economies are likely to be greater or smaller on the basis of the existing size of units relative to the minimum efficient scale. We can also show where conflicts in technical standards or public procurement policies have prevented industries expanding across national borders. What we cannot explain so easily is why available scale economies have not been exploited in many other industries where these constraints have not existed. There is, therefore, a real conflict between the two views on the ability to realize scale economies.

Furthermore, attempts to realize scale economies at a European scale immediately bring into play further worries about the anti-competitive implications of such moves, against which the European Commission has been sharpening its powers through more rigorous monopoly and merger legislation. Perhaps the most important factor, however, is how far firms actually view the European Market as a Single Market. Modelling it as a market as homogeneous as the US internal market clearly ignores the differences of culture and language which affect, if not the goods which are bought in each national market, at least the way in which they need to be sold. For this reason, much of the initial development of firms across national borders has been secured in Europe either by acquisition or by some form of joint venture or industrial cooperation.

The advantage of the cooperative route is that it minimizes the risk for a company entering new markets where they may be unfamiliar with local needs or working practices whilst getting access to that market. At the same time it secures the defensive advantage that the joint venture partner cannot become a predator in the home company's market. One survey, by KPMG Peat Marwick McLintock, recorded 669 partnerships in the last quarter of 1989 alone (*Independent*, 2 January 1990) involving British and other European companies.

Acquisitions may be a riskier strategy in that they involve a greater initial outlay, may invite scrutiny from either or both national and EC anti-trust agencies and may lead to considerable resentment by the customers of the acquired company. The outcry at French acquisition of interests in UK water companies is the best example of this. Nevertheless, cross-border acquisitions have been big business, led by Anglo-French mergers. In 1989 French companies made more than 40 acquisitions in the United Kingdom to a value of 4 billion ECU whilst British companies acquired 70 French firms for 1.7 billion ECU (*Financial Times*, 9 May 1990).

Of course there is no guarantee that such figures are evidence of a search for scale economies – cooperation and acquisition are as likely to be driven by defensive motives – but they do suggest that in advance of the completion of the Single Market there is an upwards trend in corporate activity.

5.2.4 *Improving competition and efficiency*

One of the basic indicators of the lack of the competition which would be present in a genuine Single Market is the presence of substantial variations in the prices of otherwise identical goods in the different countries. Again, part of this is due to the continuing existence of restrictions on trade which public procurement policies and technical standards impose, thus fragmenting the market and preventing arbitrage. The primary way in which this works is to channel all trade in goods through companies' designated importers and prevent so-called parallel importing.

Technically, parallel importing for most goods is not only allowed, but attempts on its restraint are in contravention of the Competition Policy. Despite many celebrated cases, this type of anti-competitive restriction does still exist. It is in practice very easy for firms to avoid the competition of parallel imports and hence to be able to set different prices in different national markets. Exclusive dealerships, restrictions on warranty provisions, etc. are all ways in which firms can control the sale of their product in any market.

Nowhere has this been more noticeable than in the automobile market where pre-tax prices for the same model have varied by up to 50 per cent between countries and by a factor of 2 for different models of the same basic type of car between countries. The United Kingdom has always come at the head of this list with the highest pre-tax prices, occasioned partly by the obvious difference in technical specification for cars in the United Kingdom (and Ireland) which drive on the left. It is not that this makes the cars significantly more expensive to produce, simply that it is easier to control parallel imports given the different specification. The growth of parallel importing by individuals led to manufacturers both refusing to supply UK specification cars to dealers in Belgium (a country with some of the lowest pre-tax prices) and to issue the type-approval certificates necessary to register the vehicle on import to the United Kingdom. Ford was one manufacturer taken to the European Court over its actions, but it is extremely difficult to prove individual cases.

Another example of great diversity in product prices can be found in pharmaceuticals where the most expensive prices (Germany) are over 2.25 times the cheapest (France). Pharmaceuticals are affected by differences in national health care systems, since prescription drugs are typically not bought by the final consumer, but as a result of prescription by a medical practitioner.

It is not only in industrial products where price variations are great – two other instances are agricultural products and financial services. We have already discussed financial services at some length in terms of harmonization of standards. Agriculture is perhaps more surprising in that product diversity in terms of branding is much more difficult to achieve successfully, but even more so in that agriculture is supposedly subject to an EC-controlled common policy. The CAP sets target prices for agricultural products, and controls these via intervention buying and border taxes and subsidies (the Monetary Compensation Amounts) as a means of ensuring that changes in currency values cannot give one country's produce an artificial price advantage in another country. Within fairly small margins, therefore, the selling prices of agricultural products should approximate in all markets. In practice, substantial variations have persisted with, for example, farmers in Germany receiving up to three times the UK price for certain products, but British farmers being unable to exploit this by exporting to Germany at their lower prices.

It is not just variations in price, however, which are relevant, but also the absolute level of prices in the Community, which has a depressing effect on the level of demand. To some extent price levels reflect the lack of exploitation of scale economies, but there are further issues of relevance here. Principal amongst these is the position of small- and medium-sized enterprises (SMEs) in the Community. The exploitation of scale economies and manipulation of separate markets are essentially the prerogative of large companies. It is large companies that are already disproportionately represented in existing intra-European trade. Small companies, however, are usually the most dynamic, the most likely to be present in new expanding markets and the most likely to use new technologies. Hence they are the fastest to grow. It is new companies and growing companies that form the basis of most regional growth, whilst large, old companies in decline are responsible for much regional decline. Hence this sector is important in understanding the spatial pattern of development.

SMEs are also the most likely to suffer from barriers to trade. Their lack of size raises the unit cost of trading across national frontiers and increases their dependence on independent freight forwarders, handling agents, etc. This keeps many SMEs out of the trade sector as they do not see the cost and complexity of dealing with the bureaucratic and other problems as worth while. The removal of many of these barriers should affect SMEs differentially. The implication of this is the introduction of a much greater degree of competition, not just across national borders but into markets that had otherwise been protected – i.e. markets become contestable.

The process of internationalization is also not the exclusive preserve of larger companies. SMEs have shown considerable tendencies to internationalize in terms of the more rapid diffusion of both fashions and technologies, the greater needs for serving segmented or customized markets within countries, the shortening of the length of the product cycle and its implications for research and development and the increasing need for close producer–customer relations. Cappellin (1990) has argued that these four factors are closely related with important spatial consequences. Again there is a tension between globalization on the one hand and market segmentation on the other. The former implies large firms, the latter often more specialized firms, but the technological demands mean that for smaller firms to survive and be in a position to innovate they need themselves to seek wider links.

Research and development is clearly a major area here since it provides both the basis for achieving scale economies and the mechanism for the diffusion of new techniques, which is an important part in maintaining and promoting further competition. It has been argued that it is in the field of R&D that the Community generally has lagged behind major competition, but the bulk of the innovations from R&D occur in small, dynamic firms and not through the achievement of scale economies in larger firms. The study by Geroski (1988) attributed 17 per cent of innovations in the United Kingdom in the period 1945–83 to firms with fewer than 200 employees, 33.2 per cent to firms with fewer than 1,000 and 56.1 per cent to firms with fewer than 10,000. Moreover, this role of small firms had grown; those with under 1,000 employees generated 29.6 per cent of innovations in 1945 but 43.2 per cent in 1983.

Is it then that the competitive pressure on small firms is such that they must innovate to survive or are they just more efficient? This is difficult to prove conclusively: it may just be that smaller firms are faster innovators, but they may also be more likely to perish if the innovation goes wrong. The large firms can be content to innovate more slowly and less adventurously. If small firms take more risks it may also be advantageous to secure greater cross-border cooperation to reduce the potential losses from failed innovations. Lack of communication can result in failure to perceive the changes already found by other firms in other regions and other countries in the Community. This involves a net loss of resources to the EC as a whole.

Here cooperation and the maintenance of competition go hand in hand.

Although the Community has had a Competition Policy since its inception and a general remit in the Treaties to promote competition and prevent the restraint of trade at a European level, there has always been a tension about the most appropriate level at which to operate this policy. National governments have jealously guarded their responsibilities to look after mergers, for example. This has now changed with the Community's new policy on mergers which became effective in 1990. Under this, the Community, through a special Mergers Task Force, has become responsible for vetting all large-scale mergers. All mergers where the combined turnover of the parties exceeds 5 billion ECU and their aggregate Community turnover exceeds 250 million ECU are covered except where more than two-thirds of each party's sales are in one member state. It is planned to seek to reduce the threshold to 2 billion ECU after three years.

Where the EC Mergers Task Force is involved, its powers should override those of any member state's investigatory procedures. However, it is clear that this could lead to resentment on the part of national agencies and governments. This is especially true where there is any political sensitivity, for example in the case of newly privatized corporations, but also since the Commission has reserved powers to re-investigate mergers which have already received national approval under its general remit given by Articles 85 and 86 of the Treaty of Rome. It is also permissible for national governments to invite EC examination of bids under the threshold which could lead to the governments of small countries unilaterally calling in the EC Task Force to investigate hostile bids from companies in large countries whose own mergers authority would be prepared to acquiesce to the merger.

Clearly the ability to police anti-competitive activity is critical in promoting the sort of competition necessary to achieve the dynamic gains from the Single Market, but what are these potential gains and are they worth the effort? Estimating the gains from the greater efficiency promoted by competition is one of the most difficult parts of the Cecchini exercise.

The simplest aspect is to consider the potential for price convergence. Convergence on the lowest price would produce an estimated aggregate gain of 250 billion ECU (8.3 per cent GDP) and on the average price a gain of 64 billion ECU (2.1 per cent GDP). The potential gains from the move to an integrated market depend on the competitive response of firms to the changes. In their contribution to

the Single Market studies Smith and Venables (1988) used two basic scenarios:

1. The tariff equivalent of NTBs is assumed to be reduced by 2.5 per cent.
2. In addition, all price variations are removed as firms are assumed to operate in a completely unified market.

Within these scenarios, Smith and Venables made various assumptions concerning market structure (numbers of firms assumed fixed or freely variable); range of products (fixed or variable) and competitive behaviour (Cournot – quantity adjustment – or Bertrand – price adjustment). Partial equilibrium models are then developed for each of a series of key sectors. Welfare effects in each sector are estimated at 0.5–2 per cent under the minimalist scenario and 0.5–4 per cent under the maximalist scenario. There are considerable variations between sectors, with bigger gains generally in those where trade, potential scale economies and the potential restructuring of more highly concentrated sectors are greatest.

It is this result which has been heavily criticized as being either optimistic or pessimistic. The pessimists consider it is too high because it is a partial equilibrium result which fails to allow for the increase in concentration both by firm and region of production such that the potential gains are lost in greater monopoly control. Thus Cutler *et al.* (1989) argue first that since the gains from the removal of NTBs are relatively small, they provide relatively small barriers to entry across borders and hence firms would have sought economies of scale across them anyway. Secondly, they argue that the Commission has misread the evidence of Pratten's study which shows relatively modest scale economy gains for what would be relatively large changes in output. The estimates are based on the cost penalty at one-half the minimum efficient technical scale and a doubling of output is argued to be unlikely. Thirdly, they suggest that if economies of scale come about this will be associated with increasing concentration and hence the 'engineering' gains will be lost in inefficiency. The 1992 programme is thus branded first a 'stunt', but then more soberly as a 'political success'. The argument is that the economic arguments for the Single Market have been manufactured (and indeed distorted) as a support to the primary political objective of unification.

However, in a more thorough economic analysis which appeals to some general equilibrium modelling of world trade patterns (Shoven and Whalley, 1984) and of US–Canada trade liberalization (Harris and Cox, 1984), Baldwin (1989) has suggested gains of up to twice those identified in the Cecchini studies could be available. Harris and Cox

(1984), for example, have suggested welfare gains to Canada of the order of 16 per cent from US–Canadian liberalization. Baldwin argues that greater levels of growth can be achieved essentially because what is involved is not just a one-off shock to the system but instead a potentially permanent enhancement to long-term growth in the EC of between 0.2 and 0.9 percentage points. Over the medium term Baldwin's estimates of the impact on GDP are up to double those of the Cecchini studies.

This so-called medium-term growth bonus arises because higher productivity and output (the direct impact of the 1992 programme) raise savings and investment and hence the long-run capital–labour ratio. Increasing returns to scale are assumed, rather than the more conventional constant returns. Baldwin argues that traditional approaches based on constant returns essentially assume that technological change is exogenous to the system rather than being induced via changes in capital–labour ratios. In fact, roughly two-thirds of most per capita growth is usually taken to come from technical progress generated outside the system. The argument here is that with constant returns to scale firms will choose the capital–labour ratio on the basis of the real interest rate. If the real interest rate is constant then so must be the capital–labour and capital–output ratios, hence any observed deviation must come from outside the system as an exogenous shift.

But if returns to scale can be shown to be not constant, and Baldwin introduces evidence that points to increasing returns on average in all the major European economies, although it is far from conclusive and certainly open to empirical criticism, then some of the implications of increasing returns have to be taken seriously. Against the rather static, centralizing towards Germany, hypothesis, this evidence also points to scale economies being potentially less important in Germany than in France or Belgium. This tends to temper a little the aggregate impact of the dynamic analysis on the German economy (Table 5.2); these

Table 5.2 Potential long-term effects of 1992: The growth bonus.

	France	Germany	Netherlands	UK	Belgium
Medium-term bonus as % of static					
Low	30	36	35	24	38
High	80	119	124	93	136
Total effect % incr. in GDP					
Low	3.3–8.5	3.4–8.8	3.4–8.8	3.1–8.1	3.5–9.0
High	4.5–11.7	5.7–14.9	5.6–14.2	5.8–17.5	5.9–25

Source: Baldwin (1989).

should be compared with the Cecchini Report's range of 2.5–6.5 per cent for the EC as a whole.

Even these estimates, however, do not tell us the full story because they are aggregate projections of macroeconomic indicators and do not really allow in sufficient detail for the sectoral changes and redistributions of resources which are implicit in 1992. This is the essence of understanding the distributive effects of 1992 to which we shall turn in the next chapter when we can look at some individual sectors.

5.2.5 *Public procurement*

Excluding defence, public procurement restrictions are estimated to have cost the Community 13.9 billion ECU in 1984 or 0.5 per cent GDP, with defence contributing a further 4.0 billion ECU in potential savings. Public purchasing in total amounted to 450.5 billion ECU for the Community as a whole, 15 per cent of GDP. Between 45 and 65 per cent of this total is genuine procurement, i.e. expenditure subject to tendering or formal contract which could be controlled or restricted. The Commission estimated that only 2 per cent of supply contracts and 2 per cent of construction contracts had actually been awarded over national boundaries in the Community. This does not reflect the actual content of delivered goods but suggests that the common rules on advertising contracts in the EC's *Official Journal* and on scrutinizing tenders were being breached quite widely. Four key sectors for public procurement, energy, water, transport and telecommunications, had also not been covered by these rules.

Liberalizing public procurement should introduce more competitive tendering which would have an initial impact on prices. In sectors where public procurement dominates purchasing this would also have the effect of increasing competition and ultimately on restructuring of the industry as firms sought scale economies and adjusted to a larger single market as in other sectors. About half of the estimated benefits flowing from the liberalization depend on this restructuring. This suggests that the benefits are potentially very nebulous since they depend first on an honouring of the open rules and secondly on a positive response by firms involved. Public procurement changes may thus have more of a symbolic function than be a cause of real economic gain.

However, there are some possibly greater signs of hope. Many of the big public (or at least public-sponsored) procurement contracts are now concerned with international ventures such as new international transport infrastructures or joint ventures in other sectors. Transport infrastructures, of which the Channel Tunnel is the biggest example so far, increasingly involve joint venture collaboration at all stages. The Channel Tunnel is not strictly a public sector project, but behaves in many respects like one (Holliday *et al.*, 1991b). It involves a primary construction contract which is a joint venture between British and French construction companies and many sub-contracts for equipment such as tunnel-boring machines, electrical equipment and rolling stock which are themselves being supplied by joint ventures. Here the joint venture could be seen as a possible restraint on competition: the foreign firm gains a share of a contract at a higher price rather than forcing the local firm into a costly price reduction exercise. On the other hand, it is also a way of introducing best practice technology into a project whilst spreading the construction benefits geographically more widely.

It is interesting to note how the UK Department of Trade and Industry has used the Channel Tunnel contracts as the basis for a 'marriage bureau' as well as promoting the potential for contracts from other large construction contracts such as the Great Belt Link in Denmark.

Some of the worst cases of the disbenefits from public procurement come in areas such as telecommunications and railway equipment. Here national agencies are procuring equipment which has to meet nationally set technical standards which are incompatible. This explains why there were sixteen EC producers of railway locomotives compared with two in the United States and eleven manufacturers of telephone exchange equipment compared with four in the US. One study for the Cecchini Report put the benefits arising from standardization of telecommunications equipment at up to 1 billion ECU, with anything between a further 2.2 billion ECU and 3.7 billion ECU of further benefits from increased competition.

5.3   A European business environment

In many respects the issues addressed in the previous sections are about the minutiae of the rules governing business operation in European markets. Perhaps more critical is the way businesses perceive their general operating environment and this is governed by the framework of company law, taxation and state aids. Without a common operating environment firms are unlikely to believe they are operating in a single market.

Company law has, for a long time, posed a problem to the EC. There have been numerous attempts to create a unified legal framework for establishing companies. These tend to meet the problem of different legal traditions. Cross-border activities through cooperation or establishing subsidiaries also run into problems of the requirements to report company accounts and to deal with questions of taxation in different countries. Just as with technical standards, the Community has had to grapple with the question of the most appropriate route to improving the environment, a set of minimum EC standards on top of national legislation, a voluntary coordination of company law or a forced harmonization of all requirements. Any of these routes tends to founder on certain key national issues. Thus for the United Kingdom a major stumbling-block has been the desire on the part of the Commission to see this as part of the Social Charter for 1992. This would require protective legislation on worker rights and worker representation on company boards enshrined as part of company statutes and has been vigorously opposed by the Conservative government.

Progress on all of these issues has been slow, but these business environment issues do not only affect the statutory position of large companies. They are equally, if not more, important for small companies trying to operate across national frontiers and especially for individuals trying to obtain acceptance of professional qualifications. One estimate suggested that it would take 40–50 years for an accountant to acquire the necessary qualifications to practise legally in every EC country. This is not simply a restrictive practice on the part of national professional organizations, but arises from the differing accounting standards and rules governing the reporting of company accounts. Thus, operating across national borders necessitates more than one set of accounts to satisfy these requirements.

One interesting example of this is that of Eurotunnel, the company established to build and operate the Channel Tunnel. This is legally a 50–50 Anglo-French company. This is achieved by there being two public limited companies, one incorporated in Paris and the other in London, the shares of each being tied inseparably in a 'unit' made up of one share in Eurotunnel SA and one share in Eurotunnel PLC which cannot be traded separately. The holding company, Eurotunnel, operates as a single management structure and reports as a single entity to its shareholders. However, it has to produce company accounts of great complexity for each separate company, in different formats to meet local rules and reveal different points of detail. It could be argued that Eurotunnel is a classic European company, specifically established to carry on inter-state business, but hampered by the absence of genuinely European accounting standards.

The various directives so far agreed on by the Commission and

Council of Ministers are moving in the direction of more common standards and easier cross-border operations. For example, the need to publish separate accounts for subsidiary companies operating in other countries has been removed. Small companies wishing to establish locally based foreign operations will benefit from this particularly since the overhead costs of meeting administrative requirements are typically disproportionately large for small companies.

If the legal and accounting framework has posed problems for companies, then so has the fiscal environment. Both the structure and levels of tax affect where companies wish to register and how they can operate in the most tax-efficient manner – this is not necessarily the most economically efficient. High levels of corporate taxation have been one reason for German companies increasing their levels of investment outside Germany. The Netherlands and the United Kingdom, for example, have marginal tax rates on corporate profits substantially below the German level. This has led to pressures for both the reduction of levels of German tax and, more importantly, a restructuring and reform of the corporate tax system. Despite the obvious pressure, there have been no real moves towards harmonization in this area, something which will clearly have to change as pressures for Economic and Monetary Union increase after 1993.

Companies are also affected differentially by local business taxes. Companies are typically able to pass on local taxes, such as business rates in the United Kingdom, to their customers, especially where these are a larger element in costs, such as in retailing or personal services, given the location of such businesses. However, when differentials become large they can affect the location decisions of firms serving wider markets. Work on a comparison of such taxes in the United Kingdom and Germany (Bennett and Krebs, 1986) has shown how the burden in the latter had typically been greater, but in both is potentially distortionary. Later work also shows how it is important to take into account the range of regional policy incentives available to obtain a true measure of the cost of capital (Bennett and Krebs, 1989).

The recent move to Uniform Business Rates in the United Kingdom with a corresponding revaluation of commercial rateable values has been argued by the UK Government to have the effect of redressing cumulative imbalances in the tax burden on companies in different regions. In the South-East, in particular, the failure of rateable values to keep up with rental values whilst population growth maintained local authorities' incomes led to substantial falls in the real value of local business rates. In more depressed regions the need to maintain councils' incomes led to excessive rises in local tax rates, making these areas look unattractive to potential inwards investment. Under the revised system, the new rateable values reflect local economic circumstances whilst a standard uniform tax rate equalizes initial incidence per pound of rateable value. However, as Tyler *et al.* (1988) have shown, substantial local variations would still occur despite the reordering of local authorities in terms of tax burdens which the new system would produce.

If we translate this to a European level, as greater harmony is achieved between national tax systems, differentials in local tax burdens could become much more significant. In particular, however, the ability of local government to use concessions on local business tax liability as a means of attracting new business leads to considerable distortion. In France, for example, the practice of exempting inwards investors to a commune from the local *taxe professionelle* by the Mayor is a well-established practice. Enterprise Zones in the United Kingdom have more formally used the incentive of a local tax holiday for ten years as a means of encouraging new enterprise. All of these distortions are in breach of the basic principles which should apply in a Single Market.

Most concern over taxation has, however, been concentrated on VAT. This is the one form of taxation that operates under common rules throughout the Community. Since indirect taxes operating differentially could have widely varying incidences on companies, this would clearly distort rules on competitions. Thus all countries in the EC have been required to introduce a common form of indirect tax based on the French system of TVA (*taxe à valeur ajoutée*) which imposes a tax on the value added at each stage of manufacture. A company can then offset any VAT already paid on its inputs from its liability. Only final consumers or those exempt from VAT (very small companies with less than a certain threshold turnover or those engaged in the production of tax-exempt goods or services) cannot reclaim VAT paid on their purchases. Exports have been zero rated, i.e. no tax is paid but that already paid is reclaimable; imports are charged at the locally operable rate of tax, hence there is no double taxation of traded items, nor are firms of one country involved in having to reclaim tax paid in another country.

The system is the same in each country and hence the way in which the incidence of indirect taxes is felt is the same so as not to lead to the possibility of firms in one country facing advantages or disadvantages *vis-à-vis* those in another country. However, rates of tax are not the same; indeed the rate of tax on certain items can vary tremendously. Six countries employ three different bands of tax, reduced, standard and increased. One of these (Belgium) actually has five different rates, two reduced, one standard and two increased. Only one country, Denmark, has no variation in rates, but this is the second highest standard rate in the Community at 22 per cent. The United Kingdom is unique in using a zero rate as the only reduced rate on essentials such as food and children's clothing.

Standard rates, those applicable on most normal consumption goods, vary from 12 per cent in Luxembourg to 25 per cent in Ireland which has the highest reduced rate of 10 per cent. The highest increased rate is 38 per cent in Italy. Hence there is enormous variation in the actual incidence of tax; the use of the so-called destination principle (imposing the tax at the point of consumption with remission of tax on exports) has thus necessitated the retention of border controls. This is exacerbated by the even greater variations in excise duties on tobacco, alcohol and fuel – all commodities which are easy to transport over internal frontiers by final consumers. On tobacco and alcohol two features can be identified: that the northern countries tax more heavily than the southern (the tax on 100 cigarettes is 129 times higher in Denmark than in Greece, and 71 times higher in the United Kingdom, and on wine no tax at all is charged in Italy, Greece, Spain and Portugal); and countries tend to charge lower taxes on domestic production than on imports. The Germans, Danes and British tax beer less heavily relative to wine than the Italians or Greeks. The French discriminate between whisky and cognac.

Clearly any border-free Europe has major implications both for the preferred place of purchase and for government tax revenues. Denmark and Ireland – with uniformly high rates of VAT and excise duties – would lose out to neighbouring Germany and the United Kingdom. Southern Germans could benefit from lower excise duties on cigarettes, and wine and spirits in France and Italy, but the French and Italians would prefer to buy petrol and most luxury goods in Germany. It is not impossible to maintain differential rates. For example, if exports were taxed but a tax credit, operated through an EC clearing house, were granted to the importer, this would obviate the need for customs controls on trade flows. So-called parallel importing by individuals would remain a problem, but the clearing house could provide a means of compensating sudden changes in revenue.

The Commission has shifted ground on this issue. Its first plan was for a move to harmonize rates of both VAT and excise duty. Increased VAT rates would be abolished and lower and standard rates would need to be within two bands of 4–9 per cent and 14–20 per cent. Excise duties would essentially be averaged. Ireland and Denmark are the only states currently above the standard band and Spain the only one below it. The United Kingdom was the state most disturbed by these proposals since it would proscribe the use of a zero rate, which has advantages in keeping down the cost of essentials since liable producers are in the position of being able to reclaim tax paid on their imports without the output being taxed at all. This would harm the United Kingdom's cheap food policy – zero rate VAT had helped to mitigate slightly the impact of higher food prices occasioned by the Common Agricultural Policy in comparison with the United Kingdom's former policy of agricultural support which used world prices as its base. It would also be seen as politically unacceptable in certain other areas such as children's clothing. In addition, the Commission wished to tighten up on the definition of goods included in each rate. This would eliminate again some critical British exceptions, such as VAT on new housing, as well as a general introduction of VAT on travel tickets throughout the EC.

On some of this the Commission has now relented and the lower rate widened to 0–9 per cent, with a 15 per cent minimum standard rate, but in return it is being more insistent on imposing a common classification. With these sorts of variation it is felt that no formal clearing house system is likely to be needed. For most Europeans, as well, the cost of cross-border shopping will outweigh the advantages except for very major items.

Excise duties are still more problematic. A move to an average rate implies, for example, in the United Kingdom a reduction of nearly 90 per cent in the duty on wine, and over 55 per cent in the duty on cigarettes. The high-duty countries typically justify high duties on health and other social grounds and reductions in specific duties would not be thought desirable. However, it has to be recognized that the low-duty countries are often the high VAT countries and vice versa (with the exception of Denmark and Ireland) and the harmonization brings the effective total tax, especially on tobacco products, within narrower margins. More of a problem remains with alcohol since there is a question as to how far different types of product are direct substitutes for one another. The logical proposal by the Commission that duty should relate to alcohol content has not been able to be fully applied because of the implicit (national) discrimination this might give rise to.

Petrol also poses some problems. Rates of duty do not vary as significantly as for alcohol and tobacco: the highest duty per litre in Italy is some 2.5 times that of the lowest in Luxembourg. Generally, with the exceptions of Spain and Denmark, it is the southern countries with the higher rates and the northern with the lower rates. Here VAT will generally widen the differences. This has posed problems for harmonization, in addition to which different countries use a different balance of fuel duty, car tax, annual road taxes and direct charging by tolls to charge for road usage. The United Kingdom, for example, has tended, by the use of special car tax, to place the emphasis more on car ownership than car use.

Clearly there are many unresolved issues in the area of taxation, both direct and indirect, which can have a significant impact on the decisions of companies about how and where to operate in the Single Market. This includes the question of negative taxes, subsidies, such as those available in state aids to industry. We have already seen in Chapter 3 how these vary substantially and can have a very significant further impact on business decisions. These may actually pose a greater threat to harmonization than the more publicly emotive questions of tax. Certainly, evidence for the United Kingdom (Lee *et al.*, 1988) suggests that indirect tax and excise duty harmonization will not have major impacts on either consumers' expenditure overall (some redistribution towards alcohol and tobacco and away from travel) or on the government's revenue. Overall welfare of the United Kingdom could be affected much more by removal of remaining state aids to industry in partner states or at least a full equalization of their incidence.

5.4   Progress to the Single Market

Whatever the justification for the Single Market in terms of economic calculations of GDP gains and welfare benefits, its achievement has depended on agreeing the 282 measures identified as essential. The process for this depended, first, on securing agreement over a new procedure for determining European legislation and then putting the necessary measures through this. The Single European Act had two main provisions in this regard, a revision to the procedure by which measures were discussed and the introduction of majority voting rather than unanimity for more decisions in the Council of Ministers.

The cooperation procedure for decision making gave some greater power to the European Parliament. Although it is still the Commission that has the primary responsibility of proposing legislation and the Council of Ministers that takes the final decision, all proposals are sent directly to the Parliament, which can comment or suggest amendments. The Commission has the responsibility of trying to reach a compromise if any differences emerge, and if the Council of Ministers wishes to ignore the Parliament it typically has to reach a unanimous decision to do so. In this way, a greater degree of democratic accountability was ensured, though it is far from any real democratic control.

Getting agreement on a legislative proposal at the EC level can be time-consuming if there are strong vested interests, both sectoral and national, to be overcome. The use of a qualified majority voting procedure is an important step towards speeding up this process. This grants votes to the member states on the basis of (though not strictly proportional to) their size. Hence the large countries have ten votes, except Spain which has eight, and the smaller ones between two and five votes, making a total of seventy-six. To be approved a measure requires fifty-four votes, thus requiring a broad coalition to be formed which cannot be a simple coalition of either large or small countries, or of countries with more similar interests.

Nevertheless, many measures may still be approved against the wishes of one or more member states. There is no formal veto procedure, although, following the so-called Luxembourg compromise of 1966, it is open to individual member states to claim that a measure is so vital to their national interest that unanimity is required. The Commission tries to avoid this situation by renegotiating the measure; often major issues are resolved by discussion at the twice-yearly Heads of Government summit meeting, the European Council. However, this is not the end of the story: since most measures have the status of Directives or Decisions (as opposed to Regulations which pass directly into national legislation), they have to be enacted by each member government. Member states have differing records at completing this process.

By mid-1991 the Commission reported that all of the 282 measures of the 1985 White Paper had been presented to the decision-making bodies, but 89 of these remained to be agreed upon. Furthermore, an analysis of 126 measures showed a varying degree of enactment by member states (Table 5.3). Although there had been an improvement in the general rate of adoption to 73 per cent overall, this still hides a variation from 43 per cent of applicable measures in the case of Italy to 83 per cent in the case of the United Kingdom and nearly 90 per cent for Denmark. It is not just the number of outstanding measures, however, but the specific measures which are often involved which are seen as crucial to the achievement of the Single Market. Areas of particular concern cover such vital issues as free movement of people, direct taxation, financial services, transport and company law. Furthermore, agreement to defer the introduction of some measures for lengthy periods, such as the UK-influenced decision on the retention of duty-free allowances until 1999, and the inability to reach agreement on a harmonized VAT regime, have watered down some major symbols of a genuinely single market.

Table 5.3 Adoption of Single Market measures by member states to May 1991.

	Measures notified	Derogations	Measures not notified	Not applicable
Belgium	89	0	31	6
Denmark	107	0	12	7
Germany	95	0	25	6
Spain	83	2	38	3
France	103	0	18	5
Greece	87	5	29	5
Italy	52	0	69	5
Ireland	74	1	44	7
Luxembourg	81	0	37	8
Netherlands	86	0	34	6
Portugal	96	3	25	2
United Kingdom	99	1	20	6

Source: European Commission, Sixth Report on Completion of Internal Market, 1991.

It is unlikely (and probably always was) that all the measures of the Single Market would be in place by the deadline of 31 December 1992. Perhaps what is more remarkable is the progress that has been made towards this goal. What is left is, however, not just the tidying up of a few details, but some crucial decisions that affect the degree to which the estimated benefits can be achieved. To some extent even these have been overtaken by events. First, the recognition of the implications of a Single Market for both further Economic and Monetary Union and for greater political union led to the Maastricht Treaty, despite much publicised reluctance by the British government. Secondly, the renewed desire of the EFTA countries to seek closer ties with the Community leading to the accords on a European Economic Area in October 1991, coupled with the changes in eastern Europe, posed new challenges to the Community's ability to act as one in key economic negotiations.

Perhaps the most important outcome of the seven years of debate and search for agreement from the 1985 White Paper to 1992 was the opportunity this gave for reflection on the state of the Community and the recognition of the need to seek commitment to the next phase. The high profile given to the 1992 process ensured that this recognition was being made by all in the Community, since all were both threatened with loss if they did not act and tempted with possible gain if they did, although problems with ratifying the Maastricht Treaty show the degree of suspicion remaining. It is the outcome of those decisions that will determine how accurate the Cecchini studies were. It is to those decisions that we turn in more detail in the next two chapters.

6

The impact on sectors

The impact of the Single Market will be felt both by firms in individual sectors of the economy and by the regions in which those sectors are concentrated. We begin our assessment by looking at the sectors – this is essentially the microeconomic impact of the Single Market. In the following chapter we shall attempt the more macroeconomic assessment of overall impacts on the regions of the Community. To attempt to summarize the impact of the Single Market is perhaps one of the most dangerous exercises, especially when we are most interested in the process of change itself. We begin this chapter with a brief outline of the expected responses of sectors from the Commission's initial assessment, but the bulk of the chapter is taken up with a series of case studies of six contrasting sectors covering a range of traditional and new manufacturing industries and service sectors: food, drink and tobacco; textiles and clothing; motor manufacturing; high-technology industries; financial services; and tourism.

6.1 The framework of sectoral responses

The Cecchini study used a four-stage process to make assessments sector by sector of the potential for cost savings from completion of the Single Market, which could then be turned into estimates of welfare gains under specific assumptions:

Stage 1: cost of barriers affecting trade directly. Essentially these are those affected by border controls and delays.

Stage 2: cost of barriers affecting production. These operate whether or not a good is traded, and cover such items as technical standards, regulation and public procurement.

Stage 3: economies of scale. Restructuring and increased production arising from lower prices and market integration give rise to further cost savings through scale economies.

Stage 4: competitive pressure on costs and profits. Increased competition leads to improved efficiency through the removal of so-called X-inefficiencies and the excess profits (rents) associated with monopoly.

Stages 1 and 2 – the barrier effects – are essentially once and for all gains realizable in the short term. Stages 3 and 4 – the market integration effects – are medium-term effects depending on the restructuring of the economy within the Single Market.

Table 6.1 summarizes the findings for a set of sectors and for the European economy as a whole. These are only preliminary estimates depending on critical assumptions about the measurement of the size of barrier effects and the responsiveness to the changes. In particular, there is considerable doubt about the Stage 4 effects, changes in competition and how these interrelate with the search for scale economies. The Commission's estimates depended on detailed studies of certain sectors, which were seen as particularly critical, and a generalization to others. The overall estimates are therefore an aggregation from individual sectors. Despite this caution which has to be exercised over the estimates, they are based on a common set of assumptions and do give some indication of the way in which some sectors have more potential gains than others and hence involve more potential restructuring.

The Commission followed up these initial estimates with more detailed investigations of what were determined to be the industrial sectors particularly sensitive to the 1992 process. The forty most sensitive industrial sectors were selected for further study at both the aggregate level and at the level of individual member states (Commission of the European Communities, 1990a). These forty sectors actually account for about 50 per cent of industrial value added and a similar proportion of manufacturing employment in the Community. A further exercise was then undertaken to determine whether variations from this common list of sectors was necessary for understanding the situation in each member state – this was found to be necessary for the southern countries which have a rather different industrial structure from the average for the Community.

Table 6.1 Illustrative gains from selected sectors (billion ECU).[1]

	Removal of barriers	Integration of markets			
	Stages I and II Customs and technical barriers	Stage III Economies of scale	Stage IV Competition effects	Total	Alternative estimate[2]
Agriculture	0.7–3.0	1.1	0.0	1.9–4.2	0.7–3.0
Electricity, gas, water	3.3	0.6	0.0	3.8–3.9	3.3
Chemicals	2.8–2.9	7.7	4.6	15.0–15.2	9.2–9.4
Mechanical engineering	2.6–3.2	4.4–4.6	6.2	13.3–14.0	11.3–11.9
Electrical goods	2.6–3.3	5.3–5.4	11.0	18.8–19.7	15.7–16.4
Motor vehicles	2.1–3.1	4.5–4.7	10.0	16.6–17.8	14.1–15.1
Food products (not meat, dairy)	1.2–2.7	3.1	1.8	6.0–7.6	3.6–5.1
Beverages	0.4–0.5	0.9–1.0	0.5	1.9–2.0	1.3–1.4
Textiles, clothing	1.6–1.7	0.6	0.8	3.1–3.2	3.3–3.4
Timber, furniture	0.7–0.9	0.4	0.3	1.4–1.6	1.4–1.6
Building, civil engineering	4.3–4.9	2.3	0.0	6.6–7.2	4.3–4.9
Wholesale, retail trade	3.5–3.8	1.5	0.0	5.1–5.3	3.5–3.8
Inland transport	1.5	0.4	0.0	1.9	1.5
Credit and insurance	10.5–10.6	1.1	0.0	11.6–11.7	10.5–10.6
Total (all sectors)	64.8–79.8	60.3–61.5	45.6	170.8–187.0	126.3–141.3

[1] A range of estimates is given to reflect different databases. Competition effects in agriculture and service sectors are assumed to be given in barrier removal effects as separate studies were not carried out in these sectors.
[2] Alternative estimates are made on the basis of Smith and Venables (1988) who undertook a more thorough study of the restructuring and competition effects under differing assumptions about market structure.

Source: Emerson (1988).

The sensitive sectors were identified on four basic criteria for which data could be assembled:

1. The level of non-tariff barriers – including frontier formalities, technical standards, public procurement, differences in VAT and excise duties, all of which contribute to the degree of protection in the sector.
2. The degree of price dispersion.
3. The coverage ratio (share of domestic demand in each country covered by intra-EC and extra-EC imports) which measures the degree of penetration of trade and the openness of the economies to outside influences.
4. Potential scale economies – where there are cost advantages from greater integration.

On the basis of these criteria, four groups of sector were identified essentially on the basis of a cross-classification of trade intensity and price dispersion (Table 6.2). We shall return to this analysis in Chapter 7 where we look at the implications for the spatial impact of the 1992 process. In the remainder of this chapter we look at a selection of four industrial sectors, which cover the range of the various types of sector identified in Table 6.2, plus two service sectors, to assess how each of these is placed to be able to respond to the challenges posed by their sensitivity to the Single Market.

6.2 Food, drink and tobacco

Food, drink and tobacco (FDT), sometimes now referred to as the agrifood sector, is a broad sector representing the processing of raw agricultural products into goods for consumption including the canning and freezing of fresh produce and its further processing. The sector is large with about 10.5 per cent of employment and 10.7 per cent of value added as a proportion of manufacturing industry in the Community as a whole. It is particularly important in Denmark, Greece, Spain and the Netherlands where it accounts for over 15 per cent of both employment and value added, although its largest share of employment is in Ireland (28.8 per cent) where it, however, contributes only 9.1 per cent of value added. This sector also accounts for just over 25 per cent of total household budgets in the EC as a whole. Again there are variations, with food, etc. accounting for larger shares of expenditure in the poorer countries such as Greece and Portugal

Table 6.2 Classification of most sensitive sectors.

Trade intensity	Price dispersion	
	Weak	Strong
	Traditional or regulated public procurement markets	
Weak	*Characteristics* High NTBs Competition from NICs Restructuring	*Characteristics* High NTBs Weak competition in intra- and extra-EC trade High concentration and scale economies Major potential for 1992 restructuring
	Examples Electrical equipment Shipbuilding Pasta and cocoa products	*Examples* Boilermaking and railway equipment Pharmaceuticals Alcoholic and soft drinks
	Share Value added: 6.46 Employment: 7.32	*Share* Value added: 5.91 Employment: 4.36
	High technology public procurement sectors	**Products with moderate non-tariff barriers**
Strong	*Characteristics* Moderate NTBs Partly open to competition Open to extra-EC trade High concentration and scope for scale economies Low productivity of EC companies	*Characteristics* Moderate NTBs Fragmented distribution or marketing High degree of product differentiation
	Examples Telecommunications Data processing	*Examples* Motor vehicles Textiles, clothing, footwear Domestic electrical appliances, television, video Toys
	Share Value added: 7.12 Employment: 6.06	*Share* Value added: 42.06 Employment: 35.77

(about 40 per cent), and smaller shares in France and Netherlands (below 20 per cent).

Sensitive products within the sector fall into one of the two regulated market groups in Table 6.2 according to whether they display a high degree of import penetration and hence low price dispersion or the reverse.

The sector is a market characterized by low growth. The income elasticity of demand for most products is extremely low and the scope for exports to third markets, given the relatively high cost of EC-produced food inputs, is also low. Hence European producers have needed to look for increasing ways of developing new markets within the Community although this has been hindered by strong regional variations in patterns of demand. Growth in markets in southern European countries has been stronger as consumers have switched to higher value goods as incomes increase. Portugal, for example, has experienced real growth of 15 per cent per annum compared with less than 2 per cent in UK and German markets. There is also growth in new products, particularly fast food, ready-to-eat meals, and mineral waters, in northern markets. Compared to low overall growth, these types of products grew by at least 8 per cent per annum over the last three years in the United Kingdom. Thus the move is to products involving higher quality, higher convenience and higher variety, and hence a compensation for sluggish growth by going for higher productivity.

Despite the recognition of segmented markets, where variations in taste have been reinforced by technical and health standards, there has been a strong move to greater international integration and concentration in the industry. The ten largest firms had a market share of 67 per cent in the United Kingdom in 1986, in France the figure was 46 per cent, in Germany 43 per cent and in Italy 65 per cent. Five of the ten major European food companies are UK-owned and one is Anglo-Dutch; of the other four, two are Swiss and two French. The industry has also been characterized by strong vertical integration, from food production into distribution and retailing. Although many of the main actors are well-known household names such as Nestlé, Cadbury-Schweppes, United Biscuits, Suchard and Source-Perrier, a number of major multi-sector conglomerates also figure strongly in this sector, such as Hanson Trust and Unilever.

For the larger companies internationalization is an essential response to the lack of dynamism in the food market, but there are limits to the extent to which genuine economies of scale can be found given the limited scope of individual product lines. Fifty per cent of companies were selling given product lines in only one or two of the main EC markets on average and only 9 per cent were selling in all five of the main markets (France, Germany, Italy, Spain and the United Kingdom). Thus internationalization has had to be selective as adequate rates of return are only available to market leaders.

For FDT producers, the increasing power and internationalization of retailers, often using their own brand names, pose an additional problem. FDT has been, therefore, an industry with considerable recent mergers and acquisition activity with about one-third of deals involving cross-border activity. Some 25 per cent of deals have been in Germany, with a further 10 per cent in the United Kingdom, but UK firms have been the most active acquirers in cross-border deals, followed by US and other non-EC (especially Swiss) acquirers. As well as merger and acquisition activity there has been an increase in cross-border agreements for marketing, distribution and licensing and some collaborative moves to the organic development of 'Eurobrands'.

Regulations and standards are the most significant barrier to the creation of a Single Market about which there is some hopes of action. The Single Market programme cannot, of course, legislate for a greater integration of tastes and culinary preferences between different regions in Europe. Existing barriers fall into five main areas:

1. Specific ingredient restrictions, where the product must conform to certain ingredient standards or contents to be sold.
2. Content/denomination regulations, where the product must conform to certain ingredient standards or contents to be labelled a certain product.
3. Packaging/labelling regulations where packaging and/or labelling must conform to specific requirements (e.g. as to content).
4. Fiscal discrimination.
5. Specific importing regulations.

Of these, the first is essentially a general health–public welfare protection requirement where the issue is of harmonization and mutual recognition. The second and third are the regulations that have been particularly used as a means of protecting domestic industries. Hence regulations on fat content in chocolate and ice cream for these products to be called by that name are justified on the grounds of protecting the unsuspecting consumer. Laws on the purity of beer or pasta have a similar origin. Packaging regulations include the prohibition of plastic bottles for mineral water in Italy and non-recyclable bottles for beer in Denmark are even more overtly protectionist since they impose heavier costs on foreign imports for high bulk/value goods – the need to use glass and especially the need to re-export empty bottles.

The principle adopted for reform is that, as long as labelling is clear as to content, consumers should have the right to choose between, say, pure durum wheat pasta and its cheaper soft wheat alternative or real ice creams and its mass-produced British alternative with high vegetable fat content. The total impact of these changes is estimated to be of the order of 500–1000 million ECU per annum, 2–3 per cent of total value added in the sector. Over 80 per cent of these benefits are estimated to come from the removal of just six barriers and 20 per cent from just one, the German beer purity law.

These gains arise from the following:

1. The use of less expensive ingredients in products and increasing the possibility of saving from bulk purchases.
2. The reduction in packaging and labelling costs.
3. The elimination of the bureaucracy necessary to preserve the barriers.

However, there is scope for further gains: as consumer choice increases, greater efficiency results from increased competition and trade increases. Firms may be better placed to exploit new products with access to more and larger markets. The critical factor is a balance between this search for scale economies in product lines and an increasing market segmentation.

As trade barriers are reduced, however, there is greater attraction for non-EC firms to exploit the market. Swiss firms such as Nestlé and Suchard have been pre-eminent in this, but US firms have also shown a great interest in the EC market. US firms have shown particular strength in exploiting specific product scale economies such that 68 per cent of US brands are market leaders, compared to 50 per cent of Swiss brands and only 38 per cent of EC brands. Clearly only those foreign brands that are expected to do well will be marketed and this biases EC brands downwards. However, it is also the case that the non-EC brands have wider intra-EC coverage than the average for EC brands, such that 55 per cent of US and 73 per cent of Swiss brands are found in all five major EC markets compared to an average 49 per cent for EC brands.

Already fierce competition within the sector, especially where regulation has been less pronounced, has squeezed profit margins and hence the impact of scale economies and increased competition on prices is more difficult to predict. Traditionally, foodstuffs are relatively price-inelastic, but the search for new and expanding markets and products can produce remarkable results. The growth of the mineral water market in the United Kingdom has been remarkable, both in total and in terms of the market creation of one brand, Perrier, which increased sales from 3 million bottles (50 per cent market share) in 1976 to 77 million (60 per cent) in 1986.

The regional impacts of changes in the sector are also difficult to assess. Transport costs have been at about the average level for manufacturing industry at 3–4 per cent of total costs, but given low margins this means 30–50 per cent of profit. The relative gains to central and peripheral areas could have fairly major implications for location as markets are internationalized. However, foodstuffs include a major sector of perishable and fragile goods where transport requirements are more specific and reliability in delivery critical. These industries depend on inputs from the more peripheral regions of the Community including Ireland, Denmark and Mediterranean regions. Improved transport is likely to be critical within the Community to ensure that producers in these regions remain competitive with extra-EC competitors. At the less perishable level there is some evidence of UK firms moving into continental markets through acquisition or joint venture both in order to establish a more central base for operations and to forestall possible predatory attacks by continental producers on the UK market.

It must also be remembered that the basic inputs of the sector in the EC industry, agricultural products, are themselves produced in a heavily subsidized and distorted market under the Common Agricultural Policy. Moves to reduce agricultural subsidies and reduce protection could have two major effects. First, lower input prices could increase the profitability of EC industry and give it a competitive boost relative to extra-EC competitors. But, secondly, the impacts of lower levels of support to EC agricultural regions could be to increase reliance on imported agricultural produce which would push food processing industries away from agricultural regions and towards major ports.

Finally, two major sub-sectors, alcoholic drink and tobacco, are strongly implicated by fiscal changes in the Single Market programme. As we have seen, any move towards fiscal approximation will have major north–south implications on consumer prices and hence on consumption. Given the importance of employment in these sectors in the southern economies such a change could have major implications. It has also led to considerable vertical integration in affected sectors with, for example, companies in the brewing industry moving forwards more into retailing and major hotel chains moving backwards into food and drink supply sectors.

The conclusion for the food, drink and tobacco sector is, therefore, that, although basically stagnant in terms of its growth potential, it has already seen major corporate restructuring. This restructuring has aimed at securing new markets to compensate for sluggish growth in existing markets and to develop new product lines across national borders to exploit potential scale economies. This is leading to greater concentration in many areas of the sector and to the attraction of extra-EC firms into the market. The sector is dominated by a small number of conglomerates, often not identified with particular products or brands, and the practice of regular brand acquisitions and sale by these firms is widespread. This has a destabilizing effect on the industry in particular locations.

Overall the potential welfare gains in this sector may not be great in proportional terms, but the sector's size makes them important. The future is likely to be one of continuing change. One thing seems certain, that the diversity of taste and culinary practices in Europe will continue to place severe constraints on the complete move to a Single Market in this sector, even if the external pressure towards convenience and fast foods is having some effect in this direction.

6.3 Textiles and clothing

The textile and clothing sector represents two stages of a manufacturing process. The textile industry uses either natural or man-made fibres to produce yarn and fabric which is then used in various finishing industries including carpets and furnishings, industrial goods and clothing. About 50 per cent of textile output goes into clothing, however, and virtually all of clothing's input comes from textiles, giving rise to strong vertical integration. It is therefore sensible to treat the sectors together.

Textiles and clothing is a classic case of a major European industry which has faced increasing problems. These sectors fall clearly into the large group in Table 6.2 of sectors with moderate trade barriers and moderate to strong price variations despite relatively high degrees of import penetration both within the EC and from outside. Textiles were, of course, the basis of the industrial revolution in Europe, but so they have been for many newly industrializing countries. This has led to high wage, low productivity growth producers in Europe facing increasing problems. The problems for producers are compounded by the tendency for the industry to be highly spatially concentrated. The pressure for government aid has therefore been strong on an intra-EC level. The desire to avoid excessive state aid within the EC in a way that would distort internal competition led to a concentration on an external strategy to restrict competition from the new producers. Thinly disguised as a form of voluntary export restraint, the Multi-fibre Arrangement (MFA) has been used as a means of protecting EC producers. Following the expiry of the previous MFA in 1991, the hope is that it should be phased out over a fifteen-year period thereafter. However, the MFA itself has not provided a united front for the EC, as various bilateral arrangements within it have produced rather different situations in different member states.

The textile and clothing sector represents between 9 and 10 per cent of employment and just under 6 per cent of value added in the Community. These figures are typical of the United Kingdom and French also, but the industry is rather smaller in importance in Germany and rather larger in Italy. However, the German and Italian industries are the two largest in the EC in absolute terms. The textile industry is much more important in the EC than in the United States or Japan: production value in 1985 was 30 per cent greater than the United States and 75 per cent greater than Japan.

Textiles, and more particularly clothing, are also largely dominated by smaller enterprises. This is especially true of the Italian industry, where over 80 per cent of firms have less than 100 employees. Correspondingly, investment rates are relatively low compared with other industries, at around 10 per cent of value added, and productivity rates are quite low, especially in the United Kingdom. There is a distinction here between textiles and clothing, since it is the latter which is particularly affected by small-scale operations.

Since 1980 there has been a steady upwards trend in imports, especially of clothing, and a deterioration of the EC trade balance to around 6 billion ECU by 1988. Exports have also risen, but erratically, since third country purchases of EC-produced goods have been very sensitive to exchange rate movements. This seems to be one industry where UK producers in particular have suffered from fluctuations in the exchange rate prior to Britain's joining the exchange rate mechanism of the EMS.

The United Kingdom seems to be the major loser of the EC producers over both the recent and long periods, but the French and Italian industries have also lost considerable ground. Italy is still a major net exporter in both world, and especially EC, markets whilst the other major countries are net importers. The German textile industry has, however, shown an improvement in its competitive position in recent years.

The industry is already a fairly integrated one within the Community, the main pressures coming from outside. Trade barriers other than border controls are of minimal importance and arise mainly from the way quota systems operate within the MFA. Differing VAT rates affect clothing seriously as such products are classified differently by different member states, meaning that the widest range of rates is found. However, the overall reduction in unit costs from the completion of the Single Market is estimated to be only between 0.4 and 0.9 per cent.

Government aid to the textile and clothing industries within member states has continued to be strong. Although this clearly has had some impact in reducing work-forces and increasing investment to improve productivity and competitiveness, there is also a tendency for this just to be seen as cushioning the industries. The impact in the United Kingdom has been towards vertical integration and concentration. Four firms, Coats Viyella, Courtaulds, Tootal and Coloroll, accounted for 30 per cent of textile sales in 1988, but none of these has been able to reverse the long-term trend in the UK industry. German and Italian industries have taken rather different routes, and have had success in developing niche markets. The emphasis in Germany has been on extensive modernization and investment, whereas in Italy support has been given to developing the Italian tradition of small, but highly flexible, enterprises based on styling and design. It remains to be seen whether the German and Italian industries will be able to withstand tighter controls over direct government aid in the Single Market.

Distribution and marketing have become more important in this sector and internationalization of brand images has taken place, not just in high fashion, but now increasingly in High Street brands. Hence large retailers such as Marks and Spencer or franchised networks such as Benetton have been developing pan-European identities. These depend increasingly on an efficient logistic network. Transport costs are fairly insignificant for both textiles and clothing, typically less than 2 per cent of the value of output although again tight profit margins can make variations in such costs critical. Efficiency and reliability in transport are less directly important than for food, drink and tobacco, but will be important through their impact on stockholding.

The overall outlook for the textiles and clothing sector is that the Single Market programme is not the main influence on the future development of the industry. The major factor is the outcome of current GATT negotiations on the long-term arrangements to follow the expiry of the MFA. Clearly the future for the industry in the EC, except in the area of high quality and/or high fashion clothing, is not bright, especially as tighter controls over government aid in the Single Market are imposed. This has serious consequences for textile regions, especially in the United Kingdom and France, but also in Germany where the industry has been protected rather more in recent years. The Commission has attempted to cope with this by introducing the RETEX policy, similar to those already in existence for restructuring in coal, steel and shipbuilding regions, with 500 million ECU available over five years from mid 1992.

Some boost to sales may come from reductions in the higher rates of VAT used in some countries, but equally the possible loss of zero rating on children's clothing in the United Kingdom could have a negative effect. Increasing vertical integration through to the sales outlet and increasing internationalization in such distribution systems may provide some increase in efficiency by reducing sales and marketing costs. However, such retailers and distributors are also likely to be turning increasingly to cheaper goods from outside the EC.

6.4   The automobile industry

The automobile industry could be thought to be one of the key sectors providing the test of success or failure of the 1992 programme (others being pharmaceuticals, chemicals more generally and computers). It is a sector where fragmented markets have prevented the achievement of potential scale economies and the consequence of failure to exploit world markets in the face of US and Japanese competition. It is also a sector where technical standards have not been harmonized and where differential tax treatment of vehicles (both in terms of taxes on purchase and on vehicle ownership and use) has distorted markets. The classification of Table 6.2 puts it in a very similar position to textiles and clothing, but the scale economy potential and the rather stronger extra-EC trade position does differentiate it somewhat. It is also the largest single sector of all the sensitive sectors in terms of both value added and employment.

The automobile industry includes both the final assembly of vehicles, typically undertaken by a small number of large firms, and the production of components. Vertical integration has taken place to a large extent in the production of the major components (body shells, engines and transmissions), but specialist firms still survive in the production of other components such as instruments, shock absorbers, braking systems, etc. The total industry is one of the major sectors of the Community, producing nearly 9 per cent of the value added in manufacturing and employing just over 8 per cent of the manufacturing work-force. The leading country in the sector is Germany, where the sector accounts for over 13 per cent of value added in manufacturing. This is followed by France and Belgium (the latter being curious in that it has no indigenous motor vehicle industry) where the sector accounts for just under 9 per cent of manufacturing value added. There is then a further group of Spain, Italy and the United Kingdom where the sector produces around 6 per cent of value added. The industry is relatively insignificant in other member countries. It is, therefore, already a fairly highly concentrated industry. In 1988

Germany produced nearly 32 per cent of EC passenger car production and France nearly 23 per cent. Over 60 per cent of German production and over 40 per cent of French production went for export in 1987; these were the only two net exporters of vehicles.

The EC as a whole has been a net exporter of cars, but the trade surplus has been falling and amounted to just 3 per cent of production by 1987. This reflects the EC's declining share of world production. In 1970 EC production was well over twice that of Japan and 20 per cent greater than that of the United States. By 1989 Japanese production had risen to 90 per cent of the EC level and even the humbled US industry stood at nearly 93 per cent having fallen back from the peak of 1985 when it was producing 20 per cent more than the EC industry. The three major producers are then producing similar quantities of vehicles (between 12 and 14 million per annum), but the main differences are in market size. The EC market is roughly equal to production at 13.4 million in 1988 and 1989, the US market far exceeds domestic products at 16–18 million, but the Japanese market is still less than 7 million vehicles. The EC market fell sharply in 1990, by around 10 per cent in the United Kingdom and Spain, and this situation persisted through 1991.

That the EC industry has been able to maintain its position within the domestic markets of Europe is largely explained by protectionist measures against imports in many countries, especially of Japanese cars, which have thus not managed to penetrate EC markets to the same extent as in the United States. Nevertheless, where these restrictions were less stringent, or non-existent, Japanese producers easily took 20–30 per cent of the local market and had just over 9 per cent of the total market in 1988. Only in France, Italy and Spain, which had very restrictionist quotas, was there no real penetration.

The automobile industry is not only of direct importance as an employer, it is a symbol of both European and national identity. Cars are the most conspicuous consumption good and there are considerable variations in national preferences for a vehicle's characteristics which have given rise to distinct variations in national production. Hence the contrast between Italian style and German engineering quality is exploited by manufacturers to segment the market, not just for the highly specialized products of Ferrari and Porsche but also for the mass production of Fiat and Volkswagen.

This segmentation of the market, at least into the mass-produced family car and the low volume prestige car is important. However, Europe has also segmented the market by size much more than the United States, reflecting both the density of traffic and the need for greater fuel efficiency given higher fuel prices. Thus mass producers see the need to produce vehicles in at least three, if not four, class sizes: superminis, small and large family cars and executive cars. Demand for variety in performance and body shape (saloon, hatchback, estate) within each of these classes leads to a bewildering array of models and specifications. The automobile industry thus faces a similar problem to that of the food industry in producing standard products in the most efficient manner.

Its continued success as an industry is also vital to a series of supplying industries since the vehicle sector consumes roughly 20 per cent of steel production, 20 per cent of machine-tool production, 15 per cent of rubber production and 5 per cent of glass production. Typically, the products from each of these industries are at the higher end of the quality and hence value range.

The sector has not been immune to government intervention. All of the major producing countries have been prompted to step in to save their major producers from collapse at various stages, although this process has been reversed to some extent recently. Often this intervention was occasioned by problems arising after attempts to absorb smaller inefficient producers or the merger of several smaller producers. Hence in the United Kingdom, Austin and Morris merged to form BMC, later expanded to form British Leyland as it successively absorbed other small manufacturers both in the car market (Rover, Jaguar and Daimler) and in the commercial vehicle market. The Rootes Group in the United Kingdom and Simca in France were absorbed by Chrysler, Lancia by Fiat in Italy, NSU by Volkswagen in Germany and DAF in Holland by the Swedish firm Volvo. British Leyland and Renault in France were wholly nationalized. Volkswagen in Germany had a substantial state shareholding, without which it would probably never have recovered from its disastrous position in the early 1970s when it had a totally inappropriate model range.

Now the process has been reversed: British Leyland has been split up and privatized. Jaguar regained its independence only to be bought by Ford, Rover, as the remaining car division was privatized, after forming a strong joint venture link with Honda, the Japanese producer, by sale to British Aerospace in a deal which has incurred the wrath of the European Commission because of illegal payments made by the UK government to make the deal more attractive. This same fate has befallen the French government because of its policy of support to Renault. The German government has divested itself of its stake in Volkswagen, which leaves Alfa Romeo in the hands of the Italian nationalized holding company ENI and a complex set of arrangements affecting Fiat.

It will be clear from this that relatively little cross-border merger and acquisition activity has taken place in this sector amongst the major producers. The only long-established pan-European firms are the two US giants Ford and General Motors. Ford has had subsidiaries in the United Kingdom and Germany and has widened its scope to include operations in Belgium and Spain as well as moving towards greater integration of all its European operations. Factories now tend to specialize in models produced for the whole market or in the production of major components such as engines or transmissions. GM has also moved to a single range of European vehicles produced either under the Vauxhall (United Kingdom) or Opel (Germany) badges from factories in the United Kingdom, Germany and Belgium. The closest which a European-based manufacturer has come to this is the French firm Peugeot which, as well as acquiring the ailing Citroën, also picked up the pieces of Chrysler's disastrous venture with Simca and Rootes (for which it revived the old marque of Talbot). Peugeot now produces one of its models in Coventry for the European market whilst importing other models to the United Kingdom from France.

Other ventures have been small scale. Volvo acquired the car production of the small Dutch firm DAF. (Interestingly DAF later merged its truck operations with those of Leyland whilst Leyland's bus operations were acquired by Volvo.) Volvo as a Swedish firm is, of course, not an EC producer. The other major activity has been in Spain where the local producer Seat, after years of producing cars under licence from Fiat, was acquired by Volkswagen. Fiat has continued joint venture operations in eastern Europe and other countries such as Turkey. Renault has established assembly facilities in Spain as well as an existing plant in Belgium, but has recently entered a much bigger agreement with Volvo which may pave the way for an eventual merger. More recently changes in eastern Europe have led to Volkswagen taking over the former GDR producer Trabant and investing heavily in Skoda in Czechoslovakia.

The diversification of automobile manufacturers is also an important feature of their ability to survive. Hence it must be remembered that Renault, Fiat and Volvo all have major stakes in commercial vehicles whilst Daimler-Benz, the owner of Mercedes, is not only the world's largest truck producer, but is also Europe's largest arms producer following the acquisition of Dormer and MBB.

Finally, in any discussion of cross-border joint ventures comes the difficult question of Japanese involvement. The main problem for even medium-sized car manufacturers is gaining access to the research and development necessary for new models, plus the necessary production volumes to make design of engines and other components viable. Production levels of 500,000 per annum are usually necessary to achieve these scale economies. This is essentially what Japanese firms such as Honda have offered to Rover, or Nissan to Alfa Romeo: the access to both technology and scale. Hence Rover's 800 series was jointly designed and launched, and was followed by the well-received 200 and 400 series vehicles more recently. Rover now not only produce these cars themselves, but also collaborate in the production of similar Honda models in the United Kingdom. Such collaboration produced difficulties in the early days when BL (as it still was) was essentially just assembling Japanese-designed cars, largely from Japanese components. This made the cars count as Japanese rather than EC-produced for many other markets (especially Italy and France). This problem has been overcome for Rover with the latest models, but still faces Nissan and Toyota who have decided to establish in the United Kingdom in their own right instead of seeking joint venture partners.

Nissan has been producing cars in the United Kingdom since 1986 from a green field factory site near Sunderland. Output was 56,000 vehicles in 1988 and is planned to rise to 200,000 by 1992–93. Toyota's new plant near Derby is expected to reach an output of 100,000 by 1995 and 200,000 by 1997–98 whilst the new Honda plant at Swindon plans 100,000 by 1994. This would amount to a Japanese production of 500,000 in total by 1998 or a quarter to a third of likely UK production. The plan is to export some 50–60 per cent of this output, and the United Kingdom's current trade deficit in vehicles will be eliminated. This can only happen if the Japanese producers can achieve a minimum 80 per cent European content in their cars. This ready market for components in the United Kingdom has already led to European firms such as Bosch investing heavily in the United Kingdom, but is also attracting Japanese components producers such as a recently announced £65 million investment by Nippondenso.

The costs of non-Europe are fairly widespread in the car industry:

1. Fiscal barriers include:
   (a) variations in car sales taxes and VAT rates;
   (b) variations in policies on VAT refunds for company cars;
   (c) variations in state aid to 'national champions';
   (d) non-uniform cross-border registration rules;
   (e) variations in tax incentives for environmental improvements;
   (f) variations in excise duty on fuel, both in terms of rates and the relative treatment of diesel and unleaded fuel.
2. Physical barriers include:
   (a) delays in import and export of vehicles;
   (b) need for complex paperwork on temporary import and export of vehicles;

(c) complex quota rules on Japanese imports.
3. Technical barriers include:
(a) lack of uniform product testing and type-approval certification making personal imports difficult;
(b) differing standards on exhaust emission;
(c) car equipment peculiarities which make model variations necessary, such as side repeater flasher lights in Italy, rear reflectors in Germany, dim-dip headlamps in the United Kingdom and yellow headlamps in France, plus the fact that two countries (the United Kingdom and Ireland) drive on the left;
(d) the condoning of selective distribution systems by the EC in 1985 which allows for exclusive dealing contracts underwritten by manufacturers on the grounds of securing the prudence of dealers but in effect a means of segmenting markets and preserving producer control over selling prices.

On the basis of the evidence presented by Pratten (1988) it would appear that there is essentially room for five main manufacturers in the European car market operating at minimum efficient technical scale. There are actually ten that account for more than 2 per cent of the total market (just over 250,000 vehicles a year). These fall conveniently into two groups. Six stand a chance of realizing major scale economies with outputs of 1.3–2.0 million vehicles a year (VW, Fiat, Peugeot-Citroën, Ford, General Motors and Renault in order). The four smaller producers (Rover, Daimler-Benz, BMW and Volvo) are to some extent more specialized producers and achieve sales of between 250,000 and 450,000 vehicles. There are also a number of smaller, very specialist, producers which produce a total of around 350,000 vehicles. In addition the Japanese producers sold approaching 1.5 million vehicles in 1988.

This inability to achieve scale economies is to some extent the cost of providing choice in the vehicle market. However, it is clear from the amount of state aid poured into the French and Italian industries (and less successfully into the British) that it is not just consumer choice but a rather wider consideration of national interests that is being served here. It is difficult to envisage any of VW, Fiat, Renault or even Rover being allowed to disappear into a grouping dominated by any of the others.

However, joint ventures may increasingly be used as a way of exploiting modern production platform techniques. In this, expensive components such as floorpans, engines and transmissions can be jointly designed and produced, whilst the finished product can be distinctively different. This has been widely used already by some of the smaller manufacturers and for production of small volume, high capacity engines by larger manufacturers.

Design and engineering usually amounts to about 5 per cent of total cost and this is where both significant scale economies and gains from common type-approval certification, rather than having to effect this in each separate country, may be available. Together this may yield a 10 per cent saving overall, in such costs equal to 0.5 per cent of total costs. Increasing concordance of components may produce significant economies of scale in this part of the industry, although there is a reluctance to depend too heavily on single sources of supply by producers for fear of strikes, etc. However, the prospect of greater competition should reduce component costs by the order of 2–2.5 per cent or nearly 900 million ECU. Increased utilization of fixed plant, including the potential for joint use of production platforms, produces a further worthwhile saving of up to 600 million ECU. There are further sources of saving from increased efficiency in the organization of warranty, marketing and administration.

In total an estimate of 2.6 billion ECU or a saving of about 5 per cent on total unit costs has been made, representing an increase of around 12.5 per cent in labour productivity and 17.5 per cent in capital productivity. The potential appears greatest in Italy, and least in the United Kingdom and Germany.

However, whether such savings can be realized is open to question. How far will European consumers accept the reduction in choice implied which might start approaching the 'badge engineering' of the United States, where effectively identical cars are sold simply with different names? The less homogeneous European markets may still require a degree of variety more than that implied by the wholesale adoption of platform technology. Furthermore, national car markets have very different characteristics as indicated by the variations in price for otherwise identical cars, of between 15 and 90 per cent.

There are various reasons for these national variations which can be advanced. Low pre-tax prices in Denmark represent a means of maintaining sales despite the highest rates of tax which actually lead to highest post-tax prices. The high prices in the United Kingdom can only be partly explained by the need to re-engineer cars for the UK market with right-hand drive. Historically it may also be true that the inefficiency of domestic producers allowed importers to set high prices and profit take whilst still achieving acceptable market shares. Car manufacturers claim that national preferences for different levels of specification make most comparisons difficult and inaccurate, as does the need to take into account the total purchase package. One further factor is the very high share of the UK new car market taken by company cars, sold at substantial discounts to fleet buyers, which is compensated for by high pre-discount prices. Car producers have attempted to maintain these price differentials by creating major obstacles to the parallel importing of cars such as refusing delivery of UK specification cars to Belgian or German dealers and making the availability of type-approval certification, necessary for registering a new vehicle, only available through the recognized importer of that make. Despite court rulings against this practice, substantial differentials in price have been maintained. Restrictions on parallel importing, and moves to break dealer monopolies, should make such differentials harder to maintain, but the cost to the buyer is still likely to be great enough not to lead to a complete convergence to one price. No one manufacturer has the interest in breaking this effective cartel which enables all to make greater profits in certain markets.

The impact of the Single Market on the motor industry is thus substantial, because of the size of the industry, but uncertain. The real potential for gain lies in a restructuring of the industry to enable more efficient use of capital and greater production runs of components. This could imply some substantial reorganization of the industry. Transport costs are currently not a major element in costs, about 3 per cent of the value of output, but have risen somewhat on the basis of UK evidence over time. Traditionally the car industry was a spatially concentrated industry with component suppliers located close to production plants and most transport costs involving the distribution of finished vehicles. Led by the US multinationals this is changing, with spatially separated plants linking together to concentrate on certain components or model-assembly. This implies a greater use of transport, and need for efficient transport, at earlier stages of the production process. It is this process of integrating plants in different locations that seems critical to the success of change in the industry. The entry of Japanese producers directly into European production serves as a catalyst to this since they provide a major new market for component suppliers as they strive to achieve adequate local content levels.

6.5 High technology sectors

High technology industry can in many ways be thought of as the core sector in a modern, growing economy. It is a test of the Single Market whether it can both encourage the research and development necessary for innovation and allow the development of competitive products on the world market. Although the Community has put considerable emphasis on R&D and on collaborative funding of new technologies through various programmes such as ESPRIT and COMETT, the total resources devoted to this have been on a small scale. The ability to exploit this investment has been impaired through various restrictive practices; public procurement, aid to national champions and lack of harmonization in technical standards. This sector is identifiable in the terms of Table 6.2 as a sector with a unique set of problems, high non-tariff barriers, particularly related to public procurement, but high trade penetration and relatively little price dispersion. The problems of the sector are thus ones of fragmented markets, leading to higher costs and low productivity by world standards.

Whilst it is convenient to think of the high technology sector as a single entity with similar problems, in reality it is a collection of much smaller industries, each with individual characteristics and problems. In this review we shall ignore substantial parts of the sector and concentrate on just three parts: active electronic components (semi-conductors, microprocessors), computers and telecom equipment. The first of these is a vital producer of inputs to the other two which represent slightly different types of final product.

Active components production in the EC amounts to about 6.5 billion ECU per annum out of a total components output of about 14.5 billion ECU, less than half the Japanese output and less than 40 per cent of US output. Components account for 15–20 per cent of total electronics industry output. The EC has also been facing an increasing trade deficit in components; a surplus of 950 million ECU in 1981 had turned into a deficit of over 1.1 billion ECU by 1988 despite a strong growth in exports. Although the EC's share of world exports in semiconductors had fallen from 13 to 11 per cent, this compares favourably with the fall in the US share from 61 to 43 per cent as the Japanese share grew from 26 to 44 per cent (Hobday, 1989).

Three major difficulties face EC firms in components. First, US and Japanese competition is a real threat and requires increased R&D expenditure which can only be financed by profits on existing ventures, whilst rapidly falling prices mean that only early entrants in a market recoup costs fully. Secondly, public procurement restrictions have fragmented the market and inhibited both internal competition and the achievement of scale economies. Thirdly, rising R&D costs have necessitated more joint venture activity, and mergers and acquisitions. Thus recent years have seen the joint Megaproject of Siemens and Philips, the takeover of Ferranti by Plessey, the SGS/Thomson merger and the later takeover of Inmos (the privatized British venture) by ST. These European examples are, however, to be set against increasing cooperation with non-European producers such as the agreement on memory chips between Siemens, IBM and Toshiba.

Furthermore there is increasing non-EC investment in Europe in anticipation of the Single Market and to overcome the 14 per cent tariff imposed on imported semiconductors. Fujitsu, for example, has invested 60 million ECU in a wafer production plant in the United Kingdom.

In response, the EC has been active in the launching of precompetition joint projects. The 3.4 billion ECU JESSI (Joint European Submicron Silicon) research programme has involved Philips, Siemens and SGS/Thomson, plus Plessey. Even so, Philips, Siemens and ST are all struggling to fight losses and to finance components activities. In the United Kingdom there is only one major indigenous components producer following the GEC–Plessey merger, despite the United Kingdom being one of the major components markets. The gap is being filled by foreign firms. In addition to the Fujitsu investment already mentioned, recent announcements include a doubling of wafer production by Inmos (now owned by SGS/Thomson), a memory production plant with 50 million ECU by Motorola and a new chip production plant by Sprague. In a similar way to car production, the United Kingdom is becoming something of a platform for extra-EC firms to attack the Single Market.

Turning to final products, the computer industry in the EC has also faced a difficult time in the face of market domination by firms such as IBM. National champions such as ICL in the United Kingdom, Honeywell Bull in France and Siemens and Nixdorf in Germany have received substantial aid but face increasing difficulties. Now the proposed acquisition of ICL by Fujitsu raises an even bigger question about Japanese penetration into what has been seen to be a critical market for European producers. Clearly Japanese interest is in securing a base within the Community: acquisition not only provides the base, it helps to eliminate some subsidized competition and gives potential access to EC R&D funding. Earlier reluctance on the part of the Commission to give approval to such mergers now seems to be waning. There is some feeling that large parts of the 1.75 billion ECU a year spent on research in the high technology area have not been used for improving competitiveness, but rather to bolster companies against acquisition. Even in this sector it may be more costly in the long run to subsidize EC companies as a means of keeping out Japanese imports than to allow Japanese companies to become EC producers.

The telecommunications equipment sector is frequently held up as one of the best examples of the worst effects of public procurement.

Government-owned, national telecom agencies (PTTs) have monopsonistic and regulated control over purchasing of telecom equipment. Hence the internal competition has been weak and intra-EC trade insignificant. The industry is not insignificant in size, however, accounting for nearly 4 per cent of EC value added and 3.5 per cent of employment (nearly 5 per cent in the United Kingdom and over 6 per cent in Germany). Only four EC firms feature in the top ten world producers, though two of these (Alcatel of France and Siemens of Germany) are in the top three after the US AT&T. These two account for an estimated 46 per cent of the EC market which is just under 25 per cent of the world market. The EC is a net exporter of telecom equipment, although it runs a deficit with both the United States and Japan.

Telecom equipment involves three main sub-markets, switching equipment (the biggest), terminals and transmission equipment. Apart from the growth of new services necessitating new terminal equipment (e.g. the growth of fax), switching equipment and transmission equipment are the main areas affected recently by new technologies. Hence the introduction of ISDN (integrated services digital networks) from 1988 has required a major upsurge in investment absorbing 60–80 per cent of total R&D costs which will require recouping over a relatively short period given the rapidity of technological progress. Similarly, satellite technology, after a lifespan of only some 20–30 years, is giving way rapidly to fibre optics in transmission.

All of this change has been taking place on a fragmented, national basis involving the use of different standards, often incompatible. The Commission set out four basic goals for liberalization:

1. Liberalization of terminal equipment with separate independent bodies for type approval.
2. Liberalization of services with the exception of traditional voice telephone communications and telex.
3. Acceptance of competitive international bidding for the supply of switching and transmission equipment.
4. Creation of a European standard-setting mechanism, mutual recognition and Open Network Provision, giving private suppliers access to existing PTT networks.

Hence it will be seen that much of the benefit on the telecom equipment sector is seen to derive from liberalization of telecommunication service agencies, the major customers. Standardization and competition should lead both to greater scale economies and improved competitiveness against extra-EC competitors. The total effect on costs is estimated at between 3 and 4.8 billion ECU.

This programme has been supported by an EC initiative, the RACE project, to establish an integrated broad-band communication network. As well as standardization, this would involve major infrastructure investment and was seen to have an important regional development dimension since access to new communications technology was seen as a basic prerequisite to a region's connections with core networks in the Community.

The UK position in this sector is of interest since Britain was the first EC country to privatise its telecom services and liberalize the market. The two main domestic telecom equipment producers, GEC and Plessey, established a new joint venture in GPT which ranked third in the EC in terms of market share after Alcatel (France) and Siemens (Germany) in 1987. However, GPT has virtually no sales in other EC countries whilst import penetration has increased markedly since 1984, reaching 35 per cent of the UK market by 1987, mainly shared by Alcatel and Ericsson (Sweden). Thus although GPT's System X digital exchange system was the original industry standard in the United Kingdom, British Telecom has more recently turned to Ericsson with substantial orders.

The overall world standing of the EC in high technology production does not seem to be in an encouraging situation. The impact of 1992 so far has been to increase extra-EC competition and inward investment rather than a revival of the over-protected domestic industry. However, the high technology sector is not just about the production of hardware – given the negligible transport costs (1.5 per cent of the value of output or less) production can take place anywhere in the world – it is also about software development. This has been the key to the sector's rapid growth in the United Kingdom and may have to be for the future in the EC as a whole. Despite rationalization and considerable merger and joint venture activity, the higher production firms are in difficulties. The major firms are already highly vertically integrated and diversified – it is difficult to see how they can improve on their current difficult economic situation. Clearly some hard choices will face both corporate boardrooms and EC officials in handling this sector over the next few years.

In the future, the EC industry may have to recognize that its real strength is at the research and design stage and in software development. Production can more efficiently be performed outside Europe. What may be necessary is to find ways of linking European brainpower to this productive potential in the most profitable way.

6.6 Financial services

If high technology industry represents the basis of modern industry, financial services represent the equivalent in services. Banking and credit, insurance, brokerage and security services together make up a very substantial sector accounting for 5–6 per cent of GDP in Germany, France and Spain and over 12 per cent of GDP in the United Kingdom. It is also a market in which world competition has intensified with the globalization of trade and increasing liberalization of capital controls. It is convenient to consider the three sub-sectors independently since they have traditionally been separated and involve slightly different issues.

Banking and credit institutions provide the basic financial services essential to the running of an efficient domestic economy and its trade relations. Although they are dominated by large institutions (the ten largest European banks each has assets in excess of 5 billion ECU and the two largest, Crédit Agricole and Barclays, are over twice this size), most countries have large numbers of institutions (over 4000 in Germany). Even in France, which has five of the ten largest banks and the four largest account for 42 per cent of the total market, there are over 2000 institutions. The UK market, which is the most liberalized, is the only one where there is substantial foreign penetration. This involves 60 per cent of the market being in the hands of foreign banks, but UK domestic banks also have the largest share of foreign deposits in the world – 18.5 per cent of world foreign-held deposits were in UK banks in 1988 compared with 13.4 per cent in Japan and 11.9 per cent in the United States.

Profitability and attractiveness for foreign banks and deposits is typically not a reflection just of efficiency in the banking sector, but largely of domestic inflation and interest rates. However, the lack of exchange controls and withholding taxes also play a part, as do local rules on banking secrecy, which play an important role in other EC countries, especially Luxembourg. Clearly, therefore, the lack of harmonization in financial markets and in financial regulation has had important consequences for the location and relative importance of financial intermediaries. The major differences are in terms of non-EC penetration and this reflects also differential roles of financial centres as world centres. Hence, London is clearly in the world league along with New York and Tokyo, whilst other centres such as Paris and Frankfurt have been held back so far from this role.

Regulation, taxation, the competitive environment, exchange controls and state involvement in banking have all led to substantial differences in the price of banking services. However, as Table 6.3

Table 6.3 Price variations in provision of banking services (% variation from average of four lowest).

	Commercial loans	Consumer credit	Credit cards	Mortgages	Letters of credit	Foreign exchange drafts	Travellers cheques
Belgium	-4.6	-41.0	79.0	31.3	21.8	6.2	35.2
Germany	6.0	135.9	60.0	57.3	-10.0	30.9	-7.4
Spain	19.2	38.5	25.7	118.8	58.9	196.3	29.6
France	-7.3	105.1	-29.5	78.5	-7.2	55.6	38.9
Italy	8.6	121.0	88.6	-4.3	9.1	23.5	22.2
Luxembourg	6.0	-26.9	-12.4	36.5	27.1	33.3	-7.4
Netherlands	43.0	30.8	42.9	-6.3	16.5	-45.7	33.3
United Kingdom	45.7	121.5	16.2	-20.7	8.1	16.1	-7.4

Source: European Commission, 1988.

shows there is no simple pattern of these variations between countries. The United Kingdom, for example, has high costs of consumer credit but low mortgage costs, reflecting different patterns of demand and supply. Such differences are important because of the intermediary role of banking: differences in banking prices mean differences in other firms' costs and competitiveness.

There have been two banking directives. The first directive granted freedom of establishment for any EC bank in any other EC country, but subject to substantial local restrictions. These restrictions cover such factors as acquisition of local banks by foreign banks and the areas of business within which banks can operate. From July 1990 all exchange controls (except for some remaining but reduced controls in Spain, Portugal, Greece and Ireland) have been removed, thus allowing for the first step towards a common financial market, itself part of the first stage of EMU.

The remaining barriers lie not so much in overt rules, but rather in national practices which apply equally to all banks, but which affect foreign banks differentially. Hence if, for example, practices on mortgage lending differ, foreign banks cannot offer a differential service and thus increase competition. Here the second banking directive is supposed to clarify the situation by providing the framework for a single banking market. The second directive uses the principle of home country licensing and mutual recognition subject to certain minimum standards on such factors as reserve ratios.

In theory, the second banking directive implies easier cross-border banking, freer international expansion and competition, and lack of specific regulation on foreign banks and/or branches. In practice, there are still some grey areas. Banks are licensed in their home country to undertake certain specified types of business – thus, for example, a bank could be licensed for mortgage lending which would entitle it to carry on mortgage lending business in any other state. However, if there are specific local rules about how a particular service can be offered, e.g. whether fixed or variable rates are permitted, the local practice may still take precedence. Thus although banks can offer a specific service in any other market, they are likely to be restricted as to the extent to which they can innovate new ways of providing that service.

Nevertheless, banks are clearly likely to wish to expand in search of scale economies and to provide better services to their existing clients. Four ways of cross-border expansion can be identified: a cross-border branch network, merger and acquisition, joint venture links and trade. Scale economies are likely to be limited in banking and there are problems of customer recognition and trust in banking which may hamper new ventures. Nevertheless, the search for new markets and the exploitation of under-banked areas of the Community are likely to be a strong motive for the big banks.

Merger and acquisition activity has increased considerably in recent years, but relatively little of this has been across borders. That which has taken place has been largely very specific and much more common in the (generally smaller) wholesale banking sub-sector than in the retail sub-sector where local knowledge is so vital. Joint venture and share-swap activities have started to be more common. These provide cross-border access to foreign facilities without the risks of an unknown market and provide a defensive strategy as well. Examples of joint ventures or cooperative contracts include the Dresdner Bank (Germany) and Banque Nationale de Paris (France), Commerzbank (Germany) and Banco Hispano Americano (Spain), Rabobank (Netherlands) and Banco Popular Español (Spain), Cariplo (Italy) and Banco de Santander (Spain), and Westdeutsche Landesbank (Germany) and Standard Chartered (UK). In addition Danish mortgage credit banks have been expanding in Germany and the United Kingdom and British building societies in Spain. However, these seem to be more related to a search for new sources of funds than to develop new lending markets. French banks have moved further to establishing branches in other countries than banks from any other country.

UK banks do seem to have some advantages here. Wholesale banks have the experience of world financial markets, retail banks are large, have well-developed branch networks and a sophisticated range of services. However, they may face the problem that the oligopolistic structure has led to higher prices than necessary for some services which may open them to foreign competition. The natural comparative advantage which the United Kingdom has in this sector has not been able to be exploited owing to the regulatory environment. Whether this can lead to a bonanza in the Single Market is open to doubt as many of the previously protected banks in other EC countries may be in a position to retaliate in a way that previously they have had no inclination to do.

Such a situation is even more likely to happen in the insurance market. This is dominated by the United Kingdom which accounts for 30 per cent of the total insurance market of the EC and 46 per cent of the life insurance market. It has the largest number of companies operating in the home market, the largest number of companies operating across EC borders (44 per cent of all cross-border operators) and dominates the world market (64 per cent of EC companies operating in third countries are British). Of the top nine EC insurers (assets of 20 billion ECU or greater), five are British. Insurance

premiums account for over 8 per cent of UK GDP; the total for the
EC is 5.5 per cent and by contrast it is 6 per cent in Germany, 4.7 per
cent in France and only 2.2 per cent in Italy. Premiums are strongly
linked to income, however, and total per capita premiums are 20 per
cent higher in Germany than the United Kingdom.

Insurance in the private sector is also influenced by the degree of
state involvement in insurance provision through social security and
the welfare state. Lower non-life insurance in the United Kingdom is
clearly related to the system of health care. However, insurance is also
provided by state-owned insurance companies (as opposed to directly
by state provision of services or support) in a number of countries such
as France, Denmark, Ireland and Portugal.

Progressive deregulation has occurred in the insurance market.
Freedom of establishment was achieved in 1973 in non-life business
and 1979 in the life insurance business. The second non-life insurance
directive of 1988 extended this to freedom of provision using home
country rules for large industrial and commercial risks, but host
country rules for mass consumer risk where it was felt there was a
greater need for consumer protection. This approach will be followed
in the life market and a single insurance licence, paralleling that in the
banking sector, will be introduced. Some activities, such as cross-
border marketing of life assurance, will still not be allowed, but
generally competition should be increased substantially.

Nevertheless, similar problems to those of the banking market will
still exist, especially in life insurance. This is a buoyant market with
strong income-related growth and scope for product differentiation.
However, it also requires extensive sales networks and detailed local
market knowledge. The UK market offers again some clues as to
performance in a deregulated single market. There is substantial
competition, with highly innovative product development and new
methods of distribution. As a result, in comparison with more highly
regulated markets, where both premium rates and the investment
policies of insurance companies are controlled, prices are substantially
lower in the United Kingdom in all sectors except home insurance
(Table 6.4). Whether the UK economy suffers from the consequences
of this in terms of insurance companies' domination of investment
markets is more difficult to assess.

There would seem to be more scope for exploiting increased
competitiveness in markets other than the United Kingdom after 1992
and UK insurance companies should be well placed to take advantage
of this. Whether they will be able to compete against the local
knowledge of some of the major German insurers in the markets with
greatest potential is a more open question.

Table 6.4 Price variations in provision of insurance services (% variation from average of four lowest).

	Contents and house	Motor	Fire and theft	Public liability	Term
Belgium	−15.9	30.0	−8.7	13.4	77.6
Germany	2.7	14.7	42.5	47.3	5.1
Spain	−3.7	99.5	24.4	59.9	37.4
France	39.0	8.7	152.8	117.0	33.2
Italy	80.4	147.9	245.0	76.8	83.2
Luxembourg	56.9	76.6	−15.2	9.5	65.9
Netherlands	16.9	−6.8	−0.5	−16.3	−8.9
United Kingdom	89.7	−16.8	26.6	−6.5	−29.9

Source: European Commission, 1988.

The final area of financial services is that of brokerage and securities services. Security markets are highly regulated in all EC countries to ensure a proper functioning of capital markets and adequate investor protection. Regulations cover the issue of securities, the institutions able to be active on the markets, the structure and functioning of investment funds and the movement of capital. The various securities markets reflect considerable differences in the structure and size of the capital markets in the different EC countries (Table 6.5). The degree of capitalization shows major differences between Italy (the least capitalized stock market), where stock exchange capitalization amounts to only 13 per cent of GDP, and the United Kingdom (the most capitalized), where it is equivalent to 90 per cent. As Table 6.5 shows, the market value of quoted domestic companies is nearly three times as great in London as in Germany and London has a much more significant trade in foreign companies' stock, reflecting again its world role.

These differences affect the operation of companies that attempt to be genuinely European in the way they raise capital and are listed simultaneously. The problems faced by Eurotunnel, for example, were highlighted in the context of company legislation in Chapter 5. Their various share issues have had to be handled completely differently in France and the United Kingdom on the basis of differing regulations controlling what information must be given and, more problematically, what information must not be given.

The process of harmonization is aiming to cover conditions for admission, information to be published and its frequency by listed companies, and the nature and content of prospectuses for admission to the listings. One of the problems is the different role taken by different institutions in the different systems, especially the different

Table 6.5   Stock Exchange capitalization, 1988.

	BL	DK	D	E	F	GR	IRL	I	NL	P	UK	EC
Stock exchange capitalization (billion ECU)	58	23	207	75	192	4	8	115	89	5	594	–
No. of companies quoted as % Community total	5.1	5.6	8.6	7.9	13.2	2.6	1.3	4.5	5.0	3.4	42.8	100
No. of domestic companies quoted (December 1989)	n.a.	n.a.	628	368	462	n.a.	n.a.	211	251	n.a.	2015	–
No. of international companies quoted (December 1989)	n.a.	n.a.	535	0	223	n.a.	n.a.	0	229	n.a.	544	–

Source: Commission of the European Communities (1990a).

role of banks in the United Kingdom compared to Germany or France. Hence the various proposals for banks clearly affect the securities markets as well to the extent that securities are considered to be a legitimate banking activity.

London, as well as being the biggest, is also one of the least regulated stock markets in Europe. This has attracted considerable business and given securities firms on the London market substantial scale economy advantages. Whether this business will be lost back to continental markets with harmonization is perhaps doubtful, unless London also loses its world financial centre role. On this all aspects of the financial services sector stand to gain or lose together. The major new factor will not be liberalization after 1992, but moves under Stages 2 and 3 of the plan for EMU which lead to a European Central Bank. The means of operation and location of such an institution could have a much more critical effect on the re-evaluation of the benefits of different centres.

The overall impacts on the various financial services markets are summarized in Table 6.6. This is based not on the maximum theoretical price reductions which could be obtained from an assumption that markets converge on the average of the lowest prices used as a basis for Tables 6.3 and 6.4, but on the mid-point of a range which is typically around half the possible reduction in prices, depending on the weight of each service in the domestic market.

6.7 Tourism

Tourism is perhaps not a sector in the same way as the other sectors we have considered since it impinges on parts of the activities of other sectors, principally transport, hotels and catering. Nevertheless the increasing integration of these elements at the marketing and production stage makes it helpful to think of it as a sector. Furthermore, the emphasis placed on tourism as a growth sector in Europe and the increasing competition from outside Europe makes it an important sector for many regions which depend heavily on the tourist trade as the basis of their economies.

Tourism revenue is estimated at 1.66 per cent of EC GDP in 1988, the most significant deviations being Germany (0.88 per cent) and Spain (5.23 per cent). With the exception of Italy where tourist receipts declined in real terms from 1983 in the face of more competition, tourism generally showed strong growth, up 20–30 per cent by 1988 in real terms in the EC as a whole. Countries such as

Table 6.6 Estimated gains from price reductions for financial services.

	Theoretical price reductions			Indicative price reduction (all services)	Change in value-added % GDP	Gain in consumer surplus % GDP
	Banking	Insurance	Securities			
Belgium	15	31	52	11	0.6	0.7
Germany	33	10	11	10	0.5	0.6
Spain	34	32	44	21	1.4	1.5
France	25	24	23	12	0.5	0.5
Italy	18	51	33	14	0.7	0.7
Luxembourg	16	37	9	8	1.2	1.2
Netherlands	10	1	18	4	0.2	0.2
United Kingdom	18	4	12	7	0.8	0.8
Total (EUR-8)				10	0.7	0.7

Source: Emerson (1988).

Spain, France and Italy have been running strong credit balances on the tourism account. Germany and the United Kingdom, despite growth in income, were showing an increasing deficit as the industry has expanded. In France and Italy, tourism accounted for 5.4 and 7.8 per cent respectively of foreign trade earnings; in the United Kingdom and Germany it accounted for 4.7 and 7.9 per cent respectively of foreign trade expenditure.

Tourism is a labour-intensive industry and an industry employing considerable low wage labour. Thus its contribution to total employment is more substantial than its contribution to GDP. Again consistent data are difficult to obtain, but a figure of 4–6 per cent of total employment seems about right. The problem is basically of seasonality and the large amount of casual labour (Jeffrey and Hubbard, 1988). What is clear is that employment in tourism in the United Kingdom has been growing much faster than employment generally (up 14.6 per cent on the 1980 level by 1987 compared with a fall of 4.8 per cent generally) although less rapidly than in the financial services sector (up 38.2 per cent over the same period).

Generally, tourism is a sector which is relatively free of discriminatory regulatory restrictions with the exception of airline regulation. There are questions about such factors as fire safety in hotels which may affect price competitiveness if standards are lower in one country than another. It is also a sector where demand is buoyant and displays strong positive income elasticity. Furthermore, increasing leisure time is having a disproportional impact on tourism since reduced working hours are increasingly being taken as additional holiday periods. In several EC countries the norm is now a minimum six weeks' annual holiday, often taken in the form of three separate holidays. This is leading to increasingly sophisticated demands and the need to develop new markets beyond the traditional summer sun and winter snow holidays.

It is this type of market which the UK tourism industry is trying to attract, particularly from the high growth (and more anglophile) markets such as Germany and the non-European markets. These are the only two with which the United Kingdom has a positive visitor balance. These markets are potentially important since they are relatively high value trade based on cultural/historical attractions. As well as the pure holiday tourist trade, a major growth sector is business-related and conference tourism.

The blurring of distinctions between business and pleasure tourism has been exploited by major hotel chains in Europe. These seek scale economies by use of a standard format, central purchasing and central reservations services. The latter also, together with loyalty incentives, promote a standard package which reduces uncertainty to users and helps increase occupancy rates. Electronic data interchange (EDI) also links hotel reservation systems to travel agents' booking computer systems and to airline booking systems such that customers of any one have access to the services of all. The tourism trade depends essentially on marketing and maintaining loyalty. UK chains have dominated the growth of the hotel chain business in Europe; seven of the top fifteen are British chains including the largest, Trusthouse Forte, which controlled nearly 75,000 rooms in 1988 and was over twelve times the size of the fifteenth largest group. A number of the major groups have either wider leisure interests, e.g. Ladbroke, or are part of a major international group, e.g. Lonrho.

The main effects of the 1992 programme on tourism will derive from transport deregulation, tax harmonization and liberalized capital flows. In general, deregulation of air, coach and bus operations should reduce travel costs within the Community. Traditionally, airlines have been heavily regulated mainly to protect the vested interests of states in their state-owned or heavily subsidized flag carriers. The main weapon has been the requirement for state approval of each service and its fare structures – these have traditionally been granted on a reciprocal route-sharing basis. Thus between major cities scheduled flights are shared between each country's flag carrier, fares are agreed and fixed, ticketing is interchangeable and fares have typically been substantially higher than on equivalent routes in the deregulated markets of the United States.

Although increasingly charter traffic has developed as a cheap alternative to scheduled traffic, charters are essentially single-ended in that they carry the nationals of one country to a destination in another and back and are not available to nationals of the other country making the trip in the reverse direction. Charters are typically sold as part of a package holiday, although it is possible to buy seats on charters to some destinations. They use marginal airport and airspace capacity and hence often have inconvenient departure and arrival times and are the most likely flights to be delayed as a result of congestion. Deregulation has, however, set in on some markets. The United Kingdom has been at the forefront of deregulation together with the privatization of its flag carrier, British Airways. This has encouraged the growth of secondary carriers. International flights need double-ended deregulation, however, and this has been slower, with the Netherlands, Ireland and more recently Belgium following the UK lead. France and Germany have been much slower and still show great reluctance to allow in UK secondary airlines except where they serve discrete regional markets in the United Kingdom.

The main bones of contention have been over so-called fifth freedom rights (carrying passengers from one member state to another by an airline of a third member state) and cabotage (the international carriage of passengers within one country by an airline of another). This reduces efficiency since it means that a UK airline is not allowed to fly London–Frankfurt–Munchen–Milano except if restricted to carry only passengers originating in London. A further problem has been over interregional flights between different countries since these may be thought to be abstracting traffic from the trunk routes through major airports which are the major profit generators for the flag carriers.

Deregulation should ultimately eliminate these practices although the experience of US and Australian deregulation is not wholly comforting. In the United States, deregulation has often made journeys more difficult as airlines have sought to protect themselves against free competition by withdrawing to the most profitable routes and developing a network based on these links between major centres, feeding into these centres by a network of secondary routes served by older or smaller aircraft. This hub and spoke approach can often result in much more roundabout journeys for many passengers. It is also clear that deregulation has led to severe financial pressure on both some major carriers, of which Pan Am was the most celebrated casualty, and on new entrants. In the EC similar effects have been felt with the smaller flag carriers such as Sabena facing problems and new entrants being squeezed between the monopoly powers of the flag carriers and the increasing competition from deregulation. This has particularly been felt by UK second rank airlines, as the collapse of Air Europe in 1991 demonstrated. The net result is that deregulation may replace controlled competition by uncontrolled monopoly.

Even if the worst aspects of deregulation can be avoided in the EC the final result may not be the substantial fall in prices that is hoped for and that early experience with routes such as London–Dublin or London–Amsterdam has suggested. This is because tax harmonization is proposed to lead to the imposition of VAT on travel tickets whilst excise duty harmonization is to be associated with the ultimate removal of the practice of allowing duty-free concessions for air or ship travellers (but not road or rail travellers) between EC states. Duty-free sales are a major revenue earner for carriers (perhaps 30 per cent of ferry operators' income on UK–France routes) and for airports. They thus directly or indirectly (e.g. via landing fees) subsidize the cost of travel. Both of these elements could eliminate any saving from deregulation.

One of the major consequences of all of these sets of changes could be to distort the price of intra-EC tourism *vis-à-vis* other destinations and thus divert traffic away from EC destinations towards longer haul destinations in the Far East, North Africa or America.

Finally, the general liberalization of capital flows could lead to substantial international investment in the tourist sector as the industry becomes increasingly integrated at a European level. Improvements to rail and road networks will introduce competition which could reduce the dominance of air in the tourist market. This appears to augur generally well for the industry, but it must not be forgotten that this is amongst the most discretionary of all consumer expenditure, very susceptible to changes in the level of economic activity, very dependent on transport and hence on final costs and therefore very likely to suffer major swings in growth.

6.8 Conclusions

The diversity of sectoral experiences discussed in this chapter is rather difficult to summarize as a simple conclusion. What we have shown is that different sectors are likely to experience a rather differing mix of the main changes implied in the transition to the single market. In some, the harmonization of standards will dominate; in others, the search for scale economies. In some, the major changes will be internal to the EC's own markets; in others, there will be a balance between what happens internally and the impact of changing world trading circumstances. In all of the sectors, however, there is clear evidence that the process of change depends critically on the response of firms themselves to the challenges and it is this which removes the certainty of the outcome of the Single Market.

What the 1992 programme has done is highlight the scope for potential gain for any firm in any market; the search for that gain will result in a gain for the Community as a whole only if there is a resistance to the temptation to succumb to pressures for helping those that fail to make gains. Clearly, however, the scale of change in some sectors such as textiles or automobiles may require some assistance during the period of transition. It is vital that this is coordinated at an EC level to avoid introducing the wrong sort of signals. As we have seen in the airline market, the lack of clear direction and the existence of conflicting signals have produced an unsatisfactory result.

Of perhaps greater concern is the way in which the process of transition in individual sectors will have impacts in specific regions given the degree of localization of some of the sectors involved. The consequences of this concentration of sensitive sectors into sensitive regions is the subject of the following chapter.

7

The impact on regions

7.1 Introduction

In the previous chapter we looked at the sort of impacts which the 1992 process would be likely to have on individual sectors of the European economy as a whole. This is because much of the thrust of the Commission's work was on identifying the incidence of barriers, particularly technical ones, and the scope of scale economies which arise at the sectoral level. In this chapter we turn to look at the spatial consequences of the 1992 process, which has not been the subject of such consistent study, although much comment has been made on the impact on individual regions.

A first impression of this might suggest that once sectoral responses are established, the regional consequences would follow logically, simply by projecting forwards the implications for the sectors on each region's sectoral structure. Indeed many of the more gloomy forecasts of 1992 impacts, on both countries and regions within them, do just that. The argument advanced here will be fairly obvious from the discussions of earlier chapters in this book, that industrial structure is not the single, nor even the major, determinant of economic perform-ance in a region. The essence of the programme to complete the single market is to liberate regions from the potential straitjacket of their existing structure and to allow freer competition so that regions can benefit from their comparative advantages. However, this process of readjustment is clearly not costless, and these costs will not be evenly distributed – it is the purpose of this chapter to set out a framework within which individual regional evaluations can be made and to illustrate this by reference to the prospects for individual regions in differing situations.

We explore this in four stages. First, we rehearse the arguments about the way in which the completion of the Single Market will affect individual regions; secondly, we examine the additional impact that the move towards economic and monetary union will have; thirdly, we consider the response of the Commission itself to newly emerging regional problems through the Structural Funds. Finally, we look at the way in which regions in differing geographical and economic situations in the Community, core regions, regions towards the geographical centre but facing a more difficult economic transition, new industrial regions, traditional industrial regions in more peripheral locations and the less developed peripheral regions, are likely to be affected.

7.2 Regional impacts of the Single Market

Begg (1989a,b) has usefully identified that interplay between two effects will be relevant in determining the impact on any one region. Increased growth in the EC deriving from the completion of the Single Market will be divided between the regions, but the reallocation of resources implicit in that boost to growth will affect regions differentially according to their competitiveness. Competitiveness will itself depend on three sets of influences: those specific to sectors independently of their location, those relevant to the nation within which the region is located and those specific to the individual region. Whether the balance is towards concentration or deconcentration will depend essentially on where regions are along a U-shaped curve of competitiveness which sees that in a world of imperfect competition there is a relationship between the degree of concentration and trade barriers. Up to a point, a reduction in trade barriers may increase concentration, but there is a possibility of this ultimately reversing (Krugman and Venables, 1990).

Hence, the performance of a region would depend initially on the extent to which there were major changes implied for its principal sectors. Greater scope for scale economies could imply greater concentration of production, or greater specialization of individual stages in the production process, depending on the nature of the production function. The changing national macroeconomic context, through greater monetary coordination, greater stability in interest or exchange rates, or harmonization of fiscal policies or rates of taxation, will affect different regions in the Community differentially for any given structure. Region-specific factors are essentially those related to its factor endowment. This is wider than just availability and skill of labour and capital and their prices. The public capital base of the region – its infrastructure – will be an important determinant of competitiveness, and this involves both physical infrastructure, such as transport, and 'soft' infrastructure such as training, business information services, etc. Physical infrastructure can be both internal to the region and involved in connecting it to other regions. Also specific to regions, or groups of regions, is the policy environment, whether this is coordinated at Community, national or local level. We look at each of these arguments in turn.

The key question for most regions is the extent to which they are competitive in the sectors within which they are specialized and the prospects for growth in that sector. If we assume that there is to be substantial restructuring of industry in the search for greater competitiveness then, regardless of whether the industry is growing or declining, regions will be competing to maintain their existing production and employment. The faster the rate of growth of the sector, the easier this may be, especially since the costs of relocating production are not negligible. In some senses the scale of the change is so large that there is no reason to suppose that, for many industries, the present location is optimal in the context of the Single Market. To the extent that, for many of the member countries, factor endowments are very similar, most growing, modern footloose industries could be essentially indifferent between locations. It is likely that factor endowments are more varied between the regions of these countries, but nevertheless it seems likely that industries will have a wide range of potential locations to choose from.

What will, therefore, determine the potential for relocation? We can identify three main elements: the relevant size of the scale economies in the sector and the stage of the production process at which these occur, the linkages to other industries, and the degree of competition within the sector. Large scale economies do not, in themselves, require a high degree of spatial concentration. In many sectors the real scope for scale economies lies at the level of individual processes which can be linked together by efficient communications and transport systems. Often it has been the existence of borders that has prevented this taking place on a European scale and it is this which has led to fragmentation in organization rather than just in production. Indeed, for many industries there may be positive benefits to decentralization of production because of the increasing costs of congestion in some industrial regions, or other bottlenecks in the supply of factors.

Industrial linkages have often been assessed as having an importance in determining a region's success (Perroux, 1955). Linkages can be either forwards, towards the market-place, or backwards, towards an

earlier stage of the production process. The traditional argument for
growth poles or industrial complexes was that linkages were important
in minimizing the leakages from a local economy from an exogenous
increase in the demand for the final product in such a system. They
might also protect the region by reducing the probability that any
single element of the linked structure would leave the region.
However, at a time of great change this advantage is likely to be
relatively small compared to the possibility that the entire complex
suffers. Certainly regions with highly developed linkage structures in
key sectors can be seen to have suffered from this problem (see
Holliday *et al.*, 1991a, for an example of this in the Nord-Pas de Calais
region of France). In the short term, regions with well-developed
linkages should be able to avoid suffering from these problems, but in
the longer run it is not clear that highly linked industries are either
necessary or desirable for a region.

The degree of competition in a sector will depend both on the
existing structure of the industry and on the extent to which it will
come under increasing pressures in the search for greater efficiency.
Thus regions with a strong dependence on industries currently protected by technical standards or substantial public procurement may
face much stronger new competitive pressures. Regions that have a
substantial sector of small- and medium-sized enterprises may correspondingly perform much better, since it is this type of firm that is likely
to benefit most from the removal of trade barriers (Cappellin, 1990).

Steiner (1990) has suggested that regions can be clustered into three
broad groups on the basis of their ability to adapt to external changes.
These he refers to as adaptable, adapted and non-adapted regions.
Adaptable regions, those that respond positively and show greatest
growth potential, are typified by the absence of large firms with
standardized types of production, a diversified industrial sector producing products at the early stage of the product cycle (i.e. those with
considerable growth potential) and high rates of new firm entry. In an
empirical study these characteristics were found in the larger urban
areas and in regions with strengthening localization economies which
would be typical of new industrial areas. *Adapted* regions on the other
hand are those that cope with change by responding to price and cost
stimuli to adjust production methods, rather than through the entrepreneurship which characterizes *adaptable* regions. Here firms with
more standardized production methods are typical, facing low input
costs and using more unskilled and female labour. Such regions are
often rural and suggest that this type of organization may be typical of
the agri-business sector, food products and the like. *Non-adapted*
regions are those that fail to respond to changes in the environment,

typified by large firms and lack of diversity in industrial structure and strong horizontal and vertical linkages. The internal structure of such firms makes them unable to respond in either an entrepreneurial way or in an allocative way to these changes. Such features are characteristic of most old industrial regions.

It is this type of approach which lies behind the EC's identification of sectors vulnerable to 1992 (Commission of the European Communities, 1989a) as we discussed in the previous chapter. Forty manufacturing sectors covering 50 per cent of both value added and employment in the EC as a whole were identified in four basic groups (Table 6.2):

1. Rapidly growing high technology industries characterized by a high degree of import penetration both intra- and extra-EC, low price disparities, high concentration and high non-tariff barriers.
2. Traditionally regulated or public procurement dominated industries characterized by high non-tariff barriers, technical standards and public procurement but low import penetration, wide price dispersion, substantial potential for scale economies.
3. A further group of public procurement dominated industries with characteristics similar to the second group, but with greater extra-EC import penetration and hence lower price dispersion.
4. A large miscellaneous group of industries with moderate non-tariff barriers and high existing intra-EC import penetration, but relatively high price disparities and scope for scale economies.

However, the regional impact of changes in these sectors will depend on the adequacy of the firms in the sector in each region to respond. Part of this, as suggested by Steiner, is simply their ability to use the economic advantage of lower input prices. As Table 7.1 shows, there are considerable variations in labour costs in the Community.

These variations do not, however, depend solely on variations in wages so that productivity differences eliminate a large part of the disparities in wages or wage costs, but perhaps overcompensate for the poorest countries removing any competitive advantage which, for example, Greece or Ireland would otherwise have. Disparities within countries are possibly more serious, however. The United Kingdom, Germany and Italy, for example, include regions which have amongst the highest and the lowest unit labour costs in the Community.

A further study by the EC (Commission of the European Communities, 1990a) has attempted to assess the impact of the changes envisaged for each of the vulnerable sectors on each member state, but taking into account that member state's performance in that sector. Performance is based on a set of four indicators, intra- and extra-EC

Table 7.1 Regional variations in labour costs, EC 1981.

	GDP per capita		Monthly industrial labour costs		Unit industrial labour costs[1]	
	National average	Regional disparity[2]	National average	Regional disparity[2]	National average	Regional disparity[2]
Germany	121.5	16.4	113.5	6.2	108.4	6.4
France	116.2	27.2	106.0	14.8	92.8	5.7
Italy	68.8	16.7	77.9	4.7	98.1	9.3
Netherlands	109.1	17.6	109.9	5.7	100.6	6.1
Belgium	106.7	23.8	118.5	9.9	106.7	7.0
Luxembourg	114.8	–	102.6	–	103.3	–
United Kingdom	99.2	10.7	87.2	7.3	96.6	8.8
Ireland	58.3	–	72.4	–	100.8	–
Denmark	122.8	–	101.2	–	113.9	–
Greece	41.7	–	48.8	–	112.5	–
EC-10	100.0	29.1	100.0	18.4	100.0	9.7

[1] Monthly labour costs divided by output per employed person in industry.
[2] Standard deviation weighted by regional share in population or industrial employment.

Source: Commission of the European Communities (1987).

coverage ratio (i.e. the proportion of domestic demand in a sector covered by domestic production as measured by the ratio of exports to imports), export specialization (the share of the sector's exports in total exports relative to the average EC share of that sector) and production specialization (a similar measure of the share of the sector in total production relative to the average EC share for that sector). An arbitrary value is then given to each indicator of −1 if the value is less than 90 per cent, 0 if the value is between 90 and 110 per cent and +1 if more than 110 per cent; these indicators are then summed for each sector to give a score in the range −4 to +4. The distribution of these scores is given in Table 7.2.

This analysis suggests several important differences between the member states at a national level. One group of countries, the United Kingdom, France, Belgium and Spain, have a fairly balanced distribution between sectors with different global scores; the United Kingdom is interesting since it has a very small proportion in extreme categories, either positive or negative. The other countries have much less balanced distributions. Italy and Germany are very skewed towards the better performing sectors; Denmark, Ireland and the Netherlands are the opposite of the United Kingdom with sectors being either good or bad but little in the middle; and Greece and Portugal show that most sectors are either very good or very bad, but there is also a strong presence of what may be termed indifferent sectors with a zero score.

Table 7.2 Distribution of industrial employment by industry performance (%).

	Global score[1]								
	−4	−3	−2	−1	0	+1	+2	+3	+4
Germany	3.3	0.2	0.5	5.1	5.7	1.9	5.4	3.0	29.4
France	0.2	9.3	4.7	1.4	5.6	6.2	10.5	5.7	7.1
Italy	2.1	1.9	8.5	3.1	4.3	1.6	2.1	4.3	21.5
Netherlands	7.3	2.6	6.5	2.2	1.1	3.8	0	8.9	12.6
Belgium	7.0	0	3.1	0.8	10.5	6.6	6.6	8.9	6.7
United Kingdom	2.8	4.8	7.9	9.7	6.8	2.4	8.9	4.8	1.9
Ireland	8.1	6.6	0.7	2.2	4.8	1.2	10.1	0	13.0
Denmark	7.2	0	4.9	1.5	3.2	2.5	5.0	10.2	15.2
Greece	12.5	1.9	3.6	5.9	16.7	1.8	1.1	3.6	14.4
Spain	6.0	2.2	8.8	2.3	6.4	0.1	2.0	4.9	7.0
Portugal	10.6	0	5.6	0.3	23.5	0.2	1.5	0	27.9

[1]See text for explanation.

Source: Commission of the European Communities (1990a).

Simply plotting the proportions in strong sectors (those with positive scores) against the rest (zero or negative scores) produces Fig. 7.1 which identifies four clusters of countries. The main group, France, Italy, Belgium, Ireland and the Netherlands, shows a general domination of stronger sectors. The United Kingdom and Spain are together with a general domination of weaker sectors. Greece and Portugal stand out at one extreme with a substantial domination of weaker sectors, although with a larger share of stronger sectors too (i.e. more of their total employment is in sensitive sectors). Finally, Germany stands out at the other extreme with a domination of strong sectors and relatively few weak sectors.

This is, of course, an essentially static analysis of the current competitive situation; it does not demonstrate the extent to which German industry is better able to respond to the particular stimuli of 1992 than industry in Spain or the United Kingdom. This evidence is also only for manufacturing industry and does not include a similar comparative analysis of service sectors. Indeed, it might be suggested that the more successful sectors in some countries have maintained their competitive position in their own markets by the use of the various barriers which the 1992 programme is designed to abolish.

Such caveats are to encourage us not to take the estimates as indicators of what will happen; they are nevertheless clear indicators of what may happen. They must therefore form the basis of any assessment of how each country will fare in the mid 1990s. The process by which that adjustment will take place is seen as being part of the internationalization of European industry through direct investment in other countries by firms based in any one member state, or by the increasing use of joint ventures or full mergers between companies based in different member states, towards the growth of genuinely European companies. The difference in corporate cultures between firms in different countries will undoubtedly play a major role in determining both the extent and direction of that adjustment. Hence British and French firms have been the most heavily involved in cross-border activity. France has, until recently, had a more restrictive and less welcoming outlook on inward investment than other countries in Europe. This reflects the nature of corporate control in the countries; the direct involvement of banks in both Germany and France in the day-to-day running of companies contrasts with the more stand-off attitude of those in the United Kingdom. The owners of German firms are less interested in financial deals across frontiers, and more interested in direct investment opportunities. Similarly, there has been much less interest by foreign investors in Greece than in Spain and Portugal. Spanish firms have used such investment to aid

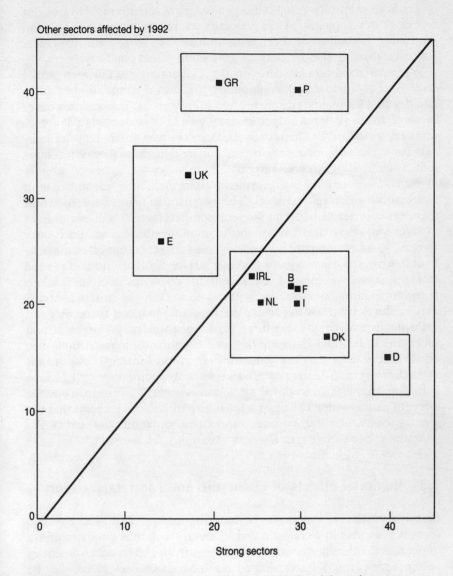

Figure 7.1   Shares of strong and weak sectors in industrial employment.
Based on data in Table 7.2 by plotting the share in strong sectors (+ve scores)
against weak sectors (−ve or 0 scores). (*Source:* Commission of the European
Communities (1990a).)

diversification of products whereas in Portugal the interest has been in technical development. This generally therefore argues against the increasing sameness of European industry or corporate structure, whilst reinforcing the difficulty of predicting gainers and losers.

We have concentrated here on the evidence collected at national level since this is the best available on the spatial distribution of gains and losses. Our real interest here, however, is in the regional response. In some cases, national responses may give us a reasonable picture of regional responses. The concentration of particular industries in particular regions, for example, will mean that the national response reflects an existing regional response. In many cases, however, the sort of adjustment implied by European changes is first identified at a national but interregional level. The need for industries to reposition themselves in terms of technology or competitiveness will cause them to investigate new locations within the same member state. This is both a springboard to compete in newly opening markets, but often more as a defensive measure against outside attack in currently protected markets. Thus we can see the extent to which firms in the United Kingdom, fearing isolation in northern locations, are looking to new sites in the South-East to protect their existing markets there. A good example is that of the Northern Irish food industry (Greenan and McHugh, 1991). This has gone further to include some relocations into northern France in conjunction with French local interests as a means of further controlling the potential increase in competition.

In some cases this regional response is clearly going to have the effect of exacerbating existing regional disparities, but it seems that the key to this is not the existing competitive situation, but rather the potential for responding to the new situation.

7.3   Regional effects of Economic and Monetary Union

In some respects, the move beyond the completion of the Single Market towards full Economic and Monetary Union is only a question of degree. The economic pressures arising from the free movement of goods, services and factors which we have examined so far will be added to by the inability to use independent monetary or fiscal policy measures as a counter to any adverse changes. It is for this reason that the enhancement of the Structural Funds of the Community, the means by which the EC as a whole can redistribute resources between different regions, has been seen as a *sine qua non* of both processes.

Opponents of EMU point to the way in which regional problems persist within member states where different regions face the same fiscal and monetary regime within the constraint of a fixed exchange rate. This includes the position of Scotland and Wales within the United Kingdom. The argument is that countries are able to use fiscal and monetary policies, adjusting the budget balance or tax rates and money supply or interest rates to favour particular groups or sectors within them in such a way that they achieve some competitive advantage. This may include greater freedom of action over exchange rates. All of these factors can enable a lack of competitiveness to be disguised and real wages to be maintained or enhanced despite a failure of productivity to grow fast enough. Within a semi-fixed exchange rate system, such as the EMS during the 1980s, freedom of action over interest rates is lost since these will be set by the need to maintain the value of the currency within its band of fluctuation. Thus a country with a balance of payments deficit due to uncompetitive industry, which is facing recession, is unable to lower interest rates to provide a boost to either domestic demand or investment. Meanwhile, the higher level of interest rates encourages an inflow of capital which ` enhances the money supply and increases inflationary pressures on the economy. Lagging regions in such a country suffer disproportionately from this. However, there is some freedom to use fiscal policy both in the aggregate by adjusting the budget balance to influence aggregate demand and by adjusting tax rates to alter patterns of behaviour of different groups in the economy. This could include the way in which fiscal policy can be regionally differentiated either through its sectoral influence or through the budgetary position of regional or local authorities.

In an EMU even the freedom to make adjustments to the exchange rate as a last resort is lost and this implies that there is central determination of monetary aggregates and hence of the budget balance. There is no freedom to attempt regionally differentiable policy; moreover, the national economy as a whole becomes like that of a region within a unified state. Lagging countries will behave like lagging regions within countries and their ability to converge will be reduced rather than increased. Within lagging countries, the lagging regions will fare the worst, since they include the sectors and firms least able to adjust without outside assistance.

The counter argument to this emphasizes the more dynamic forces in the economy which the ability to interfere in policy terms may stultify. Furthermore it emphasizes the different responses to a given set of variables which may be obtained if the EMU framework creates an environment of greater certainty. The first argument here is that the existence of nationally differentiated policies, and within these further regional differentiations, produces a climate which is not conducive to convergence. Economic agents within the regions use the ability to have their actions sterilized from outside influences as protection from not taking the correct decisions. Since the ultimate defence of devaluation is not available in EMU, it is clear to all parties that more efficient decisions must be reached. Given the greater certainty which the EMU framework should create, particularly about the likely behaviour of competitors from within the EC, economic agents should also behave in a more consistent manner in different regions. One of the reasons for the lack of convergence within countries is that the lack of such a stable environment internationally leads each country to have to concentrate on those sectors and regions where it believes it can be successful – in this scenario it is the very freedom of policy action that maintains the divergence between regions.

The performance of the EMS during the 1980s gives some support to this thesis. One of the real fears about a fixed exchange rate system is that the convergence it forces on the members implies an averaging of their performance. Thus the inclusion of high inflation, high deficit countries, such as Italy, with low inflation balanced budget countries, such as Germany, would lead to reductions in the former but increases in the latter, as the symmetry of the intervention mechanism would imply a faster rate of growth of money supply in Germany. In practice this has not happened and an asymmetric response has occurred. This has been harder on the weaker economy, but has forced a more rapid adjustment in its underlying economic position. This is due to two reasons. First, Germany has been able to sterilize its own economy more than expected from the money supply growth in the weaker economies. Secondly, and possibly even more relevant for the future, is that the weaker economies have been able to borrow credibility from the past performance of the stronger. The consistency of German economic performance over the previous period and the strength and independence of the Bundesbank encourages speculators to believe that those economies more closely tied to it will inherit aspects of German performance. This is evidenced by the degree of success we have noted in Chapter 4 in achieving some degree of convergence in monetary aggregates.

Some research for the EC by the IFO (Institut für Wirtschafts-forschung) (reported in Commission of the European Communities, 1990a,b) suggests that managers in lagging regions are generally less optimistic about the impact of the Single Market on their firms' prospects (Table 7.3). This evidence suggests a greater polarization of expectations in lagging regions with the ratio of perceived opportunities to threats being about 2 to 1 compared to 3 to 1 in the most favoured regions and somewhere between in the regions in industrial decline. There are clear national variations to this, however, as shown in Table 7.4 where the responses, relating not to the firms but to the expectations for the regions, are converted to an index taking values between −100 for a unanimously negative assessment and +100 for a unanimously positive one. This shows clearly the much less positive view taken in the United Kingdom, especially of the prospects for the prosperous regions, and that the most positive views were found in Spain and France.

Table 7.3 Managers' expectations of the completion of the Single Market.

	% managers reporting in each region type		
	Lagging regions (Objective 1)	Regions in industrial decline (Objective 2)	Prosperous regions (control group of 10 regions)
Increased opportunities	36	32	38
Opportunities and threats about equal	29	37	37
Don't know	16	18	13
Increased threats	19	14	13
	100	100	100
Total	100	100	100

Source: Commission of the European Communities (1991a).

Table 7.4 Companies' assessments of the Single Market's impacts on regions.

	Index of firms' assessments of prospects for region		
	Lagging regions (Objective 1)	Regions in industrial decline (Objective 2)	Prosperous regions (control group of 10 regions)
Belgium	–	5.0	22.4
Germany	–	6.8	30.0
Greece	13.4		–
Spain	34.5	10.5	20.9
France	34.8	35.2	43.1
Ireland	14.2	–	–
Italy	7.1	–	19.3
Netherlands	–	22.0	11.9
Portugal	12.3	–	
United Kingdom	4.4	8.1	−19.2
Total sample	14.2	9.4	23.4

Source: Commission of the European Communities (1990b).

Expressed in this way there is potentially more positive expectation from the lagging regions than from those in industrial decline. Managers also appear to see the benefits as being better for the region in general than for their firms in particular. When asked about the prospects for individual factors determining this change, the most positive assessments from all regions were in terms of economic growth, increasing accessibility of suppliers, improved communications, and completion of the Single Market in business and financial services. The most negative aspects were seen as problems with taxes (both national and local), wage and other labour costs and labour market regulations and problems in the supply of skilled labour. The biggest variations in perception between region types were for proximity of customers (negative in lagging regions, positive elsewhere), but some variations were also identified for what may be termed regional social infrastructure, such as schools, housing, training facilities, culture and leisure.

This research confirms that there are important differences in outlook between different regions and that some of these may be principally related to the lack of certainty in the general framework of economic policy. However, this is not to suggest that it is simply a matter of creating a new policy environment and persuading people that it will hold. Some of the more seriously lagging regions will need direct help of the type already identified through the increases in the structural funds, especially in providing the basic infrastructure essential for such faster growth. There is a further element to this, however. The greater alignment of fiscal policy implied by the greater limits to freedom in setting the budget also implies the need to consider a more formal way of achieving fiscal balance between regions. This is familiar to those who deal with a federal structure and is usually referred to as fiscal federalism. In brief, what is required is an adequate means of assessing the regional distribution of both tax revenues and the public sector expenditure financed by these. This has two functions: one is to remove the possibility of member states undertaking fiscal policies inconsistent with what is required; the other is to make explicit the basis for public sector transfers between regions. This policy already applies within the Federal Republic of Germany through the concept of *Finanzausgleich* (for a discussion of this in the EC context see Biehl, 1987, 1989).

The argument advanced here is essentially that the move beyond the Single Market and towards EMU is actually vital to the achievement of the principal aims of the Single Market itself, since it is only in the context of the tighter economic union that the required major change in policy stance – the so-called 'regime shift' (Commission of the

European Communities, 1990b) – will occur. This regime shift is essential to provide both the structure within which regions can compete more fairly and effectively with each other and the incentive for economic agents to modify their behaviour. In the following section we examine the main components of this policy framework.

7.4 The policy framework: Structural Funds

The Community has already embarked on a major reappraisal of the spatial aspects of its policies as part of the process towards completion of the Single Market. The reform of the existing sets of policy and financial instruments with a spatial dimension, available under the agricultural policy (the Guidance section of EAGGF), regional policy (ERDF) and social policy (ESF and various training initiatives) into a common set of structural policies targeted at specific types of region has already been discussed in Chapter 3. It will be recalled that this identified three basic types of problem region on the basis of existing regional characteristics, classified as Objectives 1 (lagging, underdeveloped regions), 2 (old industrial regions needing restructuring) and 5b (rural regions in need of development assistance). At the same time the commitment was made to double the size of the Structural Funds in the Community's budget by 1993, taking it to nearer 20 per cent of the total. Even so the current size of the total EC budget will still leave the resources devoted to redressing regional imbalances an inadequately small part of total Community GDP, less than 1 per cent. Nevertheless this was an important step forward since it highlighted the need for a clear assessment of the regional implications of any Community policy, and for the first time it was the Commission itself that was responsible for defining and designating the areas eligible for assistance.

To some extent the Structural Funds reform was only the end stage of a long drawn out process of attempting to focus regional assistance within the Community on those regions most in need and where the policy could be the most effective. The challenges of the Single Market and EMU require a more far-reaching reassessment of the policy response which we can assess from the inclusion of a specific reference to spatial policies in the documents on EMU (Commission of the European Communities, 1990b) and more directly in the assessments of the regional situation in the 1990s and the possible implications following greater integration in the 'Europe 2000' documents (Commission of the European Communities, 1991a, 1991b, 1991c).

As Table 7.5 shows, the current assisted areas include some 43 per

Table 7.5 Population in ERDF-assisted regions.

	Objective 1	Objective 2	Objective 5b	Total	Share of state in total EC population
		Share of population in regions eligible			
Belgium	–	22.1	2.7	24.8	3.0
Denmark	–	4.9	2.1	7.0	1.6
Germany (West incl. Berlin)	–	11.4	7.4	18.8	18.9
Greece	100.0	–	–	100.0	3.1
Spain	57.7	22.2	2.5	82.6	12.0
France	2.7	17.8	9.7	30.2	17.2
Ireland	100.0	–	–	100.0	1.1
Italy	36.4	6.6	5.0	47.8	17.7
Luxembourg	–	38.0	0.8	38.8	0.1
Netherlands	–	9.9	3.0	12.9	4.5
Portugal	100.0	–	–	100.0	3.2
United Kingdom	2.8	35.0	2.6	40.4	17.6
EC-12	21.7	16.4	5.0	43.0	100.0

Source: Commission of the European Communities (1991a).

cent of the total population of the Community. The bulk of the funding available, increasing to around 80 per cent of ERDF, goes to the Objective 1 regions which are almost exclusively in the peripheral regions of the Community and include about half of the total population in eligible regions. Objective 2 regions are principally concentrated in the United Kingdom, northern and eastern France and Belgium. Large parts of the former German Democratic Republic have also been made eligible for assistance under a Community Support Framework (Commission of the European Communities, 1991d) with funding of 3 billion ECU for the period 1991–93. Additional funding may be made available to border regions under the INTERREG scheme, even where the regions may not otherwise be eligible. As Table 7.6 shows, the emphasis on Objective 1 regions has disadvantaged the United Kingdom in particular which, except for western Germany and Belgium, receives the lowest allocation of Structural Fund money relative to its share of population in assisted regions. Ireland, in particular, Greece and Portugal have benefited most under this, receiving a much larger share of the Funds than they have population. Spain receives approximately the same share of Funds as it has assisted region population.

Funding available under the Structural Funds is subject to the additionality principle in that money provided by the Community is expected to be additional to, and not a replacement for, funding provided by the appropriate national government. Thus budgetary constraints within a region can inhibit the ability to benefit from EC funding. EC competition policy rules also prevent money being given

Table 7.6 Relative distribution of Structural Funds.

	GDP/capita (EC-12 = 100)	% share Structural Funds	% share eligible population	Ratio	% share funds / % share eligible
Belgium	100.7	0.8	1.72		0.47
Denmark	112.5	0.3	0.26		1.15
Germany					
(West incl. Berlin)	113.6	3.1	8.26		0.38
Greece	54.8	14.2	7.21		1.97
Spain	73.6	24.3	23.05		1.05
France	109.3	7.3	12.07		0.60
Ireland	64.5	7.8	2.56		3.05
Italy	103.5	18.5	19.67		0.94
Luxembourg	121.7	0.05	0.09		0.56
Netherlands	104.2	0.8	1.35		0.59
Portugal	53.6	14.9	7.44		2.00
United Kingdom	106.5	7.9	16.53		0.48

in such a way as to imply a sector-specific subsidy to firms in a region. Thus direct subsidies to firms are not usually given, and EC rules also limit the ability of national or local subsidies of this type being given. This means that the bulk of assistance will typically be what may be termed 'generic', available to all firms and all sectors. It is not surprising, therefore, that infrastructure support has dominated, both in the form of physical productive infrastructure such as roads, bridges, etc., but also more social infrastructure, in the form of hardware such as sports or cultural facilities and software such as training or business advice.

However, it is recognized that the needs for policy are changing, both in terms of the definition of problem areas and the sort of instruments most appropriate for dealing with these changing problems. The main pressures on individual regions are seen to be demographic and infrastructural. Demographic issues arise both in terms of the overall change in the population and its age structure and in terms of the educational and training needs of the resident population. This relates to the pressures for migration both internally within the Community and increasingly from external pressures. It was seen how dramatic this could be during the last quarter of 1989 when the upheavals in eastern Europe led to enormous pressures on EC countries, especially Germany. The other source of such pressures is on the southern fringes of the Community where the relative affluence of even the poor regions of southern Italy and Spain has proved attractive to, often illegal, immigrants from North Africa. The concern here is that the achievement of a genuinely free Single Market for people in the EC will encourage even more widespread internal and external migrations.

Infrastructure issues are more complex than just the need to complete a basic integrated physical infrastructure network for the Community if it is to function as a single economic entity. They are about the need to develop a genuine Common Transport Policy as originally foreseen in the Treaty of Rome, but also to see the development of a framework for information technology and telecommunications, energy and the environment. The information economy is often seen as the basis for future economic development, regions that are excluded from this new technology will be those that lose out in the next wave of economic development. Since information technologies and telecommunications are often easier to use as the basis for integrating otherwise far-flung regions of the Community into the core of the economy than traditional transport infrastructures, they may provide the scope for allowing the most remote regions of the

Community access to the mainstream of economic growth. However, they also require the identification of an adequate rate of return, implying a sufficient scale of operations, before they are worth while. Energy and the environment go together, although not necessarily in harmony in any one region. New technologies can often be expensive in terms of their needs to protect scarce energy resources and the environment. Remote regions may often find that providing a given level of energy is less cost effective than in more central regions for a given degree of conservation, and potentially more damaging to the natural environment which is often of a higher intrinsic level in some of the more remote regions.

All of these considerations emphasize the interregional nature of the problem. Spillover between regions abound in terms of congestion and pollution. These spillovers are not just between adjacent regions. It is increasingly recognized that regions with common interests may be spatially separated, whilst those that are inflicting adverse externalities may also be some substantial distance away. It is this that argues strongly again for the existence of an authority at the EC level which can improve the allocational efficiency of resources and also effect the resource redistributions between regions that this implies.

This has led to an attempt to define a new set of regional types for use in such analysis and policy information. The first round of this was to identify the common characteristics of regions with similar functions, urban areas, old industrial regions, rural areas, upland areas, border areas, coastal areas and islands. The second was to use these to define rather broader macro-regions of the EC for further analysis. Seven such macro-regions have been identified:

1. Atlantic arc – the western fringe of the Community running from northern Scotland through the United Kingdom and Ireland, France, Spain and Portugal.
2. Central capitals – the core regions of the EC including SE England, northern France, Belgium, southern Netherlands and central western Germany, including the big EC industrial areas of London, Paris, Brussels, Randstad Holland, the Rhein–Ruhr and Frankfurt, but also featuring a large number of separate regions with specific cross-border problems.
3. North Sea coasts – northern and eastern England, Denmark, north-western Germany, northern Netherlands.
4. Alpine regions – mountain areas in France, Italy and southern Germany (together with the potential new members in Switzerland and Austria).

5. Western Mediterranean – southern coastal regions of Spain and France and the northern west coast of Italy.
6. Central Mediterranean – the Italian Mezzogiorno and Greece.
7. Inland continental regions – mainly in Spain and France.

To these seven has been added an eighth region of the five new German *Länder*, the former GDR, which given its history and its location cannot be easily integrated with the others.

The most important features of these new macro-regions is that they transcend many of the traditional groupings by regional policy status or geographical proximity. The concept is to be able to consider the way in which new developments in industry, technology, transport, communications, etc. will affect these contrasting regional groups. Many of them include regions of contrasting economic fortune, but these will be regions which depend on each other in a closer way than those outside. Thus far the definition of the regions is somewhat arbitrary, but it poses major questions which future policy will have to answer. The groupings also build on the increasing desire of regional authorities within Europe to seek out similar regions in other countries with which to form valuable pressure groups.

For the first time the Community's entire spatial development can be assessed within a common framework which aims both to curb the negative aspects of over-concentration and over-development as much as to promote the positive aspects of growth in lagging regions. However, it is clear that the resources requiring to be transferred to effect such a shift in the spatial balance are greater than those available. It is also clear that it is more than just a question of a central shift of resources between regions, it is also a question of self help by those regions, but self help within an environment of greater certainty and greater potential reward. The EC's policy document on Europe 2000 (Commission of the European Communities, 1991c) suggests that 'widening the horizons of regional and local actors is one of the keys to successful economic and social development', but points out that this can only be achieved in an environment of cooperation between regions.

This leads us to re-emphasize the question of the appropriate level at which decision making takes place within the Community. If we abandon the separate notions of national and regional policy making within the Community, which is the logical outcome of the move to greater integration, and refer instead just to spatial policy, we can treat the question of subsidiarity more objectively than when it becomes confused with the idea of sovereignty. In the context of the intergovernmental negotiations leading up to the Maastricht Summit of December 1991 as the basis of new treaties on both Economic and Monetary Union and Political Union, the UK government in particular has stressed the extent to which closer union, so-called deepening of the Community, implies an unacceptable loss of control over key policy areas and its replacement by decision making at a Community level. This move towards a federal structure for the Community has been strongly resisted by the United Kingdom, mainly playing on the implication of transferring power to an unelected body, the Commission, whilst also being reluctant to see greater powers transferred to the European Parliament. Whilst the 'democratic deficit' is an undoubted problem, a satisfactory resolution of this problem is not just to use the subsidiarity argument to keep all control at one particular level, essentially the national level, but rather to seek an appropriate reallocation of powers between all levels of government. This needs to be done within a framework which not only allocates responsibilities and powers, but also establishes a structure of intergovernmental responsibilities and financing to enable each level not only to be subject to the lowest level of democratic control and provide the lowest level of efficient delivery of services (which is the essence of subsidiarity as a concept), but also to provide each level with sufficient resources to enable it to deliver without imposing negative spillovers on other jurisdictions. This is perhaps the real test of the success of greater integration in the 1990s and involves the transition from conventional regional policy to a genuine Community spatial policy affecting the whole territory of the Community.

There is a sense in which the UK government's fears are well founded here, since in such a situation the level of government which appears least logical is the national level. Many of its powers could be better discharged at a regional or local level, within the framework of a spatial policy which clearly transcends existing national frontiers and is better shaped at a Community level. National politicians in a state such as the United Kingdom, where there is less need for such politicians to have a local power base than in many other European countries, could clearly see this as a considerable threat to their own survival. It is here that we can see the parallel between events in both western and eastern Europe – it is not the contrast which the anti-federalists in the United Kingdom have tried to draw between the desire for independence in the east and the attempt to impose central control in the west, but in both a desire to seek a structure within which regional (cultural and economic) diversity can flourish without regional economic divergence. However, in both there is a need for a strong international organization to provide both physical security and a lessening of economic risk to a level that will enable local entrepreneurship to flourish.

7.5 Diversities in regional impacts

Thus far in this chapter we have outlined the general issues affecting regions, and the changing definition of appropriate regions for spatial policy. In this section we shall discuss the likely direct impact of greater European integration on different types of region in different spatial situations in the Community. We shall identify five types of region:

1. Core regions.
2. Centrally located regions dependent on core regions but facing greater economic problems.
3. New fast-growing regions outside the core based largely on new industries.
4. Old industrial regions in less central locations.
5. Lagging peripheral regions.

The use of this typology, which is transitional between the traditional definitions of regions for regional policy and the new definition of macro regions, enables us to use traditional measures of performance, but also to set the regions in their wider spatial context in the Community. In particular, we need to establish the functional relationships between regions as part of this definition. This term is used to describe the extent to which a region has economic independence of others in the system and the types of linkage that tie it in to the rest of the economic system. Economic independence, as discussed in more detail in Chapter 3, comes from the relative importance of the base sectors of the economy, those sectors which provide a base for exogenous economic development of the region. Clearly in a highly integrated European economy, even the leading regions will have no real independence of the others since they will depend on the rate of growth of other regions in the system. This is not just a question of observed economic flows, but also of the decision flows. Decision makers are mainly in the core regions and these are the people responsible for issuing the instructions which govern the performance of the other regions and on which their growth depends.

The key point to note in this discussion is that it is neither a region's economic structure nor its location which is seen as the determinant of its likely future in the Single Market, but a combination of these, together with its functional position in the overall economic system.

7.5.1 Core regions

The core regions are those that form the major international decision-making centres of the Community and that are traditionally the dominant centres of the Community in terms of output, productivity and wealth. Geographically they are largely synonymous with the major metropolitan centres of Europe, London, Paris, Brussels, Randstad Holland, Frankfurt. It is important to recognize that this term is not intended to define the complete area enclosed by these major metropolitan centres as we must distinguish carefully between the core urban regions and their highly dependent hinterlands, including not just the outer metropolitan areas of each centre but also the substantial geographical areas which lie between the major centres.

These centres are distinguished by a number of unique features: a high proportion of service employment, in both market and non-market (governmental) services, reflecting their functional role as decision-making centres; a concentration on high value added activities, including important research and development functions; they are important transport nodes with the highest level of service at three levels, to other world core regions, between each other and to those regions dependent on them. On the negative side, these regions are characterized by high costs, including increasing costs of congestion and pollution, and this makes them the centres for inflationary pressure for transmission to the rest of the system.

The completion of the Single Market has major implications for these regions in a number of different dimensions which intersect with each other in differing ways in different locations. At a sectoral level they depend on the sorts of responses in sectors such as high technology industry and financial services discussed in Chapter 6. The removal of barriers to trade in financial services and in research and development activity, and the boost given to small firms which often form an important part of the economy of large metropolitan areas where they can benefit from the positive externalities, will all boost their economies. Each of these core regions has traditionally enjoyed a near monopoly position in each country, with the exception of the unique situation in Germany (although even there the functional specialization of the main centres meant that there was less internal competition between centres than might have been expected).

The question arises of whether there is space in the Single Market for such a number of core regions and thus whether the opening of competition will lead to a major reallocation of activities between these centres. This reallocation will depend on the relative efficiency with which each centre can fulfil its functional position. For such centres this may depend less on the productivity of the private factors of production than on the productivity of the more public factors, those urbanization economies which are so vital to the functioning of large metropolitan areas. These will depend on the degree of linkage into the core region itself, of which a good example is the quality of transport service as given by airports and the emerging high-speed railway network. Cities with severe airport congestion and no good alternative will start to lose functions. It also depends on the quality of internal transport systems since these will be a major contributing factor to the overall level of productivity. Regions, such as London, where the evidence suggests that the lack of infrastructure has been a constraint on their overall productivity (Biehl, 1991), are clearly less well placed than competitors, even if all such regions tend to display over-use of factor inputs as a characteristic.

7.5.2   *Central dependent regions*

These regions contrast markedly with the close-by core regions. They lie in a central geographical location in Europe, in south-east England, northern and eastern France, Belgium, southern Netherlands and western border regions of Germany, but have levels of economic performance below that of the core regions and of the faster-growing new regions. They include some old industrial regions (such as Nord-Pas de Calais or Hainaut), some predominantly agricultural regions (such as Champagne-Ardenne) and some mainly commuter-dependent regions (such as Kent and Picardie). The principal distinguishing characteristic feature of these regions is their dependence on the core regions. New industries which have developed are there because of proximity to such core regions rather than any intrinsic property of these regions; they are often used as distribution centres given the lower price of land than in the neighbouring metropolitan regions and their strategic location. However, they often do not escape the deteriorating competitive position of the core regions since negative externalities, such as congestion and inflationary pressure, tend to spill over into them because of their location and functional dependence.

The future of these regions in the Single Market is rather uncertain. At a sectoral level they depend currently on sectors such as food, drink and tobacco and also textiles and clothing. They may also have received implants of motor vehicles given their location. They typically have not attracted high technology industry. Their sectoral future is thus uncertain as they face increased intra- and extra-EC competition in these sectors. Although the older industrial regions among them do benefit currently from regional assistance, it is not clear that these regions will be able to continue to do so and this places them under increasing competitive pressure from the more peripheral old industrial regions and from peripheral lagging regions. Theoretically they should benefit disproportionately from the removal of internal borders since many of them lie on such borders and will see an increase in their natural hinterlands. However, this will simply increase the competition between these regions.

These regions are quite well integrated into the Community's transport system at the moment, although this is mainly through their proximity to the core regions since the internal borders tend to present barriers and channel communications unequally in different directions. As already noted, they do face problems of increasing congestion since they are the main transit regions of the Community. Improvements to communications along these main transport corridors may actually reduce accessibility, as the need to segregate high value traffic between the core regions from lower value traffic to or within these regions leads to roads with fewer access points, or the development of high speed rail routes without intermediate stations. The traditional activity which derived from the operation of frontier controls will also be lost.

A very good case study of the tensions between these various forces is provided by the French region of Nord-Pas de Calais. This is a traditional industrial region based on coal, iron and steel and textiles, serving also as a major frontier region with strong industrial links with the neighbouring Belgian regions and the transport centre for trade between much of continental Europe and Britain, as well as an important deep-sea trade. The decline of the traditional industries has reduced the region's independence. The growth of trade within the Community has increased pressure on the infrastructure given the region's location at the intersection of two major European axes of communications, a north-west to south-east axis from industrial Britain through the industrial heartlands of France, Belgium and Germany to northern Italy, and a north-east to south-west axis from the Baltic and Netherlands through Paris to new growth centres in Spain. The region has abundant cheap land, but despite a young and naturally growing population, strong out-migration and a skills deficit typical of an old industrial region. This has failed to be attractive to new industries, and despite a reasonable rate of inward investment, the region has been outperformed by many of its competitors in less favourable locations.

Now emphasis is being placed on the construction of the Channel Tunnel and TGV-Nord high speed railway line, which will form part of an emergent high-speed railway system linking together the main core regions of north-west Europe, at the centre of which is the regional capital of Lille. A new city centre station developed in conjunction with a new business district is intended to reposition the city and make it part of the core. So far the evidence is not strong that this is being achieved (see Holliday *et al.*, 1991a, for detailed evidence) despite the considerable public and private confidence in the venture in the region. The competition from the surrounding core regions is potentially too strong and the distances to the other centres too short for Lille to lose its dependent status.

Even if Lille achieves this, the danger is that it will be at the expense of the rest of the region such that intraregional tensions will replace the interregional ones. This has been recognized to some extent by the investment in regional infrastructure linking to the new interregional infrastructure in the hope of spreading the potential gains. However, it is also fairly clear that too much emphasis on spreading the benefits around the region may reduce the scope for achieving such benefits for the region at all. As we have already seen in the case of the core regions, their gains are typically at the expense of surrounding regions. Time will tell whether Lille can separate itself from its region and join the core, but the competition will be very strong and the chances are not great.

Of all of these regions, however, this is the only one with a real chance of achieving such a repositioning; for the rest the future is of continuing dependence, with worsening competitiveness as the negative spillovers from the core regions increase. The danger is that these regions are overlooked in policy terms and become the empty heart of the Community.

7.5.3 New technopole regions

The new technopoles, sometimes called the 'motor regions', are perhaps the direct antithesis of the central dependent regions. Geographically these are typically a similar distance from the core regions, but 'outside' rather than 'inside'. Essentially they have achieved emerging independence by becoming the favoured regions for investment in new industries and have been rewarded by improvements in their infrastructure and links to the core, which has enhanced this independence, whilst not suffering from the costs to the same extent since they are not required to serve as transit regions between core regions. Rather, they can emerge as the bridgehead regions for the development of more peripheral regions.

These regions should be favoured by the Single Market integration process: they will typically have a smaller proportion of employment in the sensitive sectors likely to be negatively affected and should be most competitive in the rest. At a sectoral level, they are most represented by the fortunes of high technology industry.

Regions falling into this category include East Anglia and parts of the south-east region to the north and west of London in the United Kingdom, Rhône-Alpes in France, the Stuttgart region in Germany, Lombardia in Italy and emerging regions such as Cataluña in Spain. These are characterized by relatively high levels of economic performance, especially in terms of growth in recent decades. This is particularly true of indicators that take into account labour market performance as well as output per capita, since they are characterized by low levels of unemployment and high levels of in-migration and skill. One of the main features of these regions is the extent to which they are in a position to take over certain functions from core regions. In particular there has been a decline in the ability of core regions to continue to serve as incubators or nurseries for new firms and new industries as rising costs of land, labour and urban public goods reduce their attractiveness in terms of the positive externalities they possess. These new regions have been able to replace the traditional externalities of the core regions with an attractive environment and as newer industries have been able to replace the traditional requirement for physical accessibility to other industries with one of using telecommunications for many service functions, the lower levels of physical accessibility are more than adequately compensated.

Nevertheless the other feature of many of these regions has been the extent to which they have benefited disproportionately from new infrastructure linking them into the traditional core. For example, Lyon and Stuttgart were each among the first regions in France and Germany to gain new high speed rail infrastructure. The Rhône-Alpes region is a good case study of this type of region, especially since it has been the subject of considerable research trying to assess the balance of advantage between the region and the core region, Paris, deriving from the completion of the first French high-speed rail line, TGV-Sud Est, in the early 1980s. Throughout the 1980s the Rhône-Alpes region outperformed the French economy as a whole, growing at an average rate of between 3 and 4 per cent per annum (between one-half and one percentage point faster than the national rate). The industrial sector is both large and diversified, with a base in older industries such as textiles and engineering which has spread into newer industries in the last thirty years, especially electrical and electronics industries. A major contrast with old industrial regions, such as Nord-Pas de Calais considered above, is the greater prominence of small- and medium-sized firms which have proved more conducive to adaptation and change. The region is second only to the Paris region for research and technology transfer. One city alone, Grenoble, with 1 per cent of total population, has 10 per cent of all French research jobs and produces 14 per cent of the French output of engineers.

The region has certainly benefited from being the first region linked to a new high-speed rail network, the TGV-Sud Est. This new line, opened between 1981 and 1983, reduced the journey time from Lyon to Paris from over four hours to just two hours. This led to an enormous growth in rail traffic in the first few years of about 50 per cent, of which nearly half was newly generated traffic. However, more important than this is the way it has put the region, especially Lyon as the main city, at the centre of a developing network with proposals to extend the line southwards to the Mediterranean with connections westwards to Spain, the first part of which is already under construction, together with a direct link to the region's main airport, the major French airport outside Paris. There is a further proposal for a new line between Lyon and Torino, linking the region to the growth regions of northern Italy and a further proposal for a Rhine–Rhône link providing access to Strasbourg and south-west Germany. This appears to place the region in good stead to face the challenges of the 1990s, although again there are potential problems associated with intra-regional disparities where the main 'motor' centres with the new industries and the direct link to the TGV network benefit further whilst other centres lag behind.

Within the Single Market such regions will face increasing competition, but with largely new industries and new infrastructure they are well placed to succeed against core regions and old industrial regions. They should also benefit from their strategic location relative to developments in peripheral regions, both in terms of their industrial base to supply new developments, and also in many cases from their locations on the key routes into such regions. Lyon, for example, lies at the gateway to the emerging western Mediterranean growth corridor from which Lombardia and Cataluña control the access to more peripheral regions in Italy and Spain. Stuttgart faces competition from traditional core regions such as Köln and Frankfurt for access to emerging regions in eastern Europe, but is well situated at a crossroads between east–west routes and trans-Alpine routes. Moreover the increasing linkages between regions such as Rhône-Alpes, Baden-

Württemberg, Lombardia and Cataluña shows how the regions themselves see their future as a network of highly advanced regions. This is particularly important in a global context since these regions have prospered in the protected environment for high technology industries in Europe to date; they now need to survive not only in the new, more open, European market, but also, critically, in the more competitive world market.

7.5.4 *Old industrial regions*

Such regions, which lie geographically outside the core, are at the moment principally those of the United Kingdom, although we could also include the Ruhr area of Germany as distinct from the Köln–Düsseldorf regions, and the remaining industrial regions of northern Germany. We have already suggested that other industrial regions of Belgium and France are better considered in view of their geographical location amongst the central dependent group of regions. This leaves the older industrial areas of northern Italy around Milano and Torino, but these seemed to fit better into the previous group of regions in view of the growth potential of the Mediterranean belt. We also need to think how this group would be affected by the eastwards extension of the Community. Clearly the industrial areas of Saxony from the former GDR should be included and any future extension of the European Economic Space or the Community itself would bring in the industrial regions of Bohemia and Silesia.

This group of regions presents major problems for the Community. The principal economic difficulty is the dominance of old industries which are uncompetitive in both intra- and extra-EC terms. At a sectoral level they are best represented by the problems of textile and clothing, but will also have some of the less competitive firms in other sectors. Within the Community new technologies in the technically advanced regions and lower costs in more peripheral regions are squeezing these traditional regions, which are not seen to have the locational advantages of the more central old industrial regions. The UK perspective on 1992 (Cutler *et al.*, 1989; TUC, 1988) certainly paints a rather gloomy portrait of these regions' prospects, and these are echoed to some extent by studies of the prospects for other industrial regions in the Community, including those in Germany (Sinz and Steinle, 1989). Studies of the impact of the Channel Tunnel on UK regions have also suggested that the partial improvement of communications will not assist these regions, but rather act as a means of draining economic activity towards more central locations (for a summary of these see Holliday *et al.*, 1991b).

These regions do have advantages, however, which can be exploited. First it has to be recognized that their advantages are not necessarily in the same sectors. Typically these regions are competing in sectoral terms with newly industrializing countries. It will be difficult, if not impossible, to effect adequate protection for their industries in the current climate for both economic reasons (the simple cost of protection) and political reasons (the pressures to reduce protectionism within GATT). This implies the potential for large amounts of available resources as long as adequate transitional measures can be provided. Labour and land costs will thus be lower than in core areas and congestion costs will be lower than in central old industrial regions. However, transport costs will remain higher to the current core areas of the Community and this implies a need for investment in key transport links to improve accessibility for these regions. A good example of this is the need to resolve the continuing difficulties posed for UK exporters by congestion in and around London and the lack of adequate investment in alternative routes to the east coast ports. Even a strategy based on improved accessibility implies a reliance on the economic centre of gravity of Europe, and of all its potential markets, remaining fixed. The extension of the European Economic Space and the potential for growth in more peripheral regions of the present and future Community suggest that those regions that have a greater diversity of access may be able to exploit such changes better.

The German old industrial regions clearly have advantages in this way, given their location relative to new markets in eastern Europe, and the greater inclusion of Scandinavia in the trading area will provide additional boosts to northern Germany. Changes in the former Soviet Union present an unknown long-term challenge and opportunity. However, it must not be forgotten that Spain continues to offer considerable advantages for new investment, as does the whole Mediterranean area. Global trade with North America and the Pacific region will continue to be one of the fastest, if not the fastest, growing sectors of trade. Regions which are strategically placed to be able to trade effectively in any or every direction should be attractive to footloose investment during this period.

A good case study of a region which does appear to have had some success in this way, repositioning itself for multi-directional trading, often in non-traditional sectors, is Wales. Rather like Nord-Pas de Calais, Wales is a traditional industrial region that has lost its traditional industries, but has had some success in diversifying. Part of the success of this region compared with others is the existence of a coordinated policy through special agencies, such as the Welsh Development Agency which could provide an all-region basis for attracting new investment and promoting the region. In the later 1980s the economy grew considerably faster than that of the United Kingdom as a whole and will probably continue to outperform the national economy during the early 1990s. Much of the key to this is in inward investment. Wales with just over 4 per cent of the UK work-force has attracted over 20 per cent of foreign direct investment such that nearly a quarter of all employment in manufacturing is in foreign-owned companies, albeit at the price of considerable assistance (about 50 per cent of all regional aid goes to such companies). North American firms dominate this investment, but both Japanese and other European firms were increasing their share markedly during the 1980s and the US share of new employment fell from around two-thirds to one-half. One of the major effects of this has been to speed up diversification – this is similar to the experience of Rhône-Alpes, but driven by external rather than internal factors. The main factors attracting such investment are seen as the availability and adaptability of the labour force, but above all, lower labour costs. If Wales cannot keep this competitive edge it may clearly lose out to other regions in Europe that can.

The conclusion for these regions in the Single Market is that they face the greatest challenges for readjustment. However, it would be wrong to think of them as automatically the main losers since they do have considerable scope for advantage over more centrally located regions. The important issue is the need to avoid a static view of the regions in structural terms and of the EC in geographical terms. The fact that these regions have been successful in the past, but have lost that advantage, demonstrates both of these changes, but also that there is scope for further change. The worst enemy of these regions is a retrenchment into a protectionist stance which would work against achieving the restructuring essential to their future success.

7.5.5 Underdeveloped peripheral regions

The peripheral regions are currently the poorest regions of the Community. Although there are some such regions in most countries, except for the Benelux countries, the problem is their domination of four member states, Ireland, Portugal, Spain and Greece, and virtually a separable half of another, the Mezzogiorno of Italy. Objective 1 regions occupy (prior to German unification), 39 per cent of the land area of the EC and 22 per cent of its population. On average these regions have a level of GDP per inhabitant only some 67 per cent of the Community's average, and, per worker, 75 per cent of the average, and an unemployment rate over 70 per cent greater than the EC average. Twenty-seven regions fall below the average for Objective 1 regions; these are all in Greece, Portugal, Spain, Italy and Ireland, except for the French overseas territories (DOM).

Although the temptation is to think of these regions as agricultural, and they do have much larger shares of agriculture in both employment (particularly) and output than the rest of the Community, the industrial sector is still the most important for most of them. At a sectoral level they are represented by food, drink and tobacco and textiles and clothing, of the sectors discussed in Chapter 6, although they may also have received car plants, usually as a deliberate policy measure. What is typically least developed is the tertiary or service sector since it is this that is symptomatic of more economically advanced regions. The tourist industry may be seen as an important sector, but typically will not involve such high value spending as in other areas. This suggests that it is not just a question of an overdeveloped sector which cannot expand sufficiently in these regions, which is preventing expansion of other sectors, but a failure to achieve competitiveness across the full range of sectors.

The other temptation is to concentrate just on the regions' peripherality as the key issue. Again, this is clearly an issue that affects the ability of these regions to compete on equal terms with more centrally located regions. From a policy perspective, the relevant national governments see themselves as often being thwarted by other member states' governments in a desire to achieve an improvement in accessibility. Access to the core regions typically involves transit passage across at least one other member state which itself has peripheral regions whose interests it wishes to protect and promote.

It is perhaps even more difficult to generalize about these peripheral regions than about the other types of region discussed, but it is nevertheless useful to take a brief look at the problems faced by one region, Ireland. This highlights the difficulties felt by the others because of Ireland's virtually unique geographical position after 1993, lacking any fixed link access to continental Europe. Ireland is also unusual in the Community in being treated in its entirety as a single region (only Luxembourg at less than one-tenth the population is similarly treated), although with a population of 3.5 million it is smaller than the other regions we have looked at except for Wales.

The Irish economy is extremely open, exports represent over 60 per cent of GDP, of which about 34 per cent by value goes to the United Kingdom (over 55 per cent by volume). This dominance of the United

Kingdom in Irish trade has fallen dramatically since entry into the EC in 1973 when it was nearly 55 per cent. Germany is the second major market. The changing direction of trade reflects also a changing composition of trade away from the traditional low value trade in agricultural and food products specialized for the UK market, towards electronics and chemicals which are less sensitive to transport costs. These latter two product groups now represent nearly 40 per cent of export value, with foodstuffs accounting for a further 25 per cent. The industrial sector is still a relatively small employer with 27.5 per cent of the work-force, agriculture being large by EC standards with 15.2 per cent. Tourism is still a relatively small sector; total expenditure in 1988 totalled less than 5 per cent of the value of goods exports, but grew by nearly 50 per cent between 1984 and 1988. Again the United Kingdom dominated this with over 50 per cent of expenditure and the United States and Canada came second with nearly 25 per cent. However, it was non-UK EC markets which were again the fastest growing, up 74 per cent over this five-year period, against UK growth of 53 per cent and North American growth of only 27 per cent.

The real fear in Irish markets is that improved communications to other regions will drain away the traditional UK traffic and competing UK destinations such as Cornwall, Wales and Scotland will benefit from improved communications, whilst the traditional emigrant Irish markets in North America are increasingly sluggish. Like Wales, Ireland has benefited substantially from overseas investment, traditionally American but increasingly European, exploiting low production costs in activities where peripherality is no disadvantage. This has helped to diversify the Irish economy, but it still faces enormous problems of unemployment. The unemployment rate in the late 1980s was almost double the average EC rate at over 17 per cent, and Ireland had the fourteenth worst unemployment rate in the Community. Per capita GDP at 64 per cent of the EC average made it the twenty-fifth poorest region in the Community. Progress has been made, but there is clearly a long way to go to modernize the economy and there are great fears that peripherality will present constraints on being able to make further inroads on those sectors where there are some natural advantages such as business services and tourism, despite the small but efficient modern industrial sector continuing to prosper. This suggestion of a developing dual economy is not untypical of other purely peripheral countries such as Greece and Portugal, and may also be the future model for the development of eastern European countries.

One of the ironies of the development of the Community is that it has been these peripheral regions which have been amongst the most enthusiastic supporters of the move to greater integration. This is not just because the Common Agricultural Policy has been beneficial to them in providing a source of budgetary assistance and guaranteeing markets. They have also seen the Community as a way of providing a stable economic environment for attracting inward investment and overcoming their peripheral location, whilst being able to offer lower costs and a more attractive environment than competitor regions within the Community. Nevertheless, the gap is so large, and in absolute terms increasing, that considerable resources will continue to need to be put into these regions by the Community as compensation so that they can enjoy some part of the growth achieved from the process of integration. These regions are also facing new competition for such resources from the demand for restructuring in eastern Europe, which will continue to make progress difficult. Only if the Community can achieve growth levels in the higher part of the ranges forecast will it stand any chance of meeting these competing demands. Even so, the future is far from comforting in terms of the ability to achieve self-sustaining growth in the most peripheral regions of the Community.

7.6 Conclusions

If we could make some reasonable estimates of potential changes consequent on the achievement of the Single Market in individual sectors, it is clear that there is less certainty about where these gains and losses will occur. These are, of course, not separable issues since where successful enterprises are located will affect their competitiveness and the level of growth achieved in the EC, as well as that of their own region, and how successful regions develop will affect the costs of production and hence the competitiveness of firms located within them. The purpose of this chapter has essentially been to demonstrate how there are no natural gainers and losers and that all regions have something to play for in the 1990s.

Although interregional competition clearly has its place in achieving efficient results, and we have stressed above the dangers in protecting regions from competition, there is a major role for policy at the EC level. This has to make resources available for transfer to the poorest and least well-placed regions to ensure that they can share in the gains made and to assist in ensuring a transition that is as costless as possible to the Community as a whole. The most important role of policy is to create an environment of greater certainty by ensuring that consistent policies are followed in different regions. This applies both to neighbouring regions, whether facing similar problems or not, and to similar regions in different member states. We have seen how more peripheral regions will depend on infrastructure created in more central regions, how the infrastructure which most favours the core regions may disadvantage other geographically central regions. There may also be important complementarities between neighbouring regions which it is desirable to promote to ensure balanced development. The move to a wider regional concept as the basis for regional policy is thus an important move in securing some of these potential benefits. This remains, however, an area of great concern, without progress in which much of the potential for gain may be lost in wasteful interregional competition.

8

The new order?
Integration to 2001

The major purpose of this concluding chapter is to make some assessment of the sectoral and regional impacts discussed in the previous two chapters in order to draw some conclusions about how the 1990s are going to produce a different story from the previous periods. One overriding factor has become clear: there is no simple answer to this since much of the outcome will depend on the way that individual economic agents respond to the opportunities presented by the new order of the Single Market and the moves towards EMU during the 1990s. These agents include firms, owners of factors of production, and consumers, but also, and crucially, governments at all levels within the Community.

8.1 Sectors and regions

The sensitive sectors to the Single Market are those where, until now, barriers to free movement have been the greatest. These barriers have been particularly high in sectors involving technical standards or a high proportion of output for public procurement since it is these factors that have fragmented markets, prevented the achievement of scale economies and reduced effective competition. For a sector to be sensitive to the removal of barriers does not mean that there will be enormous change once the barriers have been removed, however. That will depend on the extent to which the different factors involved balance against one another – in particular the balance between the centralizing forces of scale economies and monopoly and the decentralizing force of competition. The balance of these forces within individual sectors will also control the balance between them at a regional level since it will be one determinant of the change in regional competitiveness.

At sectoral level the transition will be easiest for those industries where there is the prospect of growth, especially as the industries that are growing are more likely to be footloose. The global competitive position of these sectors will also require substantial progress to be made in narrowing the gap between European and Japanese or US firms. These sectors are relied on to generate the export surplus needed to support weaker sectors and achieve the degree of inter-regional redistribution necessary to maintain or enhance cohesion between regions in the EC during the transition period.

For the weaker sectors and those with weaker demand growth, typically the older industrial sectors, there will be more resistance to the process of change since it will be more likely for regions to lose out. As we have seen in the previous chapter, regions of all types have relied on a process of diversification in their industrial structure. In the weaker regions, inward investment from both inside and outside the EC has been attracted to finance this diversification; in the stronger regions there has been a greater use of internal generation of new investment, particularly through the growth of small- and medium-sized enterprises. What happens, however, when we put together the need for greater concentration in expanding sectors with a continuing desire to achieve diversification in all regions? One of the answers we have given is that a greater certainty in the policy environment will remove the need for regions to act defensively through a perceived need to spread risk.

However, it is also clear that the competition for available investment funds will become stronger. This is partly because in the run-up to 1992 there has been a desire on the part of non-EC firms to get a base inside the Community given the perceived threat of a 'Fortress Europe' mentality. The flow of inward investment has therefore been boosted in the recent past and is unlikely to be maintained at such levels, especially with continuing recession in the US economy. Secondly, the restructuring of eastern Europe is providing alternative destinations for such funds as well as for investment flows from within the EC.

Weaker sectors within the EC will continue to find strong competition from the newly industrializing countries, coupled with pressure to reduce the degree of protection given to such industries in the EC. Hence the Multi-fibre Arrangement which controls imports of textiles into the Community or the continuing support given to European steel makers in several countries will continue to be attacked through

GATT, as will the Common Agricultural Policy. Reductions in the degree of support given by the latter could have important consequences for the agrifood business which is supported to some extent by subsidized local agriculture, although any opening of European agriculture to freer trade should lead to a reduction in prices.

The most difficult group of sectors to predict are the more average group where demand growth is middling, technical change less pronounced and European competitiveness questionable. This would include a wide range of intermediate and finished products, mainly from the engineering industry, including machine tools, vehicles and consumer durable goods. These are the industries where scale economies due to harmonization of technical standards are the most important. They are also the industries where the new global divisions of labour are often the most pronounced – a process which Europe cannot insulate itself from. Again the increase in competition both inside and outside the Community will dominate.

If there is one simple conclusion that can be drawn it is that only by increasing the competitiveness of its industries will the EC be able to generate the sort of growth necessary to make the Single Market a potential success. The size of the EC market is large enough to think of domestically induced expansion from the savings generated by economizing on the costs of non-Europe – this would be a Japanese solution where the trade sector is a bonus – but not large enough to dominate economic performance. But to move to such a situation would be extremely difficult for a Europe that has depended on trade to a much greater extent than any other world economy, both individually as nation states and collectively as the Community. It also has to be recognized how much the world has changed over the period of the process of completion of the Single Market. The changing political and economic structure of the greater Europe challenges the Community's estimates of the benefits from the Single Market as perceived in the mid-1980s.

These changes will be particularly relevant at the regional level since they complicate the balance of centralizing and decentralizing forces. In the mid-1980s it was fairly clear that the new strengths of the Community would be found in tapping the potential of the Spanish economy as a new motor of growth, and in the possibility of creating a new belt of economic activity along the Mediterranean coasts of Spain and France into the industrial areas of northern Italy. Meanwhile the improvement of north–south communications, aided by such major projects as the Channel Tunnel, new links in Scandinavia and through the Alps, would serve to reinforce the traditional arc of economic activity from England through the Low Countries and Germany to northern Italy. The Community's role was thus one of tying in its western and southern periphery to these corridors of activity.

The events of 1989 in east central Europe and of 1991 in the former Soviet Union have changed this geographical perspective. For the first time Europe has two peripheries, to the west and south and to the east. The potential drift westwards of the Community's centre of gravity has been arrested. The Community's traditional motor of growth, the (west) German economy, has been put under pressure from the unification of the two Germanies, since the cost of financing unification has involved budgetary pressures which are potentially inflationary and retarding to the rate of growth in the traditional industries sectors. However, the process of reconstruction in eastern Europe does present a major opportunity for boosting growth. Already there are signs that there is a potential economic upturn in the five new German *Länder* (the former GDR) in 1992. Despite the loss of some 20 per cent of output in 1991 and an unemployment rate rising to 12 per cent with as many again on short-time working, there are forecasts of up to 10 per cent industrial growth in 1992, albeit at the cost of a stagnating economy in the western *Länder* and a continuing larger budgetary burden. If the former East German economy can be turned round within two to three years this gives hope to the prospects for the remaining east central European economies of Czechoslovakia, Hungary and Poland (probably in that order, given their relative debt burdens). This may prove a drain on the western European economies in the short to medium term, but the longer-term prospects look more encouraging.

For individual regions in the West, these prospects at first appear threatening. There will be a drain on current investment, especially that originating from Germany, to provide more competition from other regions with advantages of cheap labour and newly installed infrastructure. The growth of economic welfare and aggregate demand in the eastern regions and in the western peripheral regions stimulated by their reduction of isolation should more than compensate for this. What is, however, increasingly clear is the need for a framework within which this can take place. The dangers of anti-competitive protectionism at the regional level prompted by the fear of losing out are great enough to require a clear commitment at the Community level about the distribution of aid through the Structural Funds. There are no natural gainers and losers in this rapidly changed and still changing situation, but there are forces leading to both gains and losses in all regions.

It is tempting to think of the regional future of Europe as a balance between the two peripheries, west and east, or possibly given the further distinguishing features, between four: north, south, east and west. In the north the Scandinavian countries pose some particular problems. Although Sweden, Norway and Finland have healthy rates of economic growth historically, this has faltered somewhat in the recent past. This is one of the reasons for their seeking the increased security of EC membership in the longer term. In the east are the various former Soviet bloc countries, in three groups: the east central European countries of Poland, Czechoslovakia and Hungary already discussed above; the second group of the Baltic States, Romania, Bulgaria, Slovenia, Croatia and the other Yugoslav republics, which are in a substantially weaker position; and finally the remaining former Soviet republics and Albania. The southern and western peripheries consist of states already members of the Community, although there are long-term issues surrounding the applications of Turkey and Cyprus for membership. In this emphasis on the problems of peripheral regions, however, we must not forget the less peripheral regions, including some geographically central ones, which also face major restructuring problems.

8.2   Governing the transition

The major issue to be resolved both during the debates leading to the Maastricht Summit of December 1991 and in the process of ratifying the Treaties which will emerge from it has been that of sovereignty. In the discussions over both Economic and Monetary Union and political union, a predominant concern of opponents to further integration has been the implied handing over of power to a central authority of the Community. In this, the supposed centralizing tendencies of the Community have been contrasted with the break-up of such central power in eastern Europe and the increasing claims of individual regions for independence on historical and cultural grounds.

This argument often ignores the fact that the majority of independence claims are set in the context of a wider association of European states. The key issue is that of how detailed and pervasive that association should be, and should the EC attempt to establish the rules for a deeper association before widening its membership, or loosen the degree of harmonization in order to ensure a wider membership? The economic answer to this problem has a clear theoretical foundation, that activities should be controlled at a level of government sufficiently large to ensure the achievement of desirable scale economies and minimize spillovers between jurisdictions, but sufficiently small to allow for democratic accountability, competition in service provision between authorities and hence the potential for choice between jurisdictions on the part of individuals. This is the argument about subsidiarity and the argument which has led to calls for a 'Europe of Regions'. It would seem that this is the crucial debate about Europe's future in the 1990s.

One of the clear conclusions our analysis of the 1992 process has produced is that the differential effects of greater integration will be felt much more strongly at regional than at national levels. The example of Italy is particularly relevant here. Italy has in many respects been the success story of the European Community. It has enjoyed continuing and unprecedented rates of industrial growth, it has integrated its trade more fully into the European pattern, it has had some (albeit limited) success within the confines of the EMS at controlling traditional budgetary deficits and inflation. The result of this is a situation where ten of the twenty Italian regions fall into the two richest of the five groups of EC regions shown in Fig. 2.1 with a GDP/capita more than 114 per cent of the EC average. These cover 60 per cent of total Italian population. However, seven of the remaining ten, with 35 per cent of the population, fall into the two poorest groups (less than 86 per cent of the EC average). Integration of the Italian economy as a whole disguises successful integration by regions in the north and an increasing gap between these and the regions of the south.

This dualism is more pronounced in Italy than elsewhere, although fears that it will become more evidenced in other countries are becoming stronger. The north–south divide in the United Kingdom has been well documented, though it is far less pronounced than that in Italy. There are fears of an increasing north–south divide in Germany, with much of the former GDR falling into an increasingly less prosperous north of Schleswig-Holstein, Mecklenburg, Niedersachsen, Sachsen-Anhalt and Brandenburg, plus the two city states of Hamburg and Bremen whose apparent wealth is largely due to their restricted geographical definition, with over 25 per cent of German population. French fears concern the way in which the major centres of industrial activity in Europe are being pulled eastwards, and whilst the eastern regions of France will benefit, this will be at the expense of central and western regions.

Part of the regional problem stems from the way in which regions are defined in each member state and the relationship of this to their constitutional position. In a federal system such as that in Germany, or now emerging in Belgium, it is the federal states that form the major regional subdivisions. In the case of Germany these range from the tiny states of Hamburg, Bremen and Saarland, all with less than 2 million inhabitants, to Bayern with 11.2 million and Nordrhein-Westfalen with 17.1 million. These last two are each larger than five member states.

In the United Kingdom, the South-East region, an equivalent Level I region for EC purposes, is even larger than Nordrhein-Westfalen, but in contrast has no regional government or formal regional decision making machinery, apart from purely consultative bodies such as SERPLAN. The region is then divided into ten counties with populations ranging from 0.5 to over 1.5 million, plus Greater London with a population of 6.75 million. The latter now has no government of its own, this being divided between thirty-three separate authorities.

France, another unitary state like the United Kingdom, has spent the past decade attempting to decentralize decision making to the level of twenty-two regions. Although the definition of some of these regions was itself somewhat arbitrary, the existence of an elected regional authority has been important in securing a degree of coordination over development plans in regions such as Ile de France (the Paris region) or Nord-Pas de Calais. The regions have shown themselves to be efficient in planning such elements as infrastructure and education, within the context of a national framework.

Whilst the lack of coordination and a regional planning framework is the obvious consequence of the UK system when compared with other countries, there is also an important budgetary and financial considera-tion. In order to exercise decision making power, regional authorities need a firm income base and a degree of independence in their budgetary powers. German regions achieve this through the formal structure of a federal constitution which allocates specific duties to each level of government and provides the fiscal framework within which these duties can be financed. From this perspective it is easy to see the Community level as simply a further level to be added to the existing structure. This will attain responsibility for certain activities, but under the democratic control of an enhanced European Parliament and under the financial control of a more sophisticated budgetary system which can achieve what in German is called *Finanzausgleich*. The system of fiscal federalism in place in the Federal Republic requires an ex post assessment of the fiscal flows that have taken place to ensure that any net inflows or outflows to or from any particular jurisdiction are in accordance with agreed redistribution criteria. EC flows through the various Community policies are part of this process of effective budgetary equalization.

This system ensures a considerable degree of effective equalization, but also appears to have been associated with increasing centralization since individual states do not have the incentive to develop their own tax bases (Zimmermann, 1989). However, this centralizing tendency may be defensible on cost grounds, although the evidence is not conclusive. Biehl (1989), in a useful analysis of these trends, refers to the German case as unitary federalism, identifying the strong desire to achieve a unifying set of national policies.

How does this affect the debate at the European level? From a German perspective the concern over increasing centralization of powers to the German federal level (the *Bund*) away from the state level (the *Länder*), which the efficient fiscal redistribution system actively promotes, encourages the *Länder* to believe that federalism at a European level would be looser, of necessity, than in the unitary federalism of the Federal Republic and that this would enhance their independence. Powers would be transferred either up or down from the national level. From a UK perspective, with the absence of any real government at a sub-national level, and certainly in the absence of an economically efficient system of fiscal equalization, the transfer of powers is seen to be all one way, from the national government to the European level.

It is resolving this difficulty that lies at the heart of providing an effective means of governing the transition to a more integrated Community. Further integration must involve greater convergence at the regional level, since without this it will be impossible to demonstrate the increase in welfare to which that further integration should be leading. That integration requires a more thorough system of fiscal redistribution, albeit a system which retains some incentives for a region to compete for an increase in its tax base. The redistribution must occur across the entire Community since the resource transfers will occur across the Community – in other words there has to be a single market in government service provision so that all regional government authorities can compete on an equal basis. That local governments already recognize this is evidenced by the rapid growth in cross-border cooperation between authorities. This is not just simple cooperation by border regions across a common frontier, but also the cooperation between regions facing similar problems and wishing to present a coordinated approach directly at the European level.

It would not be sensible to conclude from this that we need a common system of local government across the entire Community. Such a system would fail to recognize the important cultural and political differences which led to the varying existing systems. As the German case illustrates, there are enormous differences in size and functional structure of that system, although city states such as Bremen and Hamburg present difficulties of not having responsibility for their

immediate hinterland, whereas large states such as Nordrhein-Westfalen may be too large and diverse for sensible inter- and intraregional
planning. Existing systems of local government, even in post-1949
Germany, are often based on outdated economic logic. By this is
meant a lack of concordance between the set of relationships which
define a functional region and the associated administrative areas. As
the work of Cheshire (see Cheshire, 1991, for a useful summary) has
shown, the performance of functional urban regions often gives a
rather different picture from that of the administrative regions with
which they are associated. This suggests that the use of a set of
consistent objective indicators may produce rather different patterns of
regionalization from those found today, and rather different changes in
different parts of the Community. The functional urban regions as such
may not be the best units for administrative purposes: some of these
are too small and their influences too overlapping. Further consideration of functional relationships between these urban regions would also
be necessary.

Although this should not attempt to produce a common pattern of
sub-national government across the Community, it does suggest that
there is a need for a consistent system of allocating competences. In
states which lack a fully developed system of regional government,
there is a need to develop this as a counter-balance to the central
power of the Community. This is suggested not because of a fear of
transferring sovereignty to some threatening power in Brussels, but
because the logic of subsidiarity, of allocating government functions to
the most efficient level, suggests the need for this balance between
different levels.

We have argued in this section that the key to a successful transition
of the Community to a more integrated economic future lies in the way
it is governed at the regional level. This also requires an improved
system of equalizing the flows of tax revenues and expenditures
between jurisdictions. This concentration on the regional level is
justified by the primary need to reduce regional disparities within the
Community.

8.3   The state of integration in 2001

The basic message of this book has been a positive one. It takes as a
starting point the benefits of creating a large Single Market in Europe
that derive from freer trade. It has shown how the removal of
remaining artificial barriers to that trade can produce overall welfare
gains, which, although the actual size may be the object of much

debate, are clearly positive. It was the clear demonstration of this that enabled the Community to carry even its most sceptical members forwards along the road to 1992. It was also the increasing recognition that the distribution of the benefits and their associated costs would cause problems in some sectors and some regions that made the Commission determined to accelerate the process towards full Economic and Monetary Union as the logical consequence of the Single Market. Our analysis of both sectors and regions has suggested that there is a need for a more consistent means of determining and implementing policy at the more local level within the Community. This is particularly true if the Community is to cope with the expansion in size for which the pressures will increase during the decade.

What will be achieved during this decade of change? Will the Community demonstrate a more integrated and coherent economic profile by 2001? In many respects the prospects are good. The amount achieved during the period from 1985 to 1992 has been substantial; however, much remains to be done. To some extent the Community is sitting on a knife edge: it can either continue down the road of greater integration with all that that entails in terms of transferring competences to different levels of government, or it can regress to a set of independent states in little more than a free trade area. It is also the case that the entry point is less than auspicious. All the economies of the Community are in some stage of coping with recession. The Community's historically most dynamic economy, that of Germany, is having to cope with the more substantial than expected problems ensuing from integrating the former GDR into its economy. This has stretched German monetary and fiscal orthodoxy to the limit. The pressures which the exchange rate mechanism transfers to other members of the EMS give a hint of the way geographically distant problems can be transmitted in a fully integrated Single Market.

However, this could also be seen as a good point from which to start. The members of the Community, and prospective members, will better understand the benefits they can derive if they see the Community cope with crises before the end of the process of integration. It is perhaps this very fact that is most likely to lead to the successful transition to a more fully integrated economy. There is still a lot of work to do to achieve this, however: if the decision to complete the Single Market heralded a period of unprecedented activity and effort, making it work once it is completed could prove to be even more challenging.

Bibliography

Armstrong, H. (1985) 'The reform of the European Community regional policy', *Journal of Common Market Studies*, **23**, 319–43.

Balassa, B. (1967) *Trade Liberalisation among Industrial Countries – Objectives and Alternatives*, McGraw-Hill, New York.

Balassa, B. (1974) 'Trade creation and trade diversion in the European Common Market', *Manchester School*, **42**, 99–135.

Balassa, B. and L. Bauwens (1988) 'The determinants of intra-European trade in manufactured goods', *European Economic Review*, **32**, 1421–37.

Baldwin, R. (1989) 'The growth effects of 1992', *Economic Policy*, No. 9, 247–81.

Beckerman, W. (1956) 'Distance and the pattern of intra-European trade', *Review of Economics and Statistics*, **38**, 31–40.

Begg, I. (1989a) 'European integration and regional policy', *Oxford Review of Economic Policy*, **5**(2), 90–104.

Begg, I. (1989b) 'The regional dimensions of the "1992" proposals', *Regional Studies*, **23**, 368–76.

Begg, I. and B. Moore (1987) 'The changing economic role of Britain's cities', in V. Hausner (ed.) *Critical Issues in Urban Economic Development*, Vol. II, Oxford University Press, Oxford.

Bennett, R. J. and G. Krebs (1986) 'Local business taxes and reform proposals in Britain and Germany', in R. J. Bennett and H. Zimmermann (eds) *Local Business Taxes in Britain and Germany*, Anglo-German Foundation, London, pp. 21–54.

Bennett, R. J. and G. Krebs (1989) 'Regional policy incentives and the relative costs of capital in assisted areas in Britain and Germany', *Regional Studies*, **23**, 201–218.

Biehl, D. (1987) 'Perspektiven für die Weiterentwicklung der EG-Regionalpolitik', in W. von Urff and H. von Meyer (eds) *Landwirtschaft, Umwelt und Ländlicher Raum: Herausforderung an Europa*, Nomos, Baden-Baden, pp. 353–68.

Biehl, D. (1989) 'Optimal decentralisation – a conceptual approach to the reform of German federalism', *Government and Policy*, **7**, 375–83.

Biehl, D. (1991) 'The role of infrastructure in regional development', in R. W. Vickerman (ed.) *Infrastructure and Regional Development*, European Research in Regional Science, Vol. 1, Pion, London, pp. 9–35.

193

Boomsma, P., J. van der Linden and J. Oosterhaven (1991) 'Construction of intercountry and consolidated EC input–output tables', paper to 31st European Congress, Regional Science Association, Lisbon.

Bröcker, J. (1980) 'An application of economic interaction models to the analysis of spatial effects of economic integration', *Environment and Planning A*, **12**, 321–38.

Bröcker, J. (1988) 'Interregional trade and economic integration – a partial equilibrium analysis', *Regional Science and Urban Economics*, **18**, 252–81.

Bröcker, J. and K. Peschel (1988) 'Trade', in W. Molle and R. Cappellin (eds) *Regional Impact of Community Policies in Europe*, Avebury, Aldershot, pp. 127–51.

Camagni, R. P. (1991) 'Regional deindustrialization and revitalization processes in Italy', in L. Rodwin and H. Sazanami (eds) *Industrial Change and Regional Economic Transformation: The experience of Western Europe*, HarperCollins, London, pp. 137–67.

Cappellin, R. (1990) 'The European internal market and the internationalization of small and medium-size enterprises', *Built Environment*, **16**(1), 69–84.

Cecchini, P. (1988) *The European Challenge 1992: The benefits of a Single Market*, Wildwood House, Aldershot.

Cheshire, P. C. (1990) 'Explaining the recent performance of the European Community's major urban regions', *Urban Studies*, **27**, 311–33.

Cheshire, P. C. (1991) 'Problems of regional transformation and deindustrialization in the European Community', in L. Rodwin and H. Sazanami (eds) *Industrial Change and Regional Economic Transformation: The experience of Western Europe*, HarperCollins, London, pp. 237–67.

Cheshire, P. C., G. Carbonaro and D. G. Hay (1986) 'Problems of urban decline and growth in EEC countries: or measuring degrees of elephant-ness', *Urban Studies*, **23**, 131–49.

Cheshire, P. C., R. P. Camagni, J.-P. de Gaudemar and J. R. Cuadrado Roura (1991) '1957 to 1992: moving towards a Europe of regions and regional policy', in L. Rodwin and H. Sazanami (eds) *Industrial Change and Regional Economic Transformation: The experience of Western Europe*, HarperCollins, London, pp. 268–300.

Clark, C., F. Wilson and J. Bradley (1969) 'Industrial location and economic potential in Western Europe', *Regional Studies*, **3**, 197–212.

Commission of the European Communities (1987) *The Regions of the Enlarged Community*, Third Periodic Report on the Social and Economic Situation and Development of the Regions of the Community, Office for Official Publications, Luxembourg.

Commission of the European Communities (1988) 'The economics of 1992', *European Economy*, No. 35, Office for Official Publications, Luxembourg.

Commission of the European Communities (1989a) *Employment in Europe 1989*, Office for Official Publications, Luxembourg.

Commission of the European Communities (1989b) *European Economy*, No. 39, Office for Official Publications, Luxembourg.

Commission of the European Communities (1990a) 'The impact of the internal market by industrial sector: The challenge for the member states', *European Economy*, Special Edition, Office for Official Publications, Luxembourg.

Commission of the European Communities (1990b) 'One market, one money', *European Economy*, No. 44, Office for Official Publications, Luxembourg.

Commission of the European Communities (1991a) *The Regions in the 1990s*,

Fourth Periodic Report on the Social and Economic Situation and Development of the Regions of the Community, Office for Official Publications, Luxembourg.

Commission of the European Communities (1991b) *Europe 2000: Outlook for the development of the Community's territory, a preliminary overview*, Office for Official Publications, Luxembourg.

Commission of the European Communities (1991c) *Europe 2000: Outlook for the development of the Community's territory*, COM(91)452 final, Office for Official Publications, Luxembourg.

Commission of the European Communities (1991d) *Community Support Framework, 1991–93 for the areas of Eastern Berlin, Mecklenburg–Vorpommern, Brandenburg, Sachsen–Anhalt, Thüringen and Sachsen, Federal Republic of Germany*, Office for Official Publications, Luxembourg.

Cutler, T., C. Haslam, J. Williams and K. Williams (1989) *1992 – The Struggle for Europe: A critical evaluation of the European Community*, Berg, Oxford.

Dixit, A. K. and J. E. Stiglitz (1977) 'Monopolistic competition and optimum product diversity', *American Economic Review*, **67**, 297–308.

Dixon, R. and A. P. Thirlwall (1979) 'An export-led growth model with a balance of payments constraint', in J. K. Bowers (ed.) *Inflation, Development and Integration: Essays in honour of A. J. Brown*, University of Leeds Press, Leeds.

EFTA (1972) *The Trade Effects of EFTA and the EEC, 1959–1967*, European Free Trade Association, Geneva.

Eichengreen, B. (1990) 'One money for Europe? Lessons from the US currency union', *Economic Policy*, No. 10, 118–87.

Emerson, M. (1988) *The Economics of 1992*, Oxford University Press, Oxford.

Eurostat (1986) *National Accounts ESA: Input-Output Tables, 1980*, Office for Official Publications, Luxembourg.

Fothergill, S. and G. Gudgin (1982) *Unequal Growth*, Heinemann, London.

Geroski, P. A. (1988) 'Competition and innovation', in *Studies on the Economics of Integration*, research on the 'Cost of Non-Europe', Basic Findings, Vol. 2, Office for Official Publications of the European Communities, Luxembourg.

Giersch, H. (1949) 'Economic union of nations and the location of industries', *Review of Economic Studies*, **17**, 87–97.

Globerman, S. and J. Dean (1990) 'Recent trends in intra-industry trade and their implications for future trade liberalization', *Weltwirtschaftliches Archiv*. **126**, 25–49.

Greenan, K. and M. McHugh (1991) 'The Channel Tunnel and the N. Ireland food industry', in R. W. Vickerman (ed.) *Infrastructure and Regional Development*, European Research in Regional Science, Vol. 1, Pion, London, pp. 115–34.

Greenaway, D. and R. C. Hine (1991) 'Intra-industry specialization, trade expansion and adjustment in the European economic space', *Journal of Common Market Studies*, **29**, 603–22.

Greenaway, D. and C. Milner (1987) 'Intra-industry trade: current perspectives and unresolved issues', *Weltwirtschaftliches Archiv*, **123**, 39–57.

Gremmen, H. (1985) 'Testing factor price equalisation in the EC: an alternative approach', *Journal of Common Market Studies*, **23**, 277–86.

Harris, R. and D. Cox (1984) *Trade, Industrial Policy and Canadian Manufacturing*, Ontario Economic Council, Toronto.

Hobday, M. (1989) 'The European semi-conductor industry: resurgence and rationalization', *Journal of Common Market Studies*, **28**, 155–86.

Holliday, I. M., M. Langrand and R. W. Vickerman (1991a) *Nord-Pas de Calais in the 1990s*, Special Report M601, Economist Intelligence Unit, London.

Holliday, I. M., G. Marcou and R. W. Vickerman (1991b) *The Channel Tunnel: Public policy, regional development and European integration*, Belhaven, London.

Jacquemin, A. and A. Sapir (1988) 'International trade and integration of the European Community – an econometric analysis', *European Economic Review*, **32**, 1439–49.

Jeffrey, D. and N. J. Hubbard (1988) 'Foreign tourism, the hotel industry and regional economic performance', *Regional Studies*, **22**, 319–29.

Jüttemeier, K. H. (1987) 'Subsidizing the federal German economy, figures and facts 1973–1984', *Kiel Working Papers*, No. 279.

Keeble, D., P. Owens and C. Thompson (1982a) 'Regional accessibility and economic potential in the European Community', *Regional Studies*, **16**, 419–32.

Keeble, D., P. Owens and C. Thompson (1982b) 'Economic potential and the Channel Tunnel', *Area*, **14**, 97–103.

Keeble, D., J. Offord and S. Walker (1988) *Peripheral Regions in a Community of Twelve Member States*, Office for Official Publications, European Commission, Luxembourg.

Krugman, P. R. and A. J. Venables (1990) 'Integration and the competitiveness of peripheral industry', in C. J. Bliss and J. Braga de Macedo, *Unity with Diversity in the European Economy: The Community's southern frontier*, Cambridge University Press, Cambridge, pp. 56–75.

Lancaster, K. (1979) *Variety, Equity and Efficiency: Product variety in an industrial society*, Basil Blackwell, Oxford.

Lee, C., M. Pearson and S. Smith (1988) *Fiscal Harmonisation: An analysis of the European Commission's proposals*, Report series No. 28, Institute for Fiscal Studies, London.

Major, R. L. and S. Hays (1970) 'Another look at the Common Market', *National Institute Economic Review*, November.

Mayes, D. (1978) 'The effects of economic integration on trade', *Journal of Common Market Studies*, **17**, 1–25.

Miller, M. H. and J. E. Spencer (1977) 'The static economic effects of the UK joining the EEC: a general equilibrium approach', *Review of Economic Studies*, **44**, 71–93.

Molle, W. (1990) *The Economics of European Integration*, Dartmouth, Aldershot.

Neuberger, H. (1989) *The Economics of 1992*, Labour Group, Socialist Group of European Parliament, London.

Neven, D. (1989) 'EEC integration towards 1992: some distributional aspects', *Economic Policy*, No. 10, 14–62.

Pelkmans, J. (1989) 'Is convergence prompting fragmentation? The EMS and national protection in Germany, France and Italy', in P. Guerrieri and P. Padoan (eds) *The Political Economy of European Integration*, Harvester Wheatsheaf, Hemel Hempstead, pp. 100–44.

Perroux, F. (1955) 'Note sur la notion de pôles de croissance', *Economie Appliquée*, **7**, 307–20.

Peschel, K. (1981) 'On the impact of geographic distance on the interregional patterns of production and trade', *Environment and Planning A*, 13, 605–22.

Peschel, K. (1982) 'International trade, integration and industrial location, the case of Germany', *Regional Science and Urban Economics*, 12, 247–69.

Peschel, K. (1985) 'Spatial structures in international trade: an analysis of long-term developments', *Papers of the Regional Science Association*, 58, 97–111.

Peschel, K. (1989) *The Effects of European Integration on Regional Development: Some lessons from the past*, Discussion Paper 24, Institut für Regionalforschung, Kiel.

Peschel, K. (1990) 'Spatial effects of the completion of the European single market', *Built Environment*, 16(1), 11–29.

Peschel, K. and J. Bröcker (1988) 'Die Arbeitsmarktentwicklung in den Raumordnungsregionen der Bundesrepublik Deutschland zwischen 1970 und 1984', in *Arbeitsmarktprobleme, Forschungs- und Sitzungsberichte der Akademie für Raumforschung und Landesplanung*, Vol. 168, Vincentz, Hannover, pp. 7–48.

Pratten, C. (1988) 'A survey of the economies of scale', in *Studies on the Economics of Integration*, Research on the 'Cost of Non-Europe' Basic Findings, Vol. 2, Office for Official Publications of the European Communities, Luxembourg.

Prewo, W. E. (1974) 'Integration effects in the EEC: an attempt at quantification in a general equilibrium framework', *European Economic Review*, 5, 379–405.

Rowthorn, R. E. and J. R. Wells (1987) *De-industrialization and Foreign Trade*, Cambridge University Press, Cambridge.

Schilderinck, J. H. F. (1984) *Interregional Structure of the European Community: Part II, interregional input–output tables of the EC, 1959, 1965, 1970 and 1975*, Tilburg University, Tilburg.

Shoven, J. B. and J. Whalley (1974) 'On the computation of competitive equilibria on international markets with tariffs', *Journal of International Economics*, 4, 341–54.

Sinz, M. and W. J. Steinle (1989) 'Regionale Wettbewerbsfähigkeit und europäischer Binnenmarkt', *Raumforschung und Raumordnung*, 1, 10–21.

Smith, A. and A. J. Venables (1988) 'Completing the internal market in the European Community: some industry simulations', *European Economic Review*, 32, 1501–25.

Steiner, M. (1990) '"Good" and "Bad" regions? Criteria to evaluate regional performance in face of an enforced internationalization of the European economy', *Built Environment*, 16(1), 52–68.

Thirlwall, A. P. (1980) 'Regional problems are "balance of payments problems"', *Regional Studies*, 14, 419–25.

Tovias, A. (1982) 'Testing factor price equalisation in the EEC', *Journal of Common Market Studies*, 20, 165–81.

Trades Union Congress (1988) *Maximising the Benefits, Minimising the Costs: TUC Report on Europe 1992*, TUC, London.

Truman, E. M. (1969) 'The European Economic Community: trade creation and trade diversion', *Yale Economic Essays*, 9, 201–57.

Truman, E. M. (1972) 'The production and trade of manufactured products in the EEC and EFTA: a comparison', *European Economic Review*, 3, 271–90.

Tyler, P., B. Moore and J. Rhodes (1988) 'The rate burden: an accounting framework for assessing the effect of local taxes on business', *Regional Studies*, **22**, 387–98.

UK Government (1970) *Britain and the European Communities: An economic assessment*, Cmnd 4289, HMSO, London.

UK Government (1971) *The United Kingdom and the European Communities*, Cmnd 4715, HMSO, London.

Ungerer, H., O. Evans, T. Mayer and P. Young (1986) *The European Monetary System: Recent developments*, IMF Occasional Paper No. 48, International Monetary Fund, Washington, DC.

Vickerman, R. W. (1984) *Urban Economies: Analysis and policy*, Philip Allan, Oxford.

Vickerman, R. W. (1987) 'The Channel Tunnel: consequences for regional growth and development', *Regional Studies*, **21**, 187–91.

Vickerman, R. W. (1991a) 'Transport infrastructure in the European Community: New developments, regional implications and evaluation', in R. W. Vickerman (ed.) *Infrastructure and Regional Development*, European Research in Regional Science, Vol. 1, Pion, London, pp. 36–50.

Vickerman, R. W. (1991b) 'Other regions' infrastructure in a region's development', in R. W. Vickerman (ed.) *Infrastructure and Regional Development*, European Research in Regional Science, Vol. 1, Pion, London, pp. 61–74.

Winters, L. A. (1987) 'Britain in Europe: a survey of quantitative trade studies', *Journal of Common Market Studies*, **25**, 315–35.

Zimmermann, H. (1989) 'Fiscal equalisation between states in West Germany', *Government and Policy*, **7**, 385–93.

Index

competitiveness, 24, 25, 41–58, 94–100,
110–13
computers, 131
congestion, 20, 60, 170
convergence, 26, 59–79, 97–8
cooperation procedure, 107–8
core regions, 20–1, 28, 169–70
Council of Ministers, 31, 107–8
coverage ratio, 113
Croatia, 186
customs, 83–5
Customs Union, 2, 8–12, 21, 60
Cyprus, 186
Czechoslovakia, 7, 20, 185–6

deindustrialization, 21–2
Delors, Jacques, 6, 44, 81, 89
democratic deficit, 167
Denmark, 3, 5
    fiscal issues, 105–6
    regulatory issues, 87, 113, 116, 118
    trade patterns, 38
Deutsche Bundesbahn, 32
devaluation, 46
devolution, 17, 186–90
Directives, 5, 108
duty-free, 145
dynamic gains, 10–12, 14, 92–3

East Anglia, 20, 173–5
Economic and Monetary Union, 2, 5, 6,
14, 44, 81, 89, 141, 156–61, 186–
90
economic potential, 59–60
efficiency gains, 94–100
employment, 23–4, 65, 111–13, 120, 122,
143
Enterprise Zones, 55, 104
ESPRIT, 130
European Agricultural Guidance and
Guarantee Fund, 48–52, 161
European Central Bank, 141
European Economic Area, 109, 175
European Free Trade Association
(EFTA), 3, 63–4, 68–9, 109
European Monetary System, 5, 75–7,
89–90, 157–8
European Parliament, 80, 107–8, 188
European Regional Development Fund,
30, 48–55, 161–3
European Social Fund, 48, 52, 56, 161
Eurotunnel, 102, 139
exchange controls, 46, 134–6
Exchange Rate Mechanism, 5, 75–7, 89,
157–8
exchange rates, 2, 46, 157–8
excise duties, 13, 73, 105–7, 145

factor endowments, 26, 66–9, 149
factor mobility, 28
federalism, 166–7, 186–90
ferries, 34, 145
financial services, 44–6, 89–91, 134–41
Finanzausgleich, 160, 188–9
Finland, 3, 186
fiscal burden, 47–8
fiscal federalism, 46–7, 160, 188–9
fiscal harmonization, 13, 31, 118, 126,
144
fiscal policy, 157–8, 160
Flanders, 17
Fontainebleau Agreement, 47
food and drink, 86–8, 113–19, 178–9
Fortress Europe, 183
France, 3
    federalism, 17, 188
    fiscal issues, 105–6
    monetary policy, 75–7
    regional problems, 24, 25, 169–77
    sectoral change, 20, 89, 114, 120–1,
122–9, 131–4, 143–5, 153–4
    trade patterns, 36–8, 61
    transport, 35
Frankfurt, 20, 35, 134, 165, 169–70, 174
free trade, 1, 7, 8–12
Free Trade Areas, 2
freight rates, 33
frontiers, 13, 17, 21, 33, 60, 83–5

GATT, 3, 121, 183–4
GDP/capita, 21, 48, 50–4, 77–8, 178
Geneva, 35
German Democratic Republic, 17, 163,
166, 175, 185
Germany, 3, 99–100, 185
    federalism, 17, 160, 187–90
    fiscal issues, 105–6, 160
    monetary policy, 75–7, 158
    regional problems, 24, 25, 49, 153–4,
163, 169–77
    regulatory issues, 87, 91
    sectoral change, 20, 23, 56–7, 116,
120–1, 122–9, 131–3, 141, 143,
144
    trade patterns, 38, 61–5
    transport, 32
globalization, 19–20, 96, 115–16, 154,
183
Greece, 5
    fiscal issues, 105–6
    regional problems, 50, 53, 153–4, 163,
177–8
    sectoral change, 20, 89, 113
    trade patterns, 38, 62
growth bonus, 98–100